THE TWO PATHS TO GOD

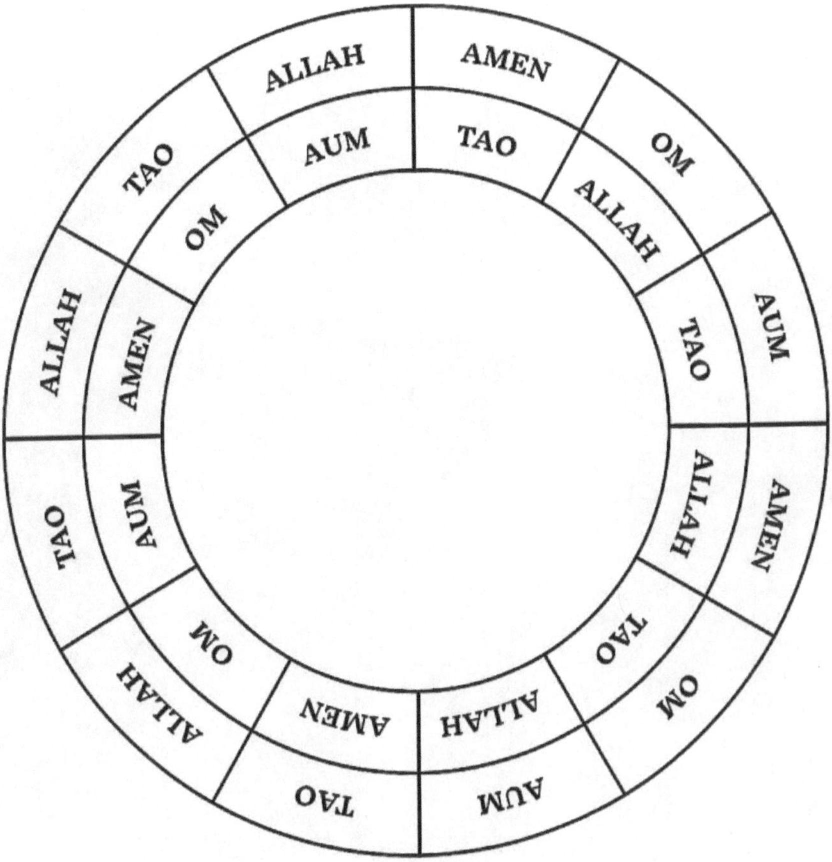

The Two Paths To God

A spiritual guide
by
XAVIER CLAYTON

Adelaide Books
New York / Lisbon
2019

THE TWO PATHS TO GOD
A spiritual guide
by Xavier Clayton

Copyright © by Xavier Clayton
Cover design © 2019 Adelaide Books

Published by Adelaide Books, New York / Lisbon
adelaidebooks.org

Editor-in-Chief
Stevan V. Nikolic

All rights reserved. No part of this book may be reproduced in any manner whatsoever without written permission from the author except in the case of brief quotations embodied in critical articles and reviews.

For any information, please address Adelaide Books
at info@adelaidebooks.org
or write to:
Adelaide Books
244 Fifth Ave. Suite D27
New York, NY, 10001

ISBN-10: 1-951214-13-7
ISBN-13: 978-1-951214-13-5

Printed in the United States of America

This book is dedicated to The Five World Mantras

Tao – Allah – Amen – Om – AUM

and to anyone who has prayed with these words that empower our Collective Consciousness.

Contents

Introduction **9**

The Age Of Religion **19**

Getting Started! – Your Equinox Journal **101**

The Five World Mantras "Om", "Amen", "Allah", "Tao", and "AUM"
The Words That Amplify Our Prayers **107**

Solar Mantras And Lunar Mantras **201**

The Clock Of The Twelve Paired Mantras In The Age Of Light **267**

The Trinities And Sacred Hearts Found Throughout Asia's Eastern Religions **323**

One Famous Example Of How Synergetic Thought Changed The World **361**

About The Supplementary Book "Exercises in Divine Science and Experiments in Multiplicative Joy" **367**

Acknowledgements **371**

About the Author **373**

Introduction

As an adolescent, I used to often go over to my Aunt's house to spend the night and have playdates with one of my cousins. Before putting us to bed, my Aunt ALWAYS made us pray. My cousin and I would put our toys away and then kneel next to our beds and press our hands together on top of the fresh-smelling sheets. Since she was a girl, I always let my cousin go first. Her prayer was always the same. Very short and sweet. "God Bless Mommy and Daddy. Amen". I can remember looking over at her and thinking "Is that it?!!". But, the effort seemed to satisfy my Aunt. Then it was my turn to pray. I got very creative with my prayers. I thanked the family… the day God created… the dinner we had… my Mother… my cousin… anything I could think of went into my prayer. As an adolescent, I did not know what I was praying to, but I felt that this nightly ritual was a moment to communicate with someone or something or some intelligence higher than my own thoughts. As I grew older, I wanted to know more about what that higher intelligence was.

Before writing this book, I had spent more than 20 years actively looking for answers to the many spiritual questions I had and still do have. I did this either on my own or with inspired men and women who taught in various spiritual centers throughout the world – whether in churches, ashrams, meditation centers, and temples. At one spiritual center in particular, in Gent, Belgium, I could ask the spiritual guide there any and every little question that came to mind about God, about man's relationship to God, and the techniques man could use to embellish the bond between Divine Intelligence and physical matter. The Siddha Shiva Yoga Center was where I grew spiritually and is where this book began.

Added to that, I also read a lot and travelled a lot. I have come to see that there are two types of spiritual writers – One that writes from the doctrine of just one religion and the other that looks at all religions from an unbiased, global, and universal perspective. I read spiritual books from both types of writers. I found myself LOVING the inspired books written by people who had a broad vision of religions role in the world for all mankind. Those were the ones that inspired me most. It is hard for me to remember a time when I did not have a book by Paul Brunton, Omraam Mikhael Aivanov, and/or Swami Muktananda by my bedside. As for my travels, Europe, Canada, The United States, India, Africa, China, Japan, Thailand, Croatia, Turkey, Montenegro, and Mexico are some of the places that have enriched me spiritually and culturally. One on one friendships and experiences with locals from different faiths does things that a book or a spiritual guide can not. These interactions open our minds and our hearts. Weaved into the text of these pages are many of those wonderful encounters I am fortunate enough to share with you.

Before consciously beginning my spiritual journey in the summer of 1993, a good part of my young adult life was spent around either atheists or scientists. My adolescent upbringing in a Baptist Church prevented me from becoming an Atheist myself. But still, I did respect the belief that there was no God that most of my friends and colleagues had. When asked my own beliefs, I was always the one in the group that said "Well… I believe that there's something, but I don't know what that something is" – Whatever that meant! I guess by saying this and believing it, I was keeping myself spiritually open.

In regards to God or anything to do with religion or spirituality, I have always been a questioner. Not the kind of questioner that interrogates a spiritualist into the folly of their faith, but more of a questioner who had an intense and open curiosity. A person who wanted to find answers and unlock mysteries. Looking back, I can see that I had this at a very young age when my Mother would take me to Sunday School and I would be the only one raising my hand in the Children's Group to ask about a word or a meaning that the Teacher had just read. When I finally met my Spiritual Guide in Gent, Belgium, he would regularly "bring up the house lights" to answer any and all questions. Again… my hand ALWAYS went up! In that same period, I learned more about Judaism, Catholicism, Taoism, Buddhism, Hinduism, Islam, and Yogas – All of which use mantras to help their followers deepen their connection to God. All of this added to my Spiritual Knowledge and would help quench my Spiritual Thirst. However, when I was suddenly inspired to write a book examining the root meanings of these mantras, I did not expect the immense joy and expansion of thought doing so would give me.

Working as a Full-Time Scientist was also an important part of how I came to look at spirituality, religion, and even God himself. This book could not have been written without the 20-year Scientific background I have had in Seattle, Antwerp, Marseille, and in The United States Army. Because of my day to day job, analytical thought was and is ingrained into my habitual thinking.

Spiritual books have been, arguably, the second most important factor in my spiritual growth – The first being my direct contact with various living spiritual guides and teachers. You might ask… "How do I know that these books and guides were spiritual at all, or even good?". Well, my answer to that is because I changed for the better after my contact with them and subsequent reflection upon them. Another set of books and teachers might be best for someone else – but these were what were best for me at the time they entered my life. Three books in particular; "The Tao Te Ching" (by Lao Tzu), "Enlightened Mind, Divine Mind" (by Paul Brunton), and "Spiritual Alchemy" (by Omraam Mikhael Aivanov) all came on my path in extremely mystical ways. The entire Siddha Shiva Yoga Center entered my life in a dynamic and mystical way over a beer at a bar. Without any of these events, and what they ultimately lead me to, I would not have been able to write the book you now have in your hands.

The experience I've had of having some books mysteriously land in my lap is what lead me to sit down for 9 years to write "The Two Paths to God". I had started collecting information on prayer techniques that I had come across – The two most Earth-Shaking (to me) being The Five Elements contained in The "Om Namah Shivaya"- mantra, written by Swami Muktananda and "The Pentacle of Virtues", written by Omraam Mikhael Aivanov. These were the two techniques I started using in my own prayers. Added to that, the many times I was present in Gent, Belgium when Sri Ganapati spoke of how certain numbers, like #23, #32, and #108, contain mystical power also got the wheels of my spiritual curiosity turning. From these guides who entered my spiritual journey, along with my habitual scientific thought at work, I began to develop my own way of praying called "The Six Steps of Scientific Prayer".

The book you have now is not the book I intended to write. My first intention was to use the large collection of prayer techniques that I've picked up along my spiritual path and to condense them down into one simple little handbook. However, when I started writing, the book just kept growing and growing. As I wrote, the ideas and words kept flowing through my hands, making the initial book larger and larger. I had to keep cutting it. Pruning it like a beautiful, thriving, and wildly abundant jasmine bush. At one time, I thought of turning my notes into a Trilogy, but friends and family advised me to focus on one of the techniques instead. Because of their advice, I've focused on the first of The Six Steps of Scientific Prayer for this book.

This book would not be what it is without the help of my husband Georges.

There are SO MANY of his suggestions sprinkled throughout these pages – both in regards to the content and the structure. He helped. If this book "flows" at all… the reader has him to thank. Not me. Questions you would have asked me about, he did – and I added the answers as a result his probing. Parts of this book that would have been "Too Christian", he helped make them more global… and even Universal.

Finally, the reason I put so much effort – JOYOUS EFFORT – into writing this book was ultimately to sell ONE COPY. Being a believer in reincarnation, I wanted to put some of the spiritual and scientific information I've gained from my travels into a structured, grounded, and physical form. The views of it were shaped and inspired by my many one-on-one talks with Catholic and Orthodox Priests, Hasidic

Jews, Avatars, A Channeler, Mormons, Avatars, Sunni Muslims, Scientists, Taoists, Buddhists, Evangelical Sunday School Teachers, Gurus, Atheists, and Spiritual Guides. My belief in reincarnation drives me when I write. It is because this book is inspired from my own thoughts, spirit, and spiritual experiences, it being written down in book form grounds that all into one place. It is my hope that even if only one copy is sold, when I reincarnate in my next life, the information I've written here will create the karmic magnetism needed to find its way back to me. My deepest intention in writing this book is to help give myself a head start in my next life.

Book Overview

My purpose for this book was to explore The Five World Mantras that the world's spiritualists use in their communication with God - "Amen", "Om", "Allah", "AUM", and "Tao". I've examined these words from their root meanings, and how the first people who used them described them. In some cases, like with The Master Jesus, I had to rely on witnesses who have described how and when this Spiritual Master routinely used the mantra, "Amen".

Each definition is taken directly from The Bible, The Vedas, The Tao Te Ching, The Talmud, The Koran, and The Gita and then analyzed on how it helps a person commune with Divine Consciousness. The Theme of the book is Spiritual Synergy. How different ideas can come together to create something greater than their individual parts.

What this book does, is it helps the reader examine other mantras than their own. At first, it classifies The Five World Mantras, based on their core meanings, into Two Universal Constants - God as "The Eternal Field" (Tao and Allah) and

God as "The Cosmic Sound" (Om, AUM, and Amen). As we continue probing the mantras further, the reader discovers through calendars and how celebrations are calculated, that Islam and Taoism (The Eternal Field Mantras) are based on The Cycles of The Moon and that Christianity, Judaism, Buddhism, and Hinduism (The Cosmic Sound Mantras) are based all, or partly, on The Cycles of The Sun.

With this new knowledge, we discover "The Twelve Paired-Mantras". These pairings are created from The Five World Mantras – That is, when a Word from The Eternal Field and a Word from The Cosmic Sound are combined. For example, "Tao-Om" or "Allah-Amen" are two of The Twelve Paired Mantras. Just like with The Trinity, these mantra-pairings use synergy to awaken our Inner Light. Through "Conscious Prayer", we learn to use mantras to resonate with our Inner Sun and our Inner Moon to form and Inner Eclipse. From this point in Divine Communion, are we truly able to create Abundance, Peace, and Pure Joy. What this practice ultimately does is trigger Transcendence our deep knowledge of the Five Mantras and their individual meanings.

The mysticism of Number 12 is shown to be one of the most powerful factors of The Clock of The Paired Mantras. It is a number that is connected to Time, Astrology, Music, and all of our Major Religions. Even in our daily lives, we find the number 12 in our Four Seasons and in the 12 major organs of the Human Body. Added to that, the latest scientific discoveries on The String Theory, says that there are 12 dimensions to The Universe. Because of the numerous twelves within and around us, this book considers twelve to be a path into The Divine Mind from here on Earth.

Finally, "The Clock of the Paired Mantras" is presented - The culmination of the entire book. Using the pattern of a regular clock, this Clock organizes all 12 Paired Mantras into one structured unit. It is a Clock that does more than tell Time. It, in conjunction with our increased mantra awareness, can trigger Light, Vitality, and Transcendence. It helps us with our thoughts. It helps us with our prayers. It expands our mind to limits of our galaxies. It takes us beyond judgement and hate and into Peace and Abundance. It is this Clock that is used with the 24 exercises found in the supplementary book - "Exercises and Experiments in Divine Science". Just as with learning how to drive a car, the first book can be viewed as theoretical, while the second book can be viewed as a practical guide to The Five World Mantras.

Throughout these pages, the word "He" is often used to describe God. God is both He and She. God, The Absolute, is both Yin and Yang. Male and Female. A Mother and a Father. God is feminine energy and masculine energy combined into Kundalini Shakti Energy. If God were just masculine, nothing would grow and nothing – including ourselves – would survive. When we think of God in both feminine and masculine aspects, our thoughts operate at the highest echelons of our Five Virtues. From here, our thoughts dance on the edges of duality. From here, we are able to trigger abundance and the elixir of spiritual transcendence. Incorporating God's feminine side into his masculine side evokes unimaginable power within us. Yet… in this book, for speed and readable ease, when God is mentioned, "She" is sometimes left out – but not forgotten!

A Guide Chart to help

The following chart is used throughout this book. Its purpose is to give you a clear overview of the section you are reading and how it fits into the body of the book itself.

THE TWO PATHS TO GOD

THE FIVE WORLD MANTRAS	Individually analyzing the one-word mantras from six major religions Christianity, Hinduism, Islam, Buddhism, Taoism, and Judaism				
	OM	TAO	ALLAH	AMEN	AUM
	The Eternal Field beyond physical matter – Tao and Allah				
	The Cosmic Sound within physical matter – Amen, Om, and AUM				
THE SOLAR MANTRAS and THE LUNAR MANTRAS	OM / AUM / AMEN		TAO / ALLAH		
	« The Cosmic Sound » THE SOLAR MANTRAS		« The Eternal Field » THE LUNAR MANTRAS		
	The SUN ☉		The MOON ☽		
	Sacred Hearts and Trinities The Poetic, The Symbolic, and The Mystical paths to God				
THE CLOCK OF THE TWELVE PAIRED MANTRAS	The Two Universal Constants: The Cosmic Sound and The Eternal Field				
	The Twelve Paired Mantras				
	Allah-AUM Om-Tao Amen-Allah	Tao-AUM Allah-Amen Om-Allah		Tao-Amen AUM-Allah Amen-Tao	Allah-Om Tao-Om AUM-Tao
	The Number 12 – Its resonance with Time, Music, and Astrology. Its link to The Earth and our World Religions.				
	△ Evolution ✡ Involution ▽ Star of David				
	The Clock of The Twelve Paired Mantras				

* Some religions are based in another religion. For example, Protestantism and Lutheranism are based in Christianity. Buddhism has the sects of Zen, Theravada, Mahayana, and Tibetan. Shintoism and Confucianism are based in Taoism. For this book, each of the six major religions may encompass other faiths. Based on their origins is why some popular religions, like Shintoism and Confucianism, are not considered separate religions in this book.

The Age Of Religion

Man's search for God is inspired from his search for who he is, where he comes from, why he is here, and what he is here to do. Religions claim to answer many of these questions. They give us the practice and the environment to delve into the deepest recesses of our hearts to explore these questions and answers. As God is limitless and incessantly active, the few pathways our world has created to reach him should be celebrated by us all.

Why Do We Need A Religion?

There have always been various doctrines and practices on how to best communicate with God. A God we believe is there, here, and eternal. We observe an intellectual and reliable Divine Force in the four seasons, our body, the constellations, Nature, and the cycles of day and night. If the signs we see of this intelligence and spiritual transcendence are correct, then after some time it slowly awakens our desire to connect with this Divine Presence. The most logical path to not only connect to, but also to feel this presence, is through thought.

Many of the first doctrines and practices our ancient mystics developed to help us (re-)unite with The Divine Consciousness within and around us have formulated the religions in our world today. Meditation, prayer, mantra repetition, and rituals are some of these techniques. All of these techniques are to help man overcome one thing – his own ego. However, in our religions today, the most important thing is not the re-unification with who we truly are, but a perpetuation that there is only one path to a God we all agree is Universal. But, when did The Age of Religion actually begin? For this book, man has always been and continues to be "spiritual". But, The Age of Religion began when religious segregation and human ego took prominence over spiritual unification through expanded knowledge.

Religions themselves have originated from the lives, teachings, and/or the works of various spiritual guides who showed us techniques to calm the mind, subdue the ego, evoke inner light, and improve our communications with Divine Consciousness. The Age of Religion is, at first glance, a period of time that started when human societies began to organize and segregate these faiths. Like-minded spiritualists who lovingly revered the same guide sometimes built temples to come together and share their aspirations, joy, and remembrance of the person giving them so much inspiration. This coming together in temples devoted to awakening thought happens on paths that are both towards Light or Darkness – and it happens on paths inspired by Truth and not. Humans congregating for metaphysical purposes have built the vast number of varied spiritual organizations we see in the world today. When people began to routinely come together, in a specific temple, using specific doctrines, to use aspirations and rituals to manifest thought-forms of a spiritual guide and/or of our Universal God, we can see this as the beginning of The Age of Religion.

Archeologists tell us that Homo erectus man started at a minimum of 200,000 years ago. Archeologists have made genetic studies dating the origins of man back 800,000 years.

One thing that we do know is that many environmental factors pre-historic man lived in we live in today. Like us, they saw the cycles of The Moon, the changing of the four seasons, as well as thunder and lightning. What did they think about these "living" and "active" elements going on in their surroundings? It must have caused a lot of fear and superstition during an earthquake or when lightning struck – as it does today. Did pre-historic man believe that there was a higher consciousness operating the elements, moon, and stars? These are some questions we can ponder.

However, what is known is that about 160,000 years ago, pre-historic man started making flake tools in huge quantities. Flake tools were sharper, simpler, and more easily repairable than stone tools. This change, arguably, shows – at the very least – a huge difference in their knowledge and discoveries. In other words, for pre-historic man to purposely seek out flake stone in order to mass-produce various tools for hunting and building shows that there was a significant change in their knowledge. Through their actions, we see that they lived a life where they co-existed with Nature, and possibly began to see various Deities found in the natural world around them. Neanderthals had to have noticed the changing of the seasons. They had to have notice the In later civilizations after pre-historic man, it is very clear that these communities began to see and communicate with various Deities in Nature. Pagans and Celtics, for instance, revered spirits found in various trees, rivers, a number of animals, The Moon, The Sun, etc. However, there was always a Supreme God that ruled over all of these spirits. In this environment, Spiritual Guides began teaching that God is also found within ourselves. This began 2,000 to 4,000 years ago. These Spiritual Masters traveled, taught, lectured, and wrote about their ponderings and Divine experiences with The One Supreme God found in us all. Many wrote poems and books such The Dhamapada, The Vedas, The Manusmriti, and The Tao Te Ching to help guide our thoughts to the One God within and around us all. The number of followers of these various guides grew. Temples were built in their honor. The particular rituals, rites, and dogmas that have ensued, and are related to a unique Spiritual Guide, have come to create the religions of our world today.

The most subtle reality that the above paragraph shows is that, from an archeological point of view, organized religion is only 1% of human kind's total existence here on Earth. All of our spiritual books, poems, and religious wars have occupied a maximum 1% in the spectrum of human existence here on Earth. Flake stone production is one of the earliest and clearest signs of humanity's change in intelligence.

The Celtics and The Pagans saw Divinity in Nature. Many of their teachers and spiritual guides were in the Stars, in the trees, in The Sun, The Moon, rivers, snakes, animals, and The Earth. Many indigenous tribes in The Americas, Australia, and Africa have connected to God through their observations of The Natural World around us. Before religion, we saw a representation of God in everything, and heard stories directly from Nature through trees, fish, birds, and rivers. We shared and lived by these stories – which helped us unify with Divine Consciousness. Polytheism is misunderstood. It is misunderstood because it is feared. Seeing God's face in multiple places and in multiple ways means that you will never forget him. In all of these ancient civilizations and tribes, there has always been a Supreme God. Yet, once we began to have human spiritual examples in the form of guides, spiritualists began to see God more and more in only one face.

THE TWO PATHS TO GOD

To go from where man saw God in multiple representations in Nature to where man sees God only through his spiritual guide, shows one of the Great Spiritual Transitions mankind has made in its 200,000 years of existence. Humanity has changed in many ways. Countless parameters of human life have evolved. For a moment, let's analyze how our ways of communicating has itself transitioned over the same period of time.

To begin with, even though our human bodies are basically the same as a Neanderthal, the way we communicate has changed dramatically. To tell another person our thoughts and feelings 50,000 to 100,000 years ago, anthropologists say that we first communicated with grunts, mumbling, and clicks of our tongues... then, slowly, we began to formulate spoken words and complex sentences. From the sentences, we built vocabularies and languages with an accepted set of rules. From there, we discovered how to make papyrus, and began to use the written word and reading. We then put pages of our written thoughts into books which helped transmit our thoughts to several people – even after our death. From there, we began to copy our books and put them into libraries. This helped us communicate our ideas to others simultaneously. Today, in our modern world, we now put our books and libraries into computers and microchips. The long progression humanity has gone through from the grunt to the SIM-card shows a definite change in how we communicate thought.

Looking at our trajectory of verbal communication can remind us of our growth in our spiritual evolution. Before we started to look and listen for our Universal Oneness through Nature, we probably didn't look for it at all. It is arguable that we progressed from not seeing God in anything... to seeing

God in The Nature around us... then to seeing God through a spiritual guide... and to finally seeing God in ourselves. Again, for this book, The Age of Religion started when we began to see God through a spiritual guide and to congregate in temples dedicated to that person's remembrance or doctrine. The Age of Religion started during the transition periods before and after our spiritual guides began teaching us. It started before and after we began practicing techniques for finding our Universal God within. We can imagine it being a very powerful changeover period, when we went from seeing God in The Nature around us to seeing God within ourselves. And too, the exalted feelings we had when we began building temples in honor of various spiritual guides out of the Love and gratitude we felt for them.

But, why do we do form religions at all? Every Saint has pointed us to God – not to a temple or a religion. So, what needs do religions fulfill within us? One need they definitely fill is the need for security. Security is a need that every living thing has. It is a major element of Nature. Animals, insects, and even plants demonstrate how they seek for security and safety. They look for a place they can flourish; A beehive, a bear cave, an ant hill, and a fox den are some examples. A secure and protected place where we can feel safe to develop in some way. Plants demonstrate this in where they thrive. For example, a Lotus flower is not a cactus and would die in a desert - and the same can be said for a cactus in a pond. Both plants thrive in a place they feel safe and secure. Our rain forests and micro-ecosystems are other ways we can see how certain plants congregate in certain environments.

Scientifically proven, is the way that plants do this by the use of sound. For instance, a plant's roots "look" for sources of water via the vibration water makes underground*. The sound waves water and insects make helps inform the plant of the safety and security of their environment. In other words, acoustics and humidity help a plant in its decision-making. If it "hears" it won't even be able to get enough water, it is possible that a plant will stay dormant as a seed. (*Michael Schoner, University of Greifswald; ScienceDirect.com - August 2016 and Monica Gagliano, Evolutionary Biologist; University of Western Australia. Oecologia, May 2017).

When we think of man, we see that we too look for security and safety. However, what sets human beings apart is that we search for security in a two-fold manner; our physical security and our spiritual security.

Let's analyze our need for physical security first. Since even before our modern-day democracies, we have always selected a leader who we felt would keep us "safe and secure". We voted for Presidents and Dictators who would protect our lives, our land, and our families. When we still lived in tribes, we wanted a chief that was strong and fearless. One that was also smart enough to keep dangerous intruders away. He or she had to have our safety at heart. When our security was threatened, we turned to that leader for a decision on what to do to make us feel safe again. To help us fulfill our need for peace. A leader who could quickly help us feel "Normal" again. But, therein lies the problem... "What is Normal?".

Normal is partly what we perceive to be normal and partly what we think, or are led to believe, is normal. Normal evolves. Normal today is different than normal 20 years ago. Anyone born since the year 1980 has seen the world change at least ten times. The world has changed and our normal has changed with it. HIV, The Internet, September 11th, the election of both Presidents Barack Obama and Donald Trump have all drastically changed our normal.

Regarding our spiritual security, unlike animals, insects, and plants, we need security not only in our physical realm, but in our spiritual realm as well. We don't see Orcas, bumblebees, and lilacs praying very often, or building a section of the beehive specifically for prayer and meditation. But, we humans do. We build those spiritual temples specifically to enrich our relationship with The Universal Mind. We pray for blessings beyond what God has naturally given us. Religion plays well into our need for spiritual security. Heaven, and feeling that we are "one of the chosen", also play well into that deep need we have.

Looking back on the conflicts our human history, many times our need for security rose when there were ships or warriors from a foreign community coming to invade our land. Fast-approaching armies on horseback heightened our fears and the threats to our safety. Our normal was threatened. Because of this, not only the protection of our normal, but also the fear of the unknown gripped us so tightly that it made us take up our weapons and fight for our lives. Fear is what made us develop better and more powerful weapons.

In our world history, this threat of our normal has happened countless times in countless places. But, today we are different. The world is smaller. Modern technology has brought us all closer together in numerous ways. Various other threats take our thoughts to impending doom; Cyber-security, Climate Change, and Martian invasions to name a few.

But, when we talk about culture and religious invasion, the so-called "invaders" are already here – and have been here for decades. The invaders work with us, marry us, live right-next door, and are starting to make up an important part of our future history. In many ways, it is already too late to ask our Kings, presidents, and prime ministers for the safety we think our grandparents and great-grandparents knew. We live in a totally different, multi-cultural world now. For decades, we have let down our guard and, by doing so, opened ourselves to abundance, growth, new energy, and knowledge. So... this is the world we live in today. We are physically, socially, politically, and technologically mixed. So now the question is... "What is the new normal?". "Where do we go from HERE, so that we all benefit and feel safe and secure?".

Traditionally, we've looked to our monarchy and political leaders to protect our "normal" and to ensure our security and safety. However, normality exists in the realm of our thoughts. It is a fluid idea we have created in our Collective Consciousness that will inevitably be changed tomorrow, in six months, or two years from now. Anything from a new politician, a new law, a new co-worker, to a pay raise would certainly change your normal. If, for example, a gang of criminals moved in next door to your house, your security would immediately change.

However, with God, we are all trying to develop a personal connection to The One Source of The Universe. We commonly see how religious conflicts have created destruction, but we can also choose to see how they were a means of spreading spiritual knowledge. As the Light of spiritual knowledge enters more and more into our world, there will be less and less need of religious war. Spiritual knowledge will bring a new norm of security and safety. There is no law that can be passed nor any document that can be signed that can make us feel as secure as evoking Light within our own hearts. It is not our Kings and politicians who can bring us to a new normal of spiritual security and true safety... It is ourselves.

The 3 Highest Known Blessings:
Being Alive, On Earth, and in Human Form

There are times when we contemplate Life, our relationship to God, and feel Light and Wonder enter our thoughts. When we look around at a sunset or a rainbow and can feel grateful and blessed. And at other times, when we are just happy to have been given another day of Life – especially, if we compare ourselves to someone who has just gone through a tragedy, or maybe has even just died. At these times, we feel blessed just for being alive.

However, to a spiritualist, we are more blessed than that. This Earth we live on is filled with wonder and abundance. We are the custodians of it. We are the keepers of how all other life on it is affected. We are at the top of the food chain. Spiritualists call our home "God's planet". Artists call it "God's Green Earth". As far as we have seen, there is no other place that has more variety of Life or reflects the abundance of Universal Consciousness more than our planet Earth. If any life form in our galaxies would want to have a fertile environment where they could re-establish their connection with the dynamic and abundant Universal Consciousness, planet Earth would be it.

As for being the custodians of Earth, we are often told that we are "Children of God" and that we are "Made in God's image". To some spiritual adepts, they remind us that it is hard to be born and that it is even harder to be born in human form. Being born in a human body says that we've agreed to the many responsibilities attached to having one. We are not only given a body with arms and legs to achieve our goals and to better our world – but we are also given a mind that we can use to re-connect to The True Source of who we are. Our mind can see this True Source beyond just ourselves – it can see that connection in others, in a plant, in animals, in our Earth, and in our Universe. That is the kind of mind we agreed to develop after birth. Even those born with mental handicaps can and do make steps to develop the human mind they were born with. Plants, animals, and insects are given a different category of mind – however, our human ones are unique and universal.

These are some of the blessings we receive from being alive, on Earth, and in human form. By being born with these three, we are able to make huge progress in our spiritual advancement. Whether you are The Elephant Man or a Supermodel, you were born with all three. Without any one of them, how could you evolve? Once we realize that, the essential key, then, is thought and spiritual practice. The best tool we can develop is a sound mind.

To progress spiritually with any technique, we use thought. Certain meditations require us to empty our minds of thought. But, even the thought not to use thought requires thought. The Universal Intelligence within and around us is Pure Thought. How else could our blood flow and our lungs inhale without our conscious participation? Even while we sleep, we are kept alive. The same incessant activity of Divine Intelligence that spins the Earth keeps us alive. The power and intelligence of this Universal Consciousness is so divinely categorized, that even though thousands of us die every second, it has never once stopped the rotation of the Earth.

Examine your hands for a moment... there are four fingers and a thumb on each... there's a mirror-like symmetry for the left and the right hand... you have your own personalized and unique fingerprints... and an intricate inner bone construction to help you type, write, grab, and scratch. Our unique hands come from Universal Thought. We exist in a universe of thought - One that extends beyond the wonder of our own hands. Our hands have two purposes; They help us achieve our dreams and desires… and they help us to pray. We evoke Light when we see that these two purposes are, in fact, the same.

We, as living human beings, were born with a Spiritual Tool Box. To gain access to the tools within that tool box, we use thought and spiritual techniques. As was said above, many people meditate to try to achieve a place where there is no thought. However, where in the universe would that place be? Divine Thought is what keeps the stars in our galaxies in order. Perhaps for a few moments in meditation we can experience feelings of ecstasy and joy, when we empty our mind of words and anxiety. But, if our blood is flowing and our hearts are beating, then there is Thought. If, by breathing, we create electro-magnetic reactions in the body, then there is Thought.

The mind is a tricky thing. It is full of imagination, plans, dreams, ideas, and desires. Most of our time is focused on some aspect of thinking. To empty the mind creates a vacuum. When we are in that fleeting, thoughtless vacuum, we open to transcendence. Light can come to fill the vacuum we've created within us. Yes, it is wonderful to feel these moments of ecstasy and joy, but why stop there? Why not also work WITH how the mind is? Why not use the natural state of the mind to harmonize it with the Universe?

Instead of struggling to achieve a few thoughtless moments in our meditation, we can also try giving the mind something to do. Something to focus on. The Universe is in incessant action and often the mind seems to also be in incessant action. From that point of view, the actions of the mind are, to some extent, already harmonized with the actions of The Universe. We just need to feed it the right thoughts so that it can merge with The Universe.

What gets further out to sea... a buoy or a rowboat? Emptying the mind is like tying it to a buoy. Merging the active mind with the active Universe is like putting it in a rowboat. The remainder of this book will help us connect to our paired mantra to help give it something transcendent and active to do. Paired mantras are like a rowboat with paddles. As we work with them, new moments of spiritual ecstasy will come... and last longer, because we have become proficient at tapping into divine joy whether our mind is active or at rest.

Even if a person is autistic or mentally handicapped, they may also be able to benefit from spiritual techniques. If these people have been taught prayer by a loved one and are able to pray on their own, then there is hope that they can develop further. Being able to pray independently partly means a person can conceptualize, imagine, feel, and love. When a caring mother or a devoted father teaches an autistic child how to pray, the most powerful tools at work are thought and love. As we will learn in the third step of scientific prayer, certain colors can be used to stimulate spiritual progress. These colors (Red, Green, and Violet) not only help the person themselves, but also those around them who are spiritually aware of their meaning. Thought transcends physical matter. Thought and prayer are powerful healers.

Religious Wars are also Vehicles of Spiritual Interchange and Faith Awareness

All told, religious wars have killed more than 340 million people throughout our human history. Contrary to famine, plagues, and many diseases, where viruses and lack of food, water, and medical care are the cause of death. In religious wars, it is our own hate and fear of an unfamiliar faith that have caused us to kill another human life. Because of fear, we miss an opportunity to grow. Religious wars close ourselves off from new knowledge. Instead of researching, we end up revolting. Instead of incorporating, we end up incarcerating. One thing we can ask to the world's faithful is…

If Christianity is so Perfect,
then why are you filled with so much hate?

If Taoism is so Divine,
then why are you filled with so much unrest?

If Judaism is so True,
then why are you filled with so much fear?

If Islam is so Loving,
then why are you filled with so much anger?

And If Buddhism is so Whole,
then why are you filled with so much jealousy?

We have spiritually failed each other because we think that what we have been taught is the only Truth. We are taught that the true spiritual answer we seek is an individualized one, instead of a conglomerate and collective one. We have been taught to seek Universal Truth from one path.

The biggest reason for this single-minded approach to our own spiritual salvation is probably because we all have death hanging over our heads. We know death is coming, but we don't know when or how. We worry that when we pass on to the next life, what funeral rituals will be performed over our body? What burial rites will be done to help ensure we reach Paradise? Am I a Hindu? Am I a Jew? Am I a Christian? Am I a Muslim? What label can I give myself so that the best funeral practices will be said over my dead body? Well... One quick thought to that is... Why can't all of them be said? Why, at our funerals, can't a Rabbi come to read Jewish rites from The Talmud, Hindu Yogis chant « Om Namah Shivaya », an Imam wrap our body in cloth and read from the Koran, an Indian Rishi give our body a benediction with water from the Holy Ganges, and a Priest walk around our coffin with a sacred incense that fills the entire room? Who would be mad? Who would be offended? And why can't this happen for all of us?

So, it is not only the fear of death that causes us to spiritually label ourselves, but it is also how we want to ensure our place in Heaven after our death. For some of us, thoughts of our impending death and Heaven in the afterlife have forced us to reflect on the path we are following. Conflicts within a faith can cause a religion to divide. If some charismatic who person does not agree with a certain aspect of a faith, they have often used their charisma to create a sect or a completely new faith. We have seen this within several particular faiths. For example, Christianity is not just Roman Catholic, but it is also Orthodox, Presbyterian, Lutheran, etc... The several yogas within Hinduism is another example. Sunni and Shiite Muslims are another example. Kabballah, Orthodox, Rabbinic, Hasidic, and Karaite Judaism is another example. These different faiths that are within the same religion were born from conflict and spiritual reflection. But, when conflict and spiritual reflection is inter-religious, war and hate are often the result. The contrast is felt to be too strong. Too shocking. Too confrontational. So, our reaction is to lash out from fear.

But yet, even though religious wars have caused so much death and destruction, they have simultaneously done a very important thing - They have given us vice-versa exposure and knowledge of other faiths and some of their practices. Even before the religious war broke out, friction and arguments arose. Through this violent exchange of information, some knowledge is gained on both sides. Even more spiritual knowledge could have been gained if the fear wasn't there. But, at the very least, vice-versa experience and visual knowledge are enhanced. There is Light and construction that can come with the fear and destruction, when spiritualists of different faiths are intermingled. We may not practice or believe in the rituals of someone else's faith, but we do get confronted with their existence. This, already, is a big advantage we have today that most of our ancestors did not have.

The majority of our ancient civilizations lived in isolation. An 11th century protestant farmer living in a small village in today's Eastern Germany probably had never heard of Zen Buddhism. The average Sunni Muslim living in 18th century Ankara, Turkey probably had never heard of Taoism. Vice-versa, etc. But in today's world, the vast majority of people are knowledgeable of different faiths. This knowledge and exposure is mainly because of religious war. The one small benefit we have from hate. A benefit we can build on to produce vast amounts of Light.

Mainstream Muslims, Jews, and Buddhists have at least heard of Christmas, The Vatican, and Easter. Mainstream Christians have at least heard of Hanukkah, Synagogues, Ramadan, Halal, and The Haj. Even a polytheist and a monotheist can learn from each other. This spiritual knowledge opens the empathetic aspects of our thoughts. We momentarily consider another point of view. As we evolve, through exposure and knowledge, we eventually reflect and start asking ourselves

> *"Aren't we all praying to "The God of Love" for blessings from "God through Love" and "God as Love" to feel "God is Love"?".*

Living next to each other, side-by-side, is not "Living as One". In today's societies, many of us have the situation that "in my house we practice this, next door they practice that, and across the street they practice another thing". This is also not living as One. This is living side-by-side in tolerance.

One area of the world where this is seen is in The Middle East. Muslims, Christians, and Jews are fighting for dominance in the same region. All three faiths descend from The Prophet Abraham (In the 7th century BC: Abraham was the first Hebrew Father. His great-grandson Judah initiated Judaism. In the 1st century A.D.: Jesus Christ led a sect within Judaism that became known as Christianity. In the 7th century AD: Islam recognizes all of the ancient Jewish and Christian prophets, of which Mohammed is considered the last in this lineage). For this reason, they are called The Abrahamic Religions. The conflicts that we see being played out there are like three triplets fighting each other. The Jewish triplet fights against the Muslim triplet and tries to manipulate the Christian triplet. The Muslim triplet fights back against the Jewish triplet and Christian triplet. The Christian triplet mistrusts the Jewish triplet and is afraid of the Muslim triplet becoming too strong – so, he tries to get his two brothers to make peace. However, with all of this constant fighting, hate, and back and forth conflict going on, the triplets forget that they are, in fact, tied at the hip. They are tied together, back to back. Each triplet struggles and fights to break free from their two brothers, but, in fact, their elbows and knees are tightly bound together. Their spiritual bonds are actually much deeper than if they were tied by rope. These three triplet brothers are Siamese. They even share the same mind and the same heart.

Spiritual lineage is not new. It does not exist only in The Abrahamic religions. The White Brotherhood, Satya Sai Baba, and Siddha Shiva yoga are some examples of how spiritual guides have a continuation for the people practicing these techniques. The Dalai Lama himself is a very clear example of a spiritual lineage. To Buddhists, he is today's representation of The Buddha himself – The Buddha himself who has incarnated into different physical forms throughout the ages. In Catholicism, The Pope is also part of a spiritual lineage.

Living as One is not only physical or geographical, in its truest sense, it is spiritual… and is ultimately global. When we begin breaking down the borders within our religions, between our religions, and between Spirituality and Science, we will start to Live as One. By bringing together the knowledge we have gained from spirituality and the various sciences into new, synergistic techniques, we start creating ways that their combined benefits can be used to help this world better connect to The Universe we live in. We begin by applying this new knowledge not only in our prayers, but also to our daily thoughts and actions. When applied to anything, knowledge is power. However, the knowledge gained from scientific poly-spirituality is Dynamic Power, because it originates from an open heart, global thought, and Universal Transcendence. That is the realm where no one and nothing is left out.

Today, we are in the final stages of "The Age of Religion". It has nothing left to teach us. More and more people are reaching out to each other. More and more of us are looking past race, religion, sex, and sexuality. Our faith in God has opened our hearts. The intermingling of The Abrahamic religions shows us that, in general, Christians are waiting for The Messiah to return, Muslims are practicing purification rituals, and Jews are waiting for The Messiah to return AND practicing purification rituals. All three are inter-connected. So, what are we fighting about? Awakening The Messiah of Light within us is the goal we all share.

There is still time to start a new beginning in "The Age of Light". We are about to begin a new chapter of human evolution. But even though we are not quite yet at that dynamic, Universal, "Living as One", global-society, we are already very far down the road. Many of us have already found ways to turn our pain into power. In regards to some degree of an international, inter-religious world faith, the seeds for it have been planted. One beautiful example of this was The Inauguration of Pope Francis (March 2013). Dozens of various religious leaders were in attendance, and the world saw the example of the new Pope's respect for other faiths.

There are many signs that we are building this society from the knowledge we already possess. New treatments in medicine, for example, where we combine technology with spirituality are quickly emerging.

Yes, there are seeds sprouting up all around us. Overcoming our complacency and fear gives water those seeds. The paired mantras we learn about in the third section of this book will shine sunlight onto those seeds. And the joy, abundance, and peace that we emanate in our lives will be the fruit that those seeds bear.

From our own collective knowledge, we are building a faith that unites us. Already, we have the mystical tools and divine techniques around us. Already, we have the transcendent knowledge and spiritual exposure within us. We are already becoming the renewed, re-born spiritual beings we were meant to be in our adult lives.

Looking at our world media, it seems that humankind is in a very dark place. But, within, we are advancing at a spiritual rate faster than we ever have! As spiritually and scientifically aware adults, we are consciously returning to the transcendent and bewondered state we spent the first few years of our lives as. We are rebuilding a renewed faith in our own collective evolution and are taking steps that are unifying our spiritual paths. Through this, we are gaining new knowledge of other paths that are complementary to our own. So, Yes… we ARE very far down the road!

Fear and religious war have given us a bad introduction to the beauty found in all spiritual disciplines. It is like when you meet someone and have a bad first impression. But after a while, if you are open, you will get to know them, see where they live, meet their parents, and have a nice dinner together. Once you "break bread", often your attitude and prejudices change. At least you have been exposed to their world… and they have been exposed to your world. In an environment of friendliness, kindness, and sharing, we are more open.

Once you have gone to their house, you invite them to your house. You show them around and break bread with them. Then your friendship improves. However, the ultimate beauty of your friendship is when you go back to their house and there is a picture of both of you on their fireplace mantle, and they have prepared one of the dishes they ate at your place. Then when they come back over to your house, there is a different photograph of you and your friend and some books they gave you as a gift. The food, photographs, and books are signs you both have changed and have benefited from the exchange.

In most all other areas of our lives, we are quite varied and inclusive in our thinking and attitude. For example, in our diet, we seek out a variety of foods; starches, meats, vegetables, fruit, dairy products, etc. Even a vegetarian needs a variety of foods. Our bodies need a variety of foods. We can also see this need for variety in our homes. We want a living room, a kitchen, a bedroom, closet space, and a bathroom (preferably with a jacuzzi tub!). We wouldn't even move into a studio if all it had was a living room and no place to cook or a toilet. In our elementary, middle, and high schools, we learn a variety of subjects; mathematics, science, reading, writing, art, and geography. Even in our universities, we are required to study a variety of topics to attain whatever degree we want. Look at our cellular phones, the books we have, the films and TV-shows we watch, our music collection, our clothes, etc. We want things, but we want the variety within those things more.

However, when it comes to religion… that way of abundant thinking *stops*. For everything else in our lives, we are VERY open – but, when it comes to developing our relationship with the One Source of Universal Abundance itself, we are often very closed. For most of us, when it comes to our spirituality, it is one thing and one thing ONLY. But, ask yourself, if God is so varied and abundant in your food, in your clothes, in Nature, and in your CD collection, why would he be scarce and singular in your spirit? "Amen", "Tao", "Allah", "Om", and "AUM" are keys to unlocking The Universe. They are mantras mankind has empowered with Transcendent Love. In defense of how we have been raised, we are quick to say "Well, God IS abundant on my path!". But, hopefully, this book will show us how our spiritual paths are complementary. Based on the mantra's own root definition, some of our religions have a strong transcendent lunar aspect, other religions have a strong abundant solar aspect – so much so, that when we consciously align two of them, we can evoke an Inner Eclipse.

But, why are we closed? We all desire for a more robust and transcendent relationship with Divine Consciousness, but what is blocking us from accepting and incorporating alchemic information from every corner of our existence? The reason is because of conditioning and fear. Fear of going to Hell and fear of being ostracized or excommunicated. Fear keeps us in line. Fear keeps us controlled. Fear keeps us predictable. Yet, God is un-predictable. God is free. God is dynamic. In today's world, religious wars, combined with the 24-hour News TV-channels, paralyzes much of our spiritual advancement. Instead of the variety and abundance we want in everything else, the spiritual region of our mind is mixed with hate and fear. It blocks the strong inner possibilities of how spiritual diversity can induce strength and of how religious diversity can induce Peace.

As for our conditioning, our genes have inherited a lot of our fears. Our lives today would be very different had our ancestors had a more open mind. To a large extent, the world we live in now is a result of the actions, thoughts, fears, and habits of our predecessors. They were our teachers. We inherited their prominent fears. These fears are reinforced by our habitual thoughts. Anxieties have become intertwined with our DNA – making many of us act out the genetic fears we feel in our body. Fear has been a big part of the world we have created. But still, the result we have created now is NOT the only result that was possible. But, even more importantly, our world's future can be changed for our next generations with Light.

Imagine our ancestors and spiritual leaders – ON BOTH SIDES OF ANY RELIGIOUS WAR – had had a more open mind when they encountered a culture with different customs and faiths. Imagine spiritual curiosity, not domination, was their driving force. Imagine their motivating factor was their own thirst for divine knowledge and universal enlightenment. Yes, there have been many invasions. Invasions for slaves, goods, material wealth, and territory. But, for a moment, imagine those invaders came looking for different interpretations and new knowledge of God to incorporate into their own spiritual practices. Imagine when they landed on some distant shore, they asked questions on why and how the people in this undiscovered civilization prayed… and vice-versa, the inhabitants asked them questions and watched how they prayed and interpreted the Nature of The Divine Mind. Imagine both sides listening to the other side with intent, interest, and openness. If this had happened in our history, more often than not, we would be living in a totally different world today.

Eventually, spiritual curiosity does occur. Eventually, questions about the spiritual practices of other cultures do get asked. But, it has never been the motivating factor. It was rarely the reason our ancestors built boats and weapons. The Romans, The Ottomans and Alexander, The Great, though they conquered lands of various faiths, their motivating factor was dominance and power. Even for Christian Missionaries today, the motivating factor is Righteous Dominance. "Righteous", meaning "One Faith". "Dominance", meaning "One Focus".

At times, our explorers set sail for dominance, but encountered unexpected transformation. These are times in our history when we have collectively broken through many internal barriers, even though we were initially looking for something else. Consider the story of Christopher Columbus's trip to America. When he landed in The Caribbean Islands, he wanted to enslave the people he encountered. His motivation was take their gold and use them as "good servants" to be "subjugated and made to do what is required of them". He felt that Mohama ("Mohammed" or Islam) was the "enemy of Catholic Christians". But, in other ways, what Columbus experienced was far beyond the gold and slaves he wanted to bring back to Spain. First of all, as he was getting his ship, crew, and cargo prepared, people constantly told him the world was flat. They warned him he would fall off the edge. But, he came back from the abyss with indigenous West Indian Tribesmen that he presented to the Queen. That must have been shocking not only to the Spanish, but also to the Native Caribbean Americans who were introduced to the Spanish elite. It had to have been a mind-exploding experience – for everyone, where both sides went into "the unknown" and then came back to tell the tale. Even from a visual angle, it was an eye-opening experience for everyone involved. Whether it was the few white Spaniards that went into the predominantly brown West Indian community, or the few brown West Indians that were brought back to Spain. The dress, the food, the language – all shocking. Everyone that took part in or even heard of this years-long, multi-voyage interchange had their world shaken. It was an unforgettable and unimaginable mind-altering encounter for both sides. Imagine the many fire-side stories the West Indian Tribesmen told their people when they got back of what they saw and experienced in Barcelona and Seville! Imagine how excited they felt, after being months away from their families, of finally landing back on their land. Imagine how excited Columbus felt to introduce them to King Ferdinand and Queen Isabella. All sides of this story are good examples of how Columbus, The West Indians, and The Spaniards inadvertently triggered spiritual curiosity and multiplicative joy.

But again, Divine Knowledge was not King Ferdinand's motivating factor then… But, it can be ours now. When all sides are open to learning about Universal Intelligence and how its laws work and affect our lives, we consciously incorporate a bit of what we learn from them and they consciously incorporate a bit of what they learn from us. When we have this mindset, there is no reason for dominance or to start a religious war. This idea of invading and conquering has led to the hate that has been passed down from generation to generation. Instead of being taught inclusion, we have been programmed to think exclusion. On this path of exclusion, we don't thirst for knowledge… we thirst for blood. And what has been the result of remaining on this path of exclusion? Revenge, murder, rape, imprisonment, terrorist attacks, mass graves, chemical weapons, drones, a refugee crisis, war, destruction, hate, fear, families torn apart, bombs, displaced communities, lost generations, abandonment, shattered lives, and countries ruined. Wasn't there… and isn't there… another more peaceful and mutually abundant way?

Whether it was our ancestors then or is us now, a more open mind would have saved and would still be saving countless lives. But, what is an open mind? What is a closed mind? How do minds open? And what are they opening to?

When we say someone has an open mind, it is, at first, given and taken as flattery. We love to hear someone tell us "You have a very open mind". It is a complement that speaks to our intellect and understanding, as well as to our empathy and feelings. It says that we are free from patterned conditioning. In some circumstances, when we are told we have an open mind, it can penetrate our thoughts deeper than hearing someone telling us "I love you". When we hear it, we reflect on ourselves in a positive and deeply universal way. Even though wonderful, "I love you" is another person's feelings about you. To hear "You have a very open mind" means your actions and words have triggered a succession of mind-expanding thoughts in the eyes of another person. That person has compared what you say and do to the many other people they have met in their lives. It means that, even though something you have said or done is normal to you, to them, the way you conduct your life, the way you reason, and the way you look at the world… is not.

The mind and the heart take us everywhere. It is from the way we think, feel, and reason that determine how we process the life experiences that happen to us. More important than reason, and deeply connected to our feelings, is our central thought – the central thought of who we are as a person. All other actions we do are connected to it. Our lives support and reinforce our central thought. It is like the center spoke of a wheel. We have reiterated our self-idea so many times – to ourselves and to others – that it has penetrated into our subconscious mind. From there, it seeps down to our conscious mind, our thoughts, our actions, and our words. If we feel we are victims within, and it is confirmed by the environment we see around ourselves, our thoughts and actions will strongly reflect that in our words and actions – even if we have a well-paid or important position. If we spiritually believe we are a king or a queen, and we believe that to be confirmed in the environment we see around ourselves, our level of consciousness and our actions will reflect that as well.

Our environment is a strong factor in supporting our central thought. Why do people advise us to get a college degree? A college degree, a job, and a home, changes our environment. Family and friends also change our environment. If we truly believe that we "have loving and robust support from family and friends", then many of their actions and words will help support our central thought. Our central thought has a cascading/domino effect on how we view the world and act in it. If we have a low self-esteem, it seems that a constant flow of new positive, successful experiences and the facing and overcoming of challenges will help change it.

Our central thought changes from situation to situation because it is not one thought, but a group of thoughts we have about ourselves when we are in different situations. It is as if one main central thought predominates the others when we are in various situations. Cooking, driving, singing, and drawing are some things that can trigger different central thoughts concerning our abilities. Even people can trigger our central thoughts. We can have one central thought for our father and a totally different central thought for our mother.

Our spirituality, too, is connected to our central thoughts. If fear, hate, or arrogance are intertwined with our spirituality, it will help your spiritual evolution if it is re-examined. Fear, hate, and arrogance are impure. They block our spiritual growth. Knowledge enriches us. Knowledge tears down walls. Spiritual knowledge enlightens us. God himself is multi-faceted and universal. As our central thought ascends closer the universal plurality that The Father-Mother God is, then our life becomes filled with non-judgement. Judgement keeps us blocked. Non-judgement sets us free.

As with anything, when we change and intensify the thoughts we have about something, we change its power in our lives - good or bad. Changing and intensifying our central thoughts about spirituality can lead us to more transcendence, more joy, more abundance, and light. Our new central thoughts are already inside us, we are just not used to using them. With a bit of knowledge and practice, they are re-activated. It is just a matter of finding the right key that turns the ignition. The right central thought that starts our engine. Similar to having a key ring with 20 different keys, we keep trying a different key until we find the one that opens the door to our true abundance.

This book is about analyzing the five different keys we have been polishing throughout this Age of Religion. The Age we live in now. These five keys are the five mantras we use to use amplify our prayers - "Om", "Allah", "Amen", "Tao", and "AUM". We not only examine these keys individually, but also when they are paired. These twelve key combinations are available to all of us. They unlock the immense power that can change our central thoughts and intensify our prayers. The keys we've discovered in this Age of Religion are the keys we will use in our new lives, living in the Age of Light.

The Role of Religion

Religions are undoubtedly an integral part of our human societies. Collectively, we have put a lot of time, effort, and money into them. We follow them for many reasons; Inner Peace, a place in Heaven after our death, or a better understanding of how to conduct our lives in harmony with the Universe are some. However, many people believe that religions are a waste of time and have been the sole cause of human destruction. They focus on the pain and suffering it has caused. Others say that the answer is no religion at all. And a few believe we should all just strive for oneness with Nature. None of these people are necessarily atheist. They want inner peace and an understanding of The Universe, as well. Often, the main difference between a follower of a religion and someone who is not is that the religious follower chooses to adhere to a fixed, laid down plan. Others choose to adhere to the freedom of their spirit and to the fluidity of Nature. The former chooses the institute. The latter chooses the instinct. Both, however, want to achieve many of the same goals.

Atheists often tell people to give up their faith, but this patronizes them and may even insult their culture and intelligence. Telling someone this is as if we know better about what they should do with their own lives than they do. Yes, it is true that many people have lost their homes, countries, and lives because of religion. But, it can also be said that, in a small way, our religions have been windows to beauty, Divinity, and the most sublime dimensions of ourselves.

Through our religions, we have added a lot of knowledge and Light to our collective consciousness. From here, on the physical plane, humanity has done a lot of work on the spiritual plane. Why are some of the happiest people those that seem to be open to expanding their knowledge and spirituality? The simple reason is because Light is food for the spirit. Through light, we gain knowledge. Through light, we expand. And through light, we feel joy.

The collective consciousness works in two ways; we feed it and it feeds us. The basic component of abundance, knowledge, joy, and transcendence is Light. Without Light, none of them would exist. Happiest are those who learn with Light, who learn of Light, who incorporate Light into their lives, and who are hungry for more Light in their lives.

Religions (like Christianity, Islam, Hinduism, and Judaism) and Spiritual practices or "Ways of Life" (like Buddhism and Taoism) don't look like they are going away anytime soon. They are some of the main components in this "Age of Faith and Religion" we are in now. Religious thought and spiritual practice have been established norms – in every new and ancient society – for the last few thousand years.

Atheists, scientists, writers, and iconoclasts often believe that the way forward is to completely give up all religions. That they have been nothing but a waste of time. They overlook the spiritual good they have brought into the world, and that to do so would mean to negate the highest aspirations we have put into our collective consciousness. How far and universally deep has an iconoclast gone into our global religions to say that they are useless?

Focusing on the purest, most non-judgmental aspects of our religion will bring out the purest, most non-judgmental aspects of ourselves. Not even our religious leaders follow everything in our spiritual textbooks. In all of the Divine Books, we are reading a wide number of contributions that have been added by various people over several decades. Like an excavator, we just need to look for the best that our faith can teach us today – The diamonds. A pure diamond would not awaken our fear. But still, some of the newest "spiritual doctrines" instill fear by declaring the impending doom of an Armageddon or an invasion Mars. Do these fears evoke Light? Why in other doctrines is the follower told he or she is part of a "secret society" or one of "God's chosen"? Is this the path of Truth… or does it lead to judgement of others? Why do certain religious groups condone excommunication? Does this path reflect The Abundant Universal Mind that cannot excommunicate anyone or anything?

On the opposite side of this same theory, is instead of the impending doom from a Martian invasion, many people believe we will, one day, gain knowledge from super-intelligent aliens who will come to the Earth and save us from ourselves. One side of the spectrum says that aliens will destroy humankind – or even the Earth itself, while the other side of the spectrum says that aliens will use their unique, super-intelligent, and mind-dazzling powers to tell us what we need to do to bring about Peace, abundance, and purification on our planet. Some people even believe that these aliens are already here – living among us. Those who believe this point to caves where alien-like depictions are painted on its walls. "Who were these people that our ancients made these drawings of?". Some point out the UFO sightings that get filmed each month by NASA – and even the ones that get accidently filmed by ordinary people – as evidence of intelligent extraterrestrial life forms. Theories abound of aliens having built The Pyramids, by using various powers to lift, polish, and put into place a pyramid's large and precisely-cut stones. Other people are convinced that space men burned Crop Circles into a number of British fields and were responsible for The Nazca Lines in Peru, as they all can only be seen from the sky. All of these extraterrestrial signs here on Earth open our minds to wonder about other life forms in the Universe – and if we are truly, in fact, alone. Many people are waiting for aliens to come down and share their infinite knowledge with us, so that mankind can be saved from its own self-destruction.

Well!... Yes, it is certainly possible that beings from The Pleiades, Sirius, and other "more evolved" E.T. life-forms may have visited Earth... but, one thing those who live in hope for an alien-intervention need to ask themselves is "If I am not open enough to accept spiritual knowledge from a Muslim, a Jew, or a Hindu... Then how am I going to be open enough to accept spiritual knowledge from a Martian?". In other words, are we even ready for this super-intelligent information? Have we even prepared ourselves with the universal knowledge we have from other human beings who look exactly like we do and even speak our own language? Are we in the habit of trading Divine Thought planetarily, to prepare us for trading

Divine Thought inter-planetarily? If you believe that aliens are, in fact, observing us, do you show yourself to be open to their superior intelligence?

For space beings to have evolved to the point of being able to fly across galaxies in UFOs, they had to have attained an incredible amount of logic. The logic in humanity's spiritual evolution needs to be provoked with questions, such as "Doesn't my spiritual filter have to first be deeply developed by the spiritual knowledge of a Christian, a Taoist, and a Buddhist before it can process the supposedly superior knowledge of a Siriusian or a Pleiadean?".

Believe it or not, when we look, we can see that we Earthlings have built a vast amount of uncompiled spiritual knowledge. We have the makings for a Universal Library here on Earth. A library for all, devoted to spirituality, Divinity, and techniques in Transcendence. Since many people believe that aliens have the ability to visit us here on Earth, they also have to believe that aliens have the ability to visit other life-forms throughout the galaxies. Surely, it was not just one-stop they made. In whatever way a UFO flew here, the fuel it used had to have been inexhaustible. In our Universe, there is only one inexhaustible fuel – Divine Consciousness. And there is only one filling station to get that fuel – The Divine Mind. These aliens either came looking for spiritual knowledge or came to share spiritual knowledge. If they had come to dominate or destroy us, as our human ancestors did when they travelled to far away regions, then we wouldn't be alive today – nor would we still have our free will.

The fact that extraterrestrial life forms may have left traces of their visits, should show us that we need to evolve. Again, we have built a vast amount of spiritual knowledge. The way we have developed the five world mantras demonstrates our own unique power. These mantras show ourselves and each other how we are able to penetrate The Divine Consciousness through thought, faith, and Love. Each day, billions of people are able to shake "The Universal Tree of Transcendent Abundance" with our human mind. Prayer, affirmations, and lists are some of the techniques countless people use every day. By shaking this tree, ripe and luscious apples fall all around us when we become adept at consciously doing it.

Waiting for higher knowledge from more evolved life forms is a wonderful idea – but, we need to first evolve ourselves planetary before anything interplanetary can happen. The most useful knowledge that aliens can share is what they have learned about and from The Divine Mind. We all come from the same God – The same Dynamic Consciousness that created ourselves, our world, and everything in existence. If aliens had the ability to leave their planet to fly all the way across the galaxy to land here on Earth, then (at the very least) that means that they are an intelligent life-form with a conscious ability to search and reflect. These capacities were surely used to build their connection to the unborn and undying transcendent realm that exists in both of our worlds. They've obviously discovered things that we haven't yet. That is knowledge we can use – when we're ready. Like them, we also use our capacities to search and reflect in order to build a dynamic relationship with Divine Intelligence. We are powerless to do anything about any other information an alien would share; for instance, if they have wars going on back on their planet or even if they live in some sort of Utopia. How would that help us much here on Earth if they told us that the 247 trillion people on their planet – 500 light years away – were being engulfed by a Black Hole?

Again… if an alien life-form has made the space trip all the way here to our tiny-little planet Earth, then an exalted type of spiritual knowledge would be their greatest resource. To navigate, calculate, travel, perceive, and even to build an alien spacecraft itself… all required the ability to access Pure Light and Pure Sound. Unbeknownst to most Earthlings, spiritual knowledge is also our greatest resource. The titanium we build into our human space ships can only take us so far – and it can only do so much. Pure Thought goes further, and can take us to the edges of our Universe. So, to evolve higher, we need to look deeper. We need to find the realm of abundance that is deeper than our own narcissism. When we see the one dynamic Eternal being within us all, we fill our hearts with that alchemic, inexhaustible fuel. Evolving past our sexism, racism, and territorialism brings us to see this Transcendent Reality. Resonating with our Divine Virtues takes us past our homophobia, Islamophobia, and anti-Semitism to where we can access the Pure Consciousness within every-one and every-living thing. This transcendent fuel fills our resources when we lose our need to stigmatize and marginalize others. It gives us a boost when we rise above these tendencies. This is the book of spiritual knowledge we are writing from here on Earth. A book we can proudly place into the shelves of God's Library. The power of transcendent thought is the theme of this Universal Library – and we have done a vast amount of research on this subject right here on our planet. This is one of the many exalted things that mankind can share or confirm with the other life-forms existing throughout our galaxies.

When we realize the blessing of being alive, on Earth, and in human form, our souls take us past the point of needing to feel we are chosen. We no longer feel we can be excommunicated. We no longer need to belong to a secret society.

Beyond excommunication and beyond a secret society, we trigger more light by remembering where all people have a common thread and the many basic Universal Laws we all share. Consider the women of the world. The mothers who carried and gave birth to us all. They are our physical portals between the un-manifested consciousness and the manifested reality. Women exist on every level of society and in every area of our world. Whether a woman is black, white, Asian, or Latino, she is reminded - once a month - of her connection to Divinity and her purest potentiality to produce life. Women are one of our commons thread and are an intricate part of many Universal Laws.

By being born human here on Earth, we all incarnated with a spiritual toolbox. When we look into those toolboxes, we see that most of the "wrenches", "pliers", and "screwdrivers" are the same. These tools are useful to each and every one of us, and can open us to the highest realms of ourselves. They enrich our connection to Divine Intelligence. There are a few tools pertaining to our talents and capacities that differentiate the toolboxes. However, the universal tools come in all of them. They are like the basic toolset – For everyone, no matter what race, religion, sex, or sexuality you are. If you were born a human being here on Earth, then you've got a set of these "Tools of Divinity".

Throughout our human history, we have used these tools to send countless thoughts and ideas into our collective consciousness. The collective consciousness is a library of thought - both good and bad. Scientific and spiritual. In comparison to our scientific thought, our religious thought collectively outweighs our thoughts on rocket science, mathematics, or anything we have developed or invented. Collectively, we probably have spent more time thinking about God than we have of food or drink. This has become the divine contributions to our collective consciousness. Divine thought is more inspired than ordinary thought because the mantras we use in our prayers and meditations come from the deep aspirations of our hearts. Mantras evoke Light and amplify our thoughts. Like a golden chariot, they carry our prayers into the fields of pure potentiality.

Religions are nothing to be frowned upon. Rather, they are like magnifying glasses that help focus the thoughts to and from the one God we all pray to. They encourage our connection to The Divine Intelligence we all want to understand. They've shown us techniques we hope will trigger blessings to our problems. Our churches, synagogues, mosques, and temples are full of spiritual energy that we have put there. Our thoughts, prayers, love, and aspirations fill all of our temples of worship with Divine Energy. And from these focused and concentrated places, we send and receive thoughts to and from Universal Consciousness - both individually and collectively.

The magnifying glass is a good metaphor for religion. When you look at one from one side, things seem smaller – and when you look at it from the other side, things appear bigger. In our temples of worship, we do the same thing with God. For example, in a mosque, a Muslim praying alone can send his thoughts to Divinity (from small to big). As well, he can receive thoughts and inspirations from Divinity itself (from big to small). Again, as human beings, we are both receptors and transmitters. Through the "magnifying glass-aspect" that the mosque has become, both directions have been activated from the Divine Energy we have empowered it with. Churches, synagogues, temples, and shrines are the same. Compared to a home or even Nature, temples of worship are highly charged places, specifically used to connect us with our own Divinity. The decorations, the symbolism, the mantras, and the mysticism all add to their highly charged attributes. Human beings are the only species we know of who build complexes to specifically enhance their communications with Divine Intelligence.

As devoted spiritualists, who are following a religious path, one thing we all have in common is a desire for more. More, in the sense of improved. More, in the sense of better. More, in the sense of a more purified body, more purified thoughts, and more purified actions to better. When we improve, we are better able to communicate with The Universal Mind. A practicing spiritualist has the desire for a clearer and more refined relationship with God. Tools and rituals to help us transform are wide and varied. Hindus have The River Ganges. Christians have communion. Muslims have Ramadan. And, Buddhists have meditation… Seen in this way, the desire for spiritual or physical purification is our central thought when we practice a religion.

Because there are so many purification practices with the same common goal, we can choose to incorporate the knowledge we have learned from our own path with new wisdom and new techniques we gain from our study of other paths. In this way, we don't lose anything, rather we gain more. We gain "the more" we seek from following a religious path. This purifies our hearts in multitude ways. We add knowledge and Light. We incorporate understanding and compassion. Our aura expands from the knowledge we are putting into practice. The wheel of joy and abundance starts turning all by itself.

There is a difference between the knowledge we have. In general, we have passive knowledge, active knowledge, and no knowledge. No one knows everything about everything. But, many of us do know something about many things. A great many things about a few things. Nothing about a great many things. Passive knowledge is when we know something about a great many things. Passive knowledge is powerful, but can only take you so far. Active knowledge is knowing a great many things about a few things. It is when a person is really involved in something. For example, most of us have passive knowledge about bread. But a baker has an active knowledge about it. Doctors, lawyers, pharmacists, and Tennis instructors all have an active knowledge we desire at times.

When a person is directly working with something, they gain active knowledge about it. They are spending a lot of their time, energy, and thoughts in the subject you are talking to them about. Any topic of conversation from politics, to cooking, to music, to 18th century Spanish writers… When the person you are talking to is actively involved in practicing or studying the subject, they are animated and full of knowledge and light. They are interested and interesting. They can often simplify many complicated theories for us. Their subject has become a part of who they are, giving them the ability to express their passion through their own words and ideas. That is one reason why "Knowledge is Power". We all see the difference between someone who is passionate about a subject and someone who is not. In spirituality, when we expand our habits and practices, we activate active knowledge. When we incorporate various techniques from the world's various spiritual discoveries, our active knowledge is triggered. Active knowledge is not only for bakers and doctors, it is also for spiritualists. Even in the realms of faith, we can apply it without feeling we are losing anything (except our prejudice and fear). Rather, we feel we are gaining more!

Active knowledge not only encompasses subjects, but it also covers experience. When we've experienced something, we've gained active knowledge of it. Compare a donator to charity to a peacekeeper in an organization. The donator donates time or money out of empathy. But, the peacekeeper has an active knowledge that goes beyond empathy. Empathy does not empower us. It might encourage us to act – But, it does not empower us with hands-on knowledge. People who donate money to organizations to help famine struck regions have a different knowledge than the peacemakers who have been to the region itself. Empathy takes us to the middle ground between passive knowledge and active knowledge. However, the problem of empathy is that it can be manipulated by the information that it is given or that the mind chooses to take in. If we only read left-wing liberal magazines, then our empathy will probably be based on left-wing liberal ideas. As in war, we feel empathy when one of our own soldiers die – but, feel nothing when an enemy soldier dies. Even for a war's fallen civilians and innocent children, we often also feel a divided empathy.

All of the warmongers of our world have ignorance or, at best, some particles of passive knowledge. Warmongers on both sides of a war operate from revenge, fear, and hate. How the Master Buddha came into enlightenment, is an example of how the power of active knowledge can transform our lives. After years of living as a prince in a palace, Buddha's curiosity took him into a nearby village where he saw people who got sick, people who aged, and people who died. These few experiences of active knowledge transformed him, to where he was determined to find a spiritual solution that transcended the deterioration of Life.

With just a few grains of active spiritual knowledge, those on all sides of a religious war can gain respect for other faiths and evoke the Light we need to create world peace. The first result of this is peace within ourselves. This kind of active knowledge leads to understanding and compassion. There can be no fear when there is understanding, and there can be no understanding when there is fear.

Since we have all put so much effort into our religious paths for so many millennia, maybe we can use some of the knowledge we have gained to help ourselves collectively evolve? The five mantras we sprinkle our prayers with - "Om", "Amen", "Allah", "AUM", and "Tao" - amplify our communion and communication with The Universal Mind. Again, there is a difference between saying "Thank you, God, for this food" and saying "Thank you, God, for this food. Amen". Through thought, love, and joy, billions of faithful souls have empowered these five mantras for thousands of years. Not only that, when we immerse ourselves in their meanings, they all are seen to have come from the same supreme and highest realms of Divine Consciousness. Each of them are gifts that we should be GRATEFUL for having manifested in our material world. Studying their root meanings reveals the beauty and uniqueness of each.

In this book, there are five mantras to explore. You are probably already well familiar with one of them. When we know more about them all, we will see how they each shine Light onto different aspect of our soul.

Each of these words has taken countless people to unimaginable heights of spiritual ecstasy. We cannot negate the work so MANY souls have done before us…and so many souls continue to do. They all take us to the same realm of Higher

Love. Buddhists and Hindus have repeated "Om" with Love. Taoists have repeated "Tao" with Love. Hasidic and Orthodox Jews have repeated "AUM" with Love. Sunni and Shiite Muslims have repeated "Allah" with Love. And Baptist, Lutheran, Protestant, Catholic, Orthodox, Methodist, and Evangelical Christians have repeated "Amen" with Love.

Because of all this faith, love, and joy, we have empowered these words. If we look without judgement, we can see that each word is a key to unlocking The Gates of Heaven. A place we unlock within ourselves where our human soul realigns with the eternal resonance of universal abundance and pure joy. Seeing, with an unbiased view, that each of these words are keys to Heaven, our thoughts are exalted and can connect to the same realm of Divine Consciousness. It's that realm of Higher Love that a Christian seeks, a Buddhist seeks, and a Muslim seeks. With an unbiased view, we evolve faster. We are able to use Om, Tao, AUM, Allah, and Amen as keys to our own evolution. It is our fear we lose... not our religion.

To bring their followers closer to God, religions, in part, teach disciples about the life, the spiritual advice, and/or the steps the saint took during their lifetimes. Apparently, when we practice and study how the saint lived during their lifetime, that will evoke Light and spiritual knowledge in ours. We assume that God will bless us with the same enlightenment that the saint him or herself knew. If this is so, then from where do all those fears that are attached to and perpetuated by our religions come? Where does the judgement that many religious leaders and followers originate? Where did we learn to hate while we were learning to love? The answer might be that these dark thoughts and habits we absorbed came from many of our misguided teachers and not from the saint. If we truly believe that the saint was filled with Divine Light, then hate could not have been any part of his or her being. The hate and judgement we picked up came from somewhere else. There are times when we see a saint get angry (Jesus in The Temple of Thieves), or when we see one get sad (Buddha's three excursions into the city), or when we see one get disgusted with the world (Lao Tzu leaving forever to the mountains before writing The Tao Te Ching) – But… these feelings ultimately transformed into a Light that is still pulsating today. To see a True Saint hate is impossible and to see one judge was probably confused with a lesson that was ultimately taught.

Again, we can trace the religious hate, fear, and judgement we have back to our misguided teachers. They are the source of it getting perpetuated throughout our pews, stools, and prayer mats. In short, we inherit The Light from The Saint and the fear from The Followers. When we are reaching for The Light with our ankles shackled with fear, we are stagnated. Our evolution is blocked. We do feel joy at times, but that joy is instantly changed whenever we see what we are taught to fear or hate. So, how true and deep is the joy we say we are feeling if it can be blocked?

There is an internet video of two adult male elk with their horns are locked together. They had apparently been fighting in a forest. At some time during their fight they had also gotten their 5-foot antlers entangled into the barbed wire fencing of a ranch. Their antlers were simultaneously interlocked with each other and intertwined with the barbed wire. Both elk were making loud cries that could be heard throughout the forest. Two brave ranchers heard the cries and came to rescue them. They wanted to help free these wild and distressed animals. Having seen the twisted mess between all four of the huge antlers, they brought wire-cutters and pliers with them. As they approached, the elk continued to struggle and charge at each other. The elk were fighting, but at the same time also trying to break free from the barbed wire. For the ranchers, it was risky. By getting close to the antlers of two confused elk, they could either be killed or maimed at any second. As the ranchers stepped closer, the elk continued struggling and pulling. For a few moments, the exhausted elk would stop and, bit by bit, the ranchers would cut one of the barbed wires. Surely, while the ranchers were cutting both the elk and the ranchers were scared – of each other! With each cut, the ranchers would have to immediately get out of the way, as they could either get stabbed, gorged, kicked, or trampled by an elk or slashed, cut, or whipped by a line of barbed wire. Finally, when one of the main inter-twisted wires was cut, one of the elk was suddenly free and immediately ran back into the forest. However, the other elk's antlers were still caught. He now seemed to pull even harder and wilder than before, as the ranchers still tried to free him. This situation was probably more dangerous than when the two elk were horn-locked. At one time, the lone elk pulled so hard his neck twisted and he fell to the ground. Both he and the ranchers were exhausted. But, the ranchers bravely approached the elk again and kept cutting the wires until... he was finally free to rise up and run back into the fields... and then back into the forest.

As for us, just like with the elk, the more fears we cut, the freer we are. What we hope will come our way is a rancher who helps free us and not one who lets us stay entangled. The more hate and judgement we eliminate, the more our vision opens. The faster our barbed wire is severed, the quicker we can rush back into the fields of pure consciousness.

In the third section, we will learn more about "The Twelve Paired Mantras" and the synergistic power they evoke within us. Each pairing takes us on a unique path into The Eternal Void – both in the way of how the pairing begins and how it ends. For example, two of them use Allah and Om together. When we are more familiar with the root meanings of both of these words, there will be a vast difference in saying "Allah-Om" and in saying "Om-Allah". With all of the pairings, our thoughts combine God as "The Eternal Field" and God as "The Cosmic Sound". With it, we see in one breath how our Universe is both "without beginning and without end" and "a universal resonance". Allah and Om together initiate a deep harmonic power rising within us. As we practice more with it, we feel the cells of our body change. We feel Light enter our hearts and expand the numerous chakras in our head. It is the same for the other eleven mantras; "Tao-Amen", "AUM-Allah", etc... The most important thing to remember is where these words take our thoughts, and what these words trigger by their root meanings. The Light we feel is because of the synergy we are consciously practicing and pondering. A paired mantra awakens a duality within us. The highest duality we know of the many ways man has contemplated The Divine Mind. Like an inner eclipse, two aspects of God align as one within.

The benefit of a paired mantra is that it takes our thoughts and prayers to new heights. We may never have even examined the root meaning of the mantra we habitually use, nor have ever even considered using it with another divinely empowered word. But, this book examines the five mantras first individually, then in two categories, and finally in the twelve pairs. Having an individual, categorized, and paired view on the five world mantras will help you find the combination that resonates best with you. It may not necessarily be the paired mantra that contains the mantra from your own religion. Their meanings, their definitions, and where they take our thoughts are what we should prioritize. Just _feel_ which one resonates most in your heart – and that will be the right one! No meaning in any of the paired mantras contain judgement or prejudice, so whichever one springs the most joy within you when you repeat it will be doing so from a pure place.

Listen to your body to feel which is best for you. Among many things, your paired mantra will become a teacher, a purifier, a pacifier, and a guide. You are opening a channel of Light between you and Divine Intelligence. As you climb, you evolve. Fears will subside, and walls will tumble. You will automatically re-build hundreds of bridges and roads throughout your inner world. You will slowly begin to lose judgement and pre-judgment, and will start to see "those people" you once were taught to hate as ones who have merely practiced seeing God in a complementary way to your own. Furthermore, when you mingle with "those people", they will surely inspire you to remember your new paired mantra. Moments of transcendent inspiration will come from the moon, the sun, any temple of worship, and "those people". As your thoughts open, they will search for inspired reasons to feel this resonance and Light again and again… Like a drug or an elixir, a paired mantra is addictive. It slowly seeps into your consciousness to where your body and mind are engulfed with bliss. Why? Because for you, you will be seeing and feeling Divine Consciousness in two ways. You will be consciously evoking a bit of each method to will feel transcendence from both The Lunar Path and The Solar Path. You cannot hate something you feel joy and inspiration from yourself. All twelve paired mantras form an inner eclipse; they bring our inner Moon and inner Sun into alignment.

Paired mantras help us consciously ascend. They help us quickly evolve back into the spiritual beings we were born as. The Light we were conceived from, though buried, is still there. We may know that it is dynamic. That it is transcendent. But, most importantly, we need to remember that it is still there. When we remember that and begin working with it, it starts to expand. We see the world in a new light because we see the world *with* a new light. We open our minds and empower ourselves when we see that God is both resonantly within every atom AND eternally pervading everything. With newer and clearer thoughts, we begin to understand that both The Eternal Field and The Cosmic Sound lead to the same Divine Source. With our paired mantra, we put two powerful tools into our hands – one is a hammer, the other is a chisel, and we are the sculptors.

One thing that we look to our religious leaders for is to interpret divine scripture for us. Most times these interpretations are explained in one way and then that one way is perpetuated over and over again… and, because of this, is eventually taken to mean the absolute truth. We should look at from what standpoint the perpetuated interpretation comes.

We often take the scriptures as purely literal. These literal interpretations do help us in practicing forgiveness, compassion, generosity, faith, Love, etc... We are taught to see God with the same human qualities we want to embellish in ourselves. People, who interpret scriptures literally, fall into the trap of giving God the same characteristics as we have ourselves. Like us, God is seen as vengeful, hateful, loving, wrathful, judgmental, compassionate, destructive, creative, prejudiced, scary, merciful, condemning, begrudging, and contemptible. If we don't toe the line, he will banish us or strike us down. For some, our sins will determine whether we will live a life of peace and will reach Paradise or live a life of torment and go to Hell. For others, our karma is the manifestation of the good and bad deeds of our past – even if these deeds come from our ancestors and have nothing to do with us. Beyond sin, how we consciously act is how we repent, and will determine if we live a life of peace or torment. Beyond karma, how we choose to respond now and react now to the circumstances that have come back to us will determine the present effect our actions from our past lives. Our reactions to our karma tell us how much purifying work we still have to do in our current life. What this book suggests is how an inclusive spiritual knowledge will help us purify exponentially. At the very least, a more broader view of The Divine Mind will intensify the purifying steps we take to eliminate our supposed sin or burn our returning karma.

When we are only focused on one path, it seems that God has more bad qualities than good. Inclusive spiritual knowledge and inclusive spiritual practice break this. Because even though the divine aspects of God are often mentioned, as humans we are apt to focus on the perceived bad aspects of God we have been taught; going to Hell, Armageddon, vengeance, persecution, etc... Because of the untrained mind's own propensity to focus on darker thoughts, we take fear instead of joy into our daily lives. In this state, we use our free will to perpetuate more hate, instead of using it to trigger more light. Our concept of how we see God operating in the world is a reflection based on how we feel him operating in our lives. If we are focused on darkness, fear, and hate, we will see hate, fear, and darkness. We will see sin. We will generate misfortune. Any fault or sign of distress is a confirmation of The Devil. But, rare is the person who can see blessings in misfortune. Rare is the person who can transform darkness into Light. We make lemonade from a lemon by first diluting it and then adding nectar. When someone can do this, what kind of karma does that person have? What kind of karma is that person generating?

When tragedy strikes, we look to our scriptures for answers. When we listen to many of our religious leaders, they often interpret the scriptures literally, instead of symbolically - or even mystically or poetically. For all of us, the answers we find are based on our own limited view of nature's mystery. But, how can we understand universal mysteries with only literal interpretations? Literal interpretations of Divine Books, combined with a view of God that is hateful, vengeful, and judgmental keeps us blocked. When these interpretations are constantly repeated and perpetuated, the followers of that religion stay blocked. Mystery reminds us of the dynamic aspect of The Divine Mind. Mystery and dynamics are catalysts in our evolution and spiritual growth. Do you see God the same way today as you did as a child… or even a year ago? This is one of the many benefits of keeping an Equinox Journal - to see how we've grown. To be witnesses of ourselves. To see right before our very eyes how our Equinox installments testify to our own spiritual evolution.

Our evolutional change directly corresponds to how we see God. Seen another way, the distance between ourselves and God corresponds to our own growth. God is unlimited and unconditional. The more we become unlimited and unconditional, the less distance we will have to God.

Ask yourself, is God looking down on the world, judging everyone from a cloud in Heaven, or is he/she within everything you see, every person you see, and in every cell of your being? Whether on the clouds of our Heavens or in the cells of our hearts, either place will generate different experiences to the spiritualist. It is up to each of us to decide which place to put him that is the more evolved, transcendent, and abundant.

For many people, how they see God is how they see Life. If, in our view, God hates something, some act, or someone, then we also have the liberty to hate the same. Literal interpretations have the danger of giving us permission to hate and judge. When we feel that God judges and hates, then we give ourselves license to judge and hate. The rest of this book investigates the transcendent power of "Love Thy Neighbor as Thine own Self.

If our Divine Books are to be read in a purely literal way, then how do they help us grow spiritually beyond our compassion and forgiveness? When God is, in your view, not only in every cell of your body but also in every cell of The Universe, God then takes on countless forms and dimensions. This God "rules" because He/She encompasses The Universe. Wherever you think God is, your mind will incorporate and encompass – whether it's from a cloud or through an all-pervasive vibrational realm throughout our Universe. Mind expansion. Growth. Evolution. Freedom. When Light replaces darkness, then judgement, fear, and hate fall away. As these erode, we merge with the One Light emanating within us all - regardless of faith or gender.

Again, we all come from and pray to the same God. We all exist in a powerful and mysterious Divine Mind we want to better understand. Even though we shake the spiritual apple tree differently, our merciful God lets some of his apples fall into our hands. It is for Love, as we are all created from his one dynamic Light. So... Would it make sense for God to hate himself? Even if he hated someone, where would he banish him?

Sacred books like The Koran, The Bible, The Talmud, The Bhagavad Gita, and The Tao Te Ching point to their own unique ways of seeing God and how we can experience him.

These books are divine because our interpretations of what we read change as we evolve. As we advance higher, the thoughts they trigger within us take us deeper. The words have more meaning. Again, we interpret their advice in the way we habitually see God in the world and experience him in ourselves. If we habitually see God as a dynamic, universal intelligence, then we will see this no matter what sacred book is placed in front of us.

What is sad is that many spiritual interpretations don't awaken sustained inner Light. If the only lesson to learn from a passage is an act of compassion or forgiveness, then the lesson is limited to situations that call for these acts. The teaching, at best, will advise us to do something sporadic to act out the lesson. If compassion or forgiveness is at the core, it means that we will need a situation outside of ourselves to act out this sacred teaching. We will have to first see suffering to act out compassion. We will have to first be wronged to act out forgiveness. There has to first be one act to trigger a second act. That is not a way to awaken sustained inner Light. Lessons from written spiritual doctrines are good when the whole passage is taken into account. When it is examined not only literally, but also symbolically, mystically, and poetically.

Light and understanding are evoked when we look at the *entire* verse, not just its ending or an excerpt of it. Viewing it as a whole, from different standpoints, helps to unlock its Truth. There is a true story that can be used to help illustrate the benefits of viewing a sacred text from different standpoints.

Two Interpretations of Mathew 25:34

Once there was a pastor who was going to start at a new parish. The congregation had not met him yet, only some of the administrators of the church had. The day he was expected to be introduced to his new assembly, he showed up dressed as a homeless man. He tried mingling with the church members, but they found him disgusting. He was disheveled and unwashed, as he was aimlessly wandering the church, talking to the members coming in, and sitting in various pews. The whole church was excited to meet their new pastor, as no one had yet seen him. But disguised as a homeless man, he saw that people thought he was a nuisance. As the church was filling up, he went around in asking people for money. Everyone refused to give him anything. People shunned and ignored him. If he sat near someone, they would move away from him or turn their backs. They all look down their noses at him. As the service was about to begin, he tried sitting in the front pew, but was asked to sit in the back. He was treated with contempt by the entire congregation.

Soon the mass began and it became time for the church to meet their new pastor. When the administrators announced his name, the disguised pastor walked from the back of the church, up to the front, and stood at the altar. People were shocked. Their mouths dropped. He then told the entire congregation what had happened to him that morning. How everyone treated him with such disdain. Both men and women in his parish were ashamed and many cried. He then read a passage from The Bible, walked off the podium, and left.

The passage he read to them was Matthew 25 :34.

Let's look at what this passage says and why it made so many devout men and women feel guilty and ashamed. The pastor apparently assumed that this would happen, otherwise he would not have gone through all of this trouble. It was a well-planned and well thought out scheme. So, let's look at his literal interpretation of this verse, and why it made his congregation cry.

Let us then compare this to another way of interpreting the same passage with a mystic, symbolic, and poetic point of view - a totally different interpretation of the same words. A way of viewing this verse with an eye on Divine Abundance as the source of ourselves and The Source of our Universe. One interpretation evokes tears and guilt, while the other interpretation evokes joy and abundance. Literal meanings are tangible meanings. Symbolic, poetic, and mystical meanings are intangible meanings. After reading the two differences, it will be for you to decide which triggers more growth for your Self.

The passage the pastor read to his congregation that day is a well-known Biblical story: "For I was hungry and you gave me something to eat..." (Matthew 25 :34).

Tangible Meaning:	Matthew 25 :34	Intangible Meaning:
Help the poor and unfortunate with money and acts of kindness		Remember your True Wealth (your inheritance) is Divine Abundance
A segregated interpretation that might awaken sporadic actions. It calls for a need before it can be implemented. Exclusive to a group.		An all-encompassing interpretation that opens The Third Eye. Sustained Inner Light and Transcendental knowledge are awakened universally
Christians.	*Come, you who are blessed by my Father...*	All human beings are blessed. Just to be alive, on Earth, and in human form, are we one of the blessed. Being born human, we are blessed.

(This part is ignored, left-out, or forgotten, as the word "Inheritance" can only mean something material.)	*Take your inheritance The Kingdom prepared for you since the creation of the world…*	The Kingdom is understood as Universal Intelligence. Divine Abundance and Transcendent Light is the inheritance that has existed and still exists since the creation of the world.
These are actions seen done by a compassionate person. Christians perform these selfless acts to act out God's Will and to be "Good Christians".	*For I was hungry and you gave me something to eat. I was thirsty and you gave me something to drink. I was a stranger and you invited me in. I needed clothes and you clothed me. I was sick and you looked after me. I was in prison and you came visit me…*	When we understand Universal Consciousness to be Pure Divine Abundance, then it will feed, nourish, befriend, and clothe us. When we see it as Transcendent Light, it will heal and comfort us. Divine consciousness is constantly nourishing us all. It sees our needs and fulfills them. It is all-pervasive, and would even be there if we were imprisoned. Divinity is constantly operating within and around us.
(Ignored, left-out, or forgotten - or, at best, seen as compassionate acts that Christians must remember to do for others).	*Then the righteous will answer him. 'Lord, when did we see you hungry and feed you, or thirsty and give you something to drink? When did we see you a stranger and invite you in, or needing clothes and clothe you?*	These are examples of those who are faithful, but have forgotten to remember their True inheritance – They are "The Righteous". We must overcome the blindness to our own Universal Abundance. The first step is to take it. To see that True Wealth is something non-material. To know that it is our birth right and to know that it is eternal.

True Christians must remember to look for opportunities to give to others. Good Christians remember to help others.	*When did we see you sick or in prison and go to visit you?...*	Before we can take anything, we have to first see it and realize that it is there. The Righteous are able to see the Lord revealing himself everywhere.
The King is speaking to Christians (The blessed and the righteous). Interpreted as meaning "We must help the poor and show compassion for those we feel are less fortunate than us". To be a good Christian you must clothe the homeless and feed the starving. No advice is given about where these people can find their own True wealth and Divine Abundance. In a subtle, yet evident way, there is confusion as to whether "My Father" in the first line and "'The King" in the last line are both meant to mean God? However, no King has ever blessed us with an "inheritance" "since the creation of the world" and God does not have "brothers and sisters". God has children, but not brothers and sisters. For this passage to make sense, "My Father" is God and a "King" is a King. A King is not God. Why would the spiritually righteous be concerned about helping the poor to please a King?	*The King will reply "Truly, I tell you whatever you did for one of the least of these brothers and sisters of mine, you did for me."*	The King is speaking to God (The Father). God is "The Father" at the beginning of this passage and the "you" here at the end of this passage. In this last line, a wealthy King is recognizing that he has a true inheritance from God and that "the least of his brothers and sisters" also have a true inheritance from God. A King is human being and can therefore have a brother or sister. God is eternal, and has no brother or sister. Rich or poor, we are the brothers and sisters of The King. To pass from being one of The Righteous to being a King or a Queen, we have to learn how to take the abundant inheritance The Father has prepared for us "since the creation of the world" – that is, since the beginning of Time. Universal Consciousness is able to fulfill the needs of us all.

Tangible Conclusion:	Combined Conclusion:	Intangible Conclusion:
Philanthropy is an important part of Christianity. By giving to those we see in need, we are acting as "Good Christians".	First remember your own True Source of Divine Abundance and Light. This unlimited source has been with us since the beginning of Time. It is within everyone who was ever and who will ever be born. Universal Consciousness provides for us all. Once we take our inheritance, we can then tap into our own divinity and help others without draining our own resources. As a giver, see yourself as a channel. Whether it is an object, money, or Light, remembering where its True Source comes from helps us transcend.	By remembering to take our Divine inheritance, all of our needs will be provided for. The needs of animals and insects are provided for by Universal Consciousness. All find food and shelter. None of God's creatures are forgotten. In this story, there is a correlation between the words "King" and "Kingdom". A King is someone who has taken their inheritance. The Kingdom is the inheritance itself. Universal Consciousness is the source of Divine Abundance. Universal Consciousness pervades everywhere, everyone, and everything. It sustains everyone, anywhere. Even if we are locked in a prison, God can come nourish us.

> When we are first connected to our True Inheritance, the act of giving becomes an act of prayer.
>
> *"Give a man a fish and he eats for a day (The Tangible Conclusion). Teach a man to fish and he eats for a lifetime (The Intangible Conclusion)".*

Sacred books are like spiritual mirrors. When we look into them, they reflect our Divinity. When we read them, we see the level of Divinity we see in ourselves. That is why they are considered sacred, and not just books. And too, that is also why we argue and debate about them. Because even though divine scriptures help focus our thoughts to the one same goal, we filter them through our individual lives, prejudices, and experiences. If our filter is clean, then the truth of the text will shine through. But, that does not mean that everyone we meet will be at the same level of understanding. We read the same passage with different filters, and because of this our interpretations vary. Our filters can get "washed" by someone who has one that is cleaner than our own, and they can also get "sullied" by someone with a dirtier one than our own. We are all at a different point on our spiritual journey than the person we are debating or taking spiritual advice from. One way to overcome this is by trying our best to incorporate every line, and sometimes every word, in a mystical, poetic, and symbolic way. If we have an interpretation that brings joy and Light into our body, we can be sure that our filter is getting washed by this elevated understand. But, if and interpretation brings animosity, guilt, and judgement of others, we can be sure that our filter is being sullied. Again, all Sacred books lead us to the one Universal all-knowing, all-encompassing Truth. We just have to be alert as to what is passing through our filter.

Ten Righteous Men and Two Ancient Cities

Many stories from The Bible have had a lot of unfortunate misinterpretations attached to them. One story, in particular, has perpetuated a lot of biased understanding. The reason for this is because half of its contents are omitted, or never fully examined. One story has led to millions of God-loving Christians, Muslims, and Jews being ostracized from their families and communities – or even being murdered. Added to that, millions – and possibly billions – more people are left feeling lost, confused, and full of self-hate. As we are all custodians of the Earth, our position in this world only gives us reasons for self-love – especially when we come to see how our fate can bring Light into the world and help keep it functioning. How could we be born from a God of Love, live our lives in this better to look at the self-hate we feel from a different angle? To see that there is nothing wrong with us. That there is nothing wrong with the book. But, there is everything wrong with our interpretation.

When read from a Universal viewpoint, this same story could bring a lot of healing and joy. It shows a way how we can filter into our world a new and much needed aspect of Divinity. It is a story that brings peace, understanding and transcendence to those who see and practice it in this way. To those who have been filled with hate and fear, they come to see that their rigid interpretations of a Divine Law is because they were led to focus on one half of this story. How can you understand a book that has only half of the pages? How can you know where you're going with only half of a map? The half-interpreted/half-examined story that has caused so much pain in the world is "The Destruction of Sodom and Gomorrah". Writers **have written about this passage in other books, like John Boswell's** *"Christianity, Social Tolerance, and Homosexuality"*. There is a beautiful and Divine Law contained within this story… But, the one that has been perpetuated for thousands of years from it is not it.

The story of Sodom and Gomorrah is actually in two parts. The reason so many homosexual men and women have been persecuted and killed because of it is because our religious leaders focus only on the second half. The first half is never examined. The first half is brushed-over. The following chart is the whole story of Sodom and Gomorrah in its entirety:

The story of SODOM and GOMORRAH	
(Genesis 18 :16 – 19 :29)	
FIRST HALF	Three angels, disguised as male travelers, went to Abraham's home to visit him. Two of the angels left and went to the cities of Sodom and Gomorrah to observe the evil that was there. The third angel, who was God himself, stayed behind (with Abraham). Abraham began bargaining with God about the fate of Sodom and Gomorrah. He wanted God to spare the cities if righteous people were found living there. He first asked God if there were 50 righteous people found, would He spare the cities? God agreed he would not destroy the cities if 50 righteous people were found.

	Then Abraham asked God if 45 righteous people are found in Sodom and Gomorrah would He spare the cities? God said yes – He would spare the cities if 45 righteous people are found living in them. Then Abraham proposed 40… then 30… then 20… with Abraham asking each time if God would spare the cities if that amount of righteous people were found living there. With each suggestion, God agreed he would not destroy the cities. Then Abraham went down to ten. If 10 righteous people are found living in Sodom and Gomorrah, would God spare the cities? God agreed. He would not destroy Sodom and Gomorrah if 10 righteous people are found living there. Then God, The Lord, departed.
SECOND HALF	The two angels that had left in the first half of the story went to Abraham's nephew's home. The nephew's name was Lot and he was living in Sodom. The angels arrived at his home in the evening and Lot fed them. Soon all the male Sodomites came to Lot's house and surrounded it. They asked the two angels, who were disguised as men, to come out of the house so that they could "have sex" with them (or to "meet" them, depending on the translation your Bible uses). Lot offered his two virgin daughters to go out instead. This infuriated the men surrounding the house. The enraged mob of Sodomites broke down the door of Lot's house. The Lot family and the two angels fled the city of Sodom, as God began destroying it with burning sulfur. As they were running away, the angels told Lot's family not to look back at the burning city. Lot's wife, however, did stop to turn and look back at Sodom's destruction. And because she did, she was turned into a pillar of salt.

That's the whole story. And even though it's short, this story – primarily the second half of it – has had a *TREMENDOUS* impact on our world. It has impacted and still impacts our actions and daily lives. Just from these few words, some people's lives are influenced partially – other people's lives are affected totally. Because only half of this story is ever spiritually analyzed (albeit falsely and subconsciously), innocent men and women have been murdered out of fear. People who could have contributed much needed Light into our world died from self-victimization. Families and friendships have been torn apart. New discoveries and inventions still lie dormant in our collective consciousness because the people who would have channeled them lived in constant fear. By focusing on the many excerpts of the second half of this story, it is no wonder as to why so many homosexual men and women have been considered:

Predators – All the male Sodomites came to Lot's house and surrounded it.

Rapists – Two virgin daughters offered to the infuriated mob.

Sex crazed – Sodomites wanting to have sex with angels.

Child molesters – Two virgin daughters.

Condemned – God destroying Sodom and Gomorrah with burning sulfur for its evil and wickedness.

Monsters – The enraged men.

Atheists – Ten righteous people not found.

Wild – The Lot family and the two angels escaping the city from the enraged mob.

Sinister – Refusing the virgin daughters over the disguised angels.

Hated by God – The cities destroyed by burning sulfur.

Perverse – The mob of homosexual men demanding group sex with the disguised angels.

Wicked – God destroying these cities because of the "unnatural" sex the men were having there.

People to be feared – The Lot family and two angels running for their lives to escape these wild and infuriated men.

To be ignored and disowned – Don't look at the Sodomites or God will turn you into a pillar of salt.

For many people, this is the whole story. And for many religious leaders, they extract and perpetuated their interpretations of it just from its second half. We are led to think that God hates gay men and gay women – and that man's unique relationship to Divine Consciousness can only exist if the person is heterosexual. However, this is what we choose to and have been led to believe… when we focus on the second half. But, what about the first half?

In the first half of this story, both God and Abraham show immense compassion. More precisely, God shows mercy and Abraham shows compassion. As is commonly known, Abraham is the father of three of our world's greatest religions – Islam, Christianity, and Judaism. They are called The Abrahamic Religions because of him. In the first half of this story, Abraham is seen advocating for both The Sodomites and The Gomorrahans. God is seen showing them forgiveness, understanding, and compassion. Both are open to finding a way to save the cities from destruction. Abraham and God are seen reaching a compromise. We watch them go through a sort of negotiation. This is not the only time in The Bible that we see God bestowing his mercy on mankind. His mercy reveals itself in many ways by showing him compromising, intervening through signs and angels, or setting laws and boundaries. In The Garden of Eden, for instance, Adam and Eve were told not to eat from The Tree of the Knowledge of Good and Evil. It was a boundary God set that gave them both a life in Paradise... All they had to do was refrain from eating an apple – but, they failed. Other examples include;

God sacrificing his Son – Jesus Christ – to save mankind.

For Christians, this is the ultimate example of God's mercy and compassion for humanity because Jesus Christ is seen as the son of God. So, for God to allow his son to be sacrificed, so that billions of others could be saved, can be seen as a way his message was spread throughout the world and has led countless people towards the Light.

Noah and The Ark

The 40 days and 40 nights of rain could have started immediately, but God shows his compassion by giving Noah the time he needed to, not only, build the Ark, but also to gather the countless pairs of animals.

Abraham and Isaac

God sending the angel and the ram just before Abraham was about to kill his son Isaac, showed his mercy and compassion for both Christians and Jews. If Abraham had, in fact, killed Isaac, the Jewish faith would probably not exist today. Jewish contributions to the world are because of God's mercy.

The Ten Commandments

Ultimately, these laws demonstrate God's compassion and mercy. They are helpful and concrete guidance for spiritually aspiring men and women.

There are many examples in other Divine Books. Hinduism's Bhagavad Gita is full of such stories, where Arjuna is shown Krishna's compassion for the families of both the Pandavas and the opposing Kauravas armies. As well, The Tao Te Ching and the Dhammapad mention either Divinity's compassion, guidance, and forgiveness – or how to be more conscious of our own.

And here, in the first part of Sodom and Gomorrah, God AGAIN shows his mercy. He and Abraham direct our thoughts into the hearts and aspirations of The Sodomites and The Gomorrahans. It is there – as it always is – that God shows his openness to saving these cities. In other words, the only thing God and Abraham are looking for in a Sodomite is faith. Not sexuality. Not race. Not whatever they did in the past. Faith now and Love now. People who were willing to step forward and express their love for our Universal Shepherd. They agreed that the love of ten righteous and spiritually aspiring Gomorrahans was enough to again trigger God's transcendent compassion and Divine mercy.

In a Christian's eyes, Jesus Christ is enough to save the world. In God's eyes, ten faithful people is enough to save two cities. In some Biblical translations, it is not ten righteous people - it is ONE. Meaning that even ONE pious person is enough to save countless others.

One other thing we have to remember is that it is Abraham that is in this story. Not Noah. Not Moses. Not Jonah. Not King David. Not even Jesus Christ. It is Abraham. Abraham, the father of three major world religions, was the one who advocated for this agreement with God on the behalf of Sodom and Gomorrah.

So, even if every word of the translation is true – despite doubts whether if The Sodomites were, in fact, all homosexual or if the mob wanted to "have sex" with the angels or just "meet" them…. what is indisputable and inextricable from this story is the fact that ten faithful men and women were enough to liberate two cities. These ten were enough to call on God and Abraham's compassion. They were enough to move mountains and inspire the Heavens. Enough to stop destruction and save lives. If ten righteous people had come forward, there would be no story… but, there would also be no lesson either. The first half and the second half resonate best when told together. One without the other does not take our thoughts to the same exalted level. By repeating and perpetuating only the second, and most-violent, half to the world only keeps the minds of the world on that same lower level. There is no Divinity in it alone. But, when the first half - the more intellectual and inspired half - is told with it, then our thoughts and hearts begin to expand.

Today, as there has always been, there are countless homosexual men and women who love God. Childless heterosexual couples are more apt to hate God than homosexuals are. However, there is possibly a spiritually higher way of looking at both situations… and that is, that it is possible that both homosexuals and childless heterosexuals have agreed to use this life to focus on their oneness with Divine Consciousness, while at the same time being part of keeping the world's overpopulation in balance. As custodians of the Earth with no predators, it would be disastrous if every human being would bear children. If that were the case, then some of us would have to voluntarily agree to give it up. It would create a lot of chaos. In today's world, it takes a very high, strong, and brave soul to agree to live their current incarnation as an out homosexual or a childless heterosexual. This is one of the many areas of life where homosexuals and heterosexuals come together – in this unique soul choice to make many great steps towards our oneness with Universal Light, without contributing to an already congested world. It would be a beautiful theme for a fabulous parade or a million-man march – one that would inspire healing to countless people who are suffering in many different ways. An event to remind us all that, for every soul (child-bearing or not), our number one focus is to re-develop our transcendent connection to The Dynamic Universal Mind.

There are many Faith-oriented homosexuals who consciously connect to the dual feminine and masculine aspects of The Father/Mother God. They use prayer and meditation to do this. Many homosexual men and women read The Bible, The Koran, and The Talmud. There are gay men and women who are Buddhists, Hindus, Taoists, healers, and religious leaders. If spiritually-oriented homosexuals came together in groups of ten to meditate and to pray, they would be performing a Divine act. Coming together to talk about their love for God, to practice experiments in Divine Science, or to examine the symbolic/poetic/mystical meanings in The Scriptures, is acting out a passage in The Bible. More precisely, these ten people would be performing a Godly act from the Genesis Chapter of The Old Testament. A divine act that both God and Abraham saw in their unique ability to perform. If inspired gay men and women felt comfortable enough to do this, they would create a new kind of transcendence. There would be Love. There would be joy and there would be healing. The source of transcendence is Light. That Light would spread through each of these ten people into their families, their friends, their communities and cities. What other interpretation can we give as to the reason why God accepted Abraham's offers?

The way heterosexuals materialize Transcendent Love is in some ways different than the way homosexuals materialize Transcendent Love. Love, as the source, is the same, of course. Overwhelmingly, the everyday acts of love between two people are the same. But still, there are a few slight differences between when a man and a woman lovingly interact and when two men or two women lovingly interact. Namely, one type of interaction is polar and the other type of interaction is non-polar. God himself is both polar and non-polar – otherwise those phenomena would not exist! Beyond scientific polarity and non-polarity, when there is Love and harmony between two components, it opens both elements up to transcendence. In physics, both polar and non-polar capacitors have the ability to transmit current. Any union becomes like a prism. A prism is used to transmit light through it. Remember that a prism comes in many shapes. They come in shapes of a diamond and they come shapes of a pyramid. But, even with so many different forms… when Light shines through a prism, the result is always a rainbow.

Is it possible that Abraham and God saw the coming together of these homosexual brothers and sisters in faith as a unique way of bringing a much-needed non-polar Light into our world? What other way can we explain the first half of this story?

Maybe you personally know ten righteous homosexuals who would be willing to come together to express their suppressed Love for God? Potentially, that could be five pairings of transcendent non-polar Light.

It is worth trying.

THE TWO PATHS TO GOD

The Caste System reflects our Inner Growth

One other belief that has led to a lot of suffering is The Hindu Caste System. This system goes beyond faith, as billions of people are placed on different hierarchies of society because of the family and the imposed class they were born into. A person's last name instantly labels them not only as higher class or lower class, but also as good or bad, saintly or despised, and godly or demonic. Your thoughts, your aspirations, your compassion, knowledge or kindness do not label you – your last name does. It is one of the world's oldest forms of creating an ordered society. Furthermore, the place you are born into in this rigid 3,000-year old hierarchy is completely out of your hands. Your last name is seen as being a result of the many past lives you and your family did in regards to your karma (work, thought, and action) and dharma (religion, duty, and faith). What causes the suffering in this system is the unfairness of it. Because no matter how much charity, faith, or work you've done in a past life and are (or are not) doing in this life, you will still stay in the same class… because you will still always be labeled by your family name.

From The Manusmritri, the most important book on Hindu Law, Hindus believe that there are four main castes - actually, there are five, if you include the "outcastes". They are categorized by trade, and are placed from head to foot on the Hindu God of Creation - Brahma:

BRAHMINS	Priests and teachers – Brahma's Head and thoughts
KSHATRIYAS	Warriors and rulers – Brahma's arms
VAISHYAS	Farmers, traders, and merchants – Brahma's thighs

SHUDRAS   Laborers – Brahma's feet.

DALITS (Outcastes) - Street sweepers and toilet cleaners –
They merit no place on Brahma's body.

From the four main castes, there are approximately 28,000 other castes and sub-castes. The Dalits are considered "untouchable", so they don't even belong to the castes system. They are known as Achhoots, and are doomed to a life of servitude and menial work.

For centuries, the caste system dominated every aspect of life in India; education, work, marriage, food, water, social activities, and the community people were allowed to live in were all dictated by the caste system. It was and still is a system that is impossible to escape. People have always thought it was unfair, unjust, and prejudiced. Honor killings and suicides are part and parcel of the caste system. For example, if two people from different castes fall in love and decide to marry, the family of the person of the higher caste will at first try to pressure their child not to go through with the wedding – even if the family of the lower caste is wealthier. If the potential groom is of the lower caste, the potential bride will have to take on his sullied, lower caste name. In Indian society, she will no longer be part of the more elite group she has always enjoyed. Grave concerns that their children will be subjected to discrimination on jobs, community, education, etc... are very real. The family will try their best to convince their child to marry someone of their own caste.

If that doesn't change their mind, the family's worry will often turn to anger and fear – more and more so if the child is steadfast on going through with an inter-caste marriage. That anger will then likely turn to hate, and the child will often be either cast out of the family or a victim of an honor killing. An honor killing is when someone in the family will murder that child to save face of the whole family. For the family, the child forced them to choose between either public humiliation or all the psychological implications of murdering someone you love. The reason the family's psychological torment can easily push them towards an honor killing is because they live in a country that wholly supports the acts for such killings. It is very likely that lawyers, politicians, judges, the media, and your neighbors will understand why you had to protect your family name and save your family from public shame. Your environment will support the terrible decision you feel your child forced you to take. Throughout the history of India's caste system, many people have gotten away with murder.

The injustice of the caste system is not only seen from higher caste to lower caste, but also from lower caste to higher caste. But, instead of it resulting in an honor killing, it often results in suicide. Living as a lower caste citizen in India is like you are living in an open-air prison. Prayers will not save you and falling in love with someone of a higher caste will not save you. The Power of Love cannot break you free from the caste system. You're trapped... forever. Often, once this deep realization hits the person of a lower caste, suicide is likely. Their poverty and daily suffering will help accelerate that decision.

The caste system is very much ingrained into the psyche of more than a billion people. Honor killings are even carried out beyond the borders of India, and are done in Europe and America. If an Indian living in the West falls in love with a European or comes out as gay, cases are seen where that person AND their partner have been killed or have disappeared. So, even outside India and the daily Indian caste system, it is very prominent in the Indian family's mind. It still remains a part of many people's everyday lives, thoughts, and actions.

Steps have been taken to correct its historical damages and injustices. But, because it is so ingrained, that is very hard to do. What is readily seen, however, is not real change to the caste system – but, rather, abuse and manipulation. Politicians, for instance, have been known to use the caste system for their own political gain. Specific promises to the different people of all four castes can influence the results of an election. In India, the different castes traditionally vote as a block. So, The Brahmins are promised changes. The Vaishyas are promised changes. The Sudras are promised changes. And even The Outcastes and The OBCs (Other Backward Classes) are promised changes. But, it is all said to grab votes and for political power.

The caste system comes from The Manusmriti, the most important book on Hindu Law. The Manusmriti is translated to mean "The Laws of Manu". Manu is the first son of Brahma, the God of Creation. This 18-volume book, also known as The Dharmashastra, proceeds the Vedas. It was written more than 1,000 years before the birth of Judaism, Islam, and Christianity. Even before it was written, it was spoken for, an unknown, hundreds and, possibly, for, an unknown, thousands of years. Manu is believed to be the progenitor of the human race. To put it into some perspective, Manu can be loosely thought of as Adam in Christianity. The first man, or the father of the human race. The one man we all descend from. The Manusmriti would be as if Adam himself had written a sacred text book on how we should conduct our actions to reach oneness with God.

However, the truth is, many people contributed to this book. Up until 200 C.E., Indian scholars and sages in pre- and post-Vedic civilizations contributed to its final form. It is a practical book, based on man's conduct and order, on how our Divine forces can be victorious over our demonic forces. But... The Manusmriti is not without human flaw and racial bias. Many of the short 1-4 sentence passages contradict each other, even in the rare times that the caste system is discussed.

For instance, in just the first three volumes, there are many conflicting passages. This is why there is a lot of criticisms and conflicts over these books.

Most of these books detail how we should act, eat, and best conduct our lives. In other words, how a man should behave and how a woman should behave, etc... Regarding the few instances these chapters mention the different castes, it says:

Chapter one -
(#2) "Deign, divine one, to declare to us precisely and in due order the sacred laws of each of the castes and of the intermediate ones".
(#91) "One occupation only the lord prescribed to the Sudra, to serve meekly even these three castes".
(#100) "Whatever exists in the world is, the property of the Brahmana; on account of the excellence of his origin. The Brahmana is, indeed, entitled to all".

Chapter two -
(#238) "He who possesses faith may receive pure learning even from a man of lower caste, the highest law even from the lowest, and an excellent wife even from a base family".
(#240) "Excellent wives, learning, the knowledge of the law, purity, good advice, and various arts may be acquired from anybody".
(#241) "A Brahmana may learn The Veda from one who is not a Brahmana in times of distress. He shall walk behind and serve such a teacher, as long as the instruction lasts".

Chapter three -
- (#17) "A Brahmana who takes a Sudra wife to his bed, will (after death) sink into hell; if he begets a child by her, he will lose the rank of a Brahmana".
- So, a Sudra (a laborer), who is born with a "contemptible name" (Ch 2, #31), can still teach a Brahmin (a priest) (Ch 2, #238).
- A Brahmin who marries a Sudra wife will go to hell (Ch 3, #17), even though he has an excellent wife (Ch 2, #238, #240).
- Brahmins cannot stay with outcastes (Ch 4, #79), but can be taught the Vedas by one (Ch 2, #241).
- A Brahmin cannot stay together with outcastes, Kandalas, Pukkasas, Fools, or Antyavasayins (Ch 4, #79), but a True Brahmana is one who befriends all creatures (Ch 2, #87).

These and other passages, can be a source of heated arguments, stress, and confusion. If a Hindu really wanted to follow the Manusmriti word for word, he could not...

- Look at the Sun – whether at sunrise, sunset, during an eclipse, reflected in water or in the middle of the sky. (So, in no way could you ever see the Sun).
- Run in the rain or look at his own image in water. (If you are caught in a sudden rainstorm or monsoon, you could not run to nearby building for shelter. You would have to walk).
- Eat with his wife or look at her if she sneezes or yawns. (Only when she is working, cooking, or in bed with you can look at her).
- Bathe naked (You would have to take a bath wearing clothes).

- Urinate on the side of the road.
- Urinate or shit however he wanted (He or she would have to defecate facing north during the day and facing south at night).
- Point out a rainbow if he sees one.
- Blow out a match or, if he is building a camp fire, he could not blow onto it with his mouth.
- Warm his feet by a fire.
- Look at a naked woman.
- Talk to a menstruating woman.
- Sleep in a house alone.
- Eat sesame seeds after sunset.
- Live in a country where The Labor or Democratic Party rules the government.
- Dance.
- Sing.
- Play a musical instrument or even slap his knee to the beat of the rhythm.
- Wear second-hand clothes or shoes.
- Bite his nails.
- Sleep naked.

(The above list comes from Chapter 4, passages 37 to 75.)

Many of these rules of conduct seem outdated – or even sadistic. However, there is another way of looking at them and the intention our Vedic ancestors might have had when proposing their addition into the Manusmriti. When we read them from the perspective that there is a realm within ourselves and the entire Universe called The Quintessence, then many of these passages start to make more sense – and even can be thought of in a more transcendental way. The vast majority of the verses in The Manusmriti do not even teach about the caste system or even karma – not enough to give it the prominence that it has become in Indian culture. The vast majority of its verses are about refining our self-discipline and practicing discrimination in order to unlock our Inner Divinity. It is not from water, food, shelter, or sex that a spiritualist evolves, it is from The Quintessence - The Five Universal Elements, The Pentacle of Akasha, and The Five Virtues of Justice, Truth, Love, Kindness, and Wisdom. Awareness of The Quintessence within ourselves is the true power of The Manusmriti.

As in Christianity, Hinduism is full of symbols and symbolism. An icon of a catholic saint holding a scepter and a globe, or of a winged archangel killing a demon, is very similar to the symbolic meanings of The Hindu God Ganesh holding a lotus flower and him stepping on a mouse, or of a Dancing Shiva displaying his infinite number of hands in full glory. So, since Vedic mystics have filled Hinduism with so much symbolism, why would that not include the caste system?

The caste system is real. But, it is not occupational, it is spiritual. It is symbolic for our spiritual evolution. That is why the Manusmriti says "The Brahmana is for all".

An outcaste can be seen as someone who is ignorant – "A fool", as it is described in the passages of The Manusmriti. These are "The street sweepers" - The Dalits, The OBCs, The Kandalas, etc... Without some kind of divine practice in our lives, we keep sweeping the streets of our inner world - only to find them filled with garbage, vermin, and dust the next day.

So, unless we learn another way to purify ourselves, we will have to start all over again – and we will remain "outcastes".

Once we start on our divine journey, we become Shudras - "The Laborers". There is a lot of work to be done in cleaning our "streets". Rites, prayers, meditation, pilgrimages, and discipleship all contain work that helps to purify our inner selves. Gurus are Spiritual Teachers that are unique to India. Finding a truly enlightened one is a blessing. When we do, these Spiritual Teachers assign us the work we need in order to wipe away much of the darker forces we have accumulated and the techniques we can use to evoke Light and abundance in our lives.

As we work with these rites and with our new spiritual knowledge, we evolve. We cultivate, we sow, we harvest, we farm, and we trade – not only on a physical level, but on a spiritual level, as well. When these techniques become habits – we become "Vaishyas", or Spiritual Merchants. We start to see that, as divine spiritual beings, we are both receptors and transmitters. When we see this, we then evolve to a higher level of the inner caste system.

Once we are spiritually strong enough, we are able to go forth into the world and rule it. We become warriors in The Vanguard Army and Rulers of Divine Law. We are able to navigate the outer world because we have created a new inner world. We are no longer street sweepers. And we know how to combine our new wisdom with Divinity and inner strength. At this point, we ascend to the level of "The Kshatriyas" - The warriors and rulers.

Once we have faith, knowledge, and inner strength, we become a "Brahmin". We become holy. We become Divine, and are able to spread that Light to others. Again... "The Brahmana is for all". It is a force and a state of being that empowers us, to where we become an active component of The

Divine Mind. It is at this point that we naturally teach others the lessons of transcendent joy we have learned. Our actions, our thoughts, our silence, and our words speak volumes. If a person has evolved through this inner caste system, then even someone with the family name of a Shudra or Vaishya can teach a person with the family name of a Kshatriyas or Brahmin. The Brahmana does not come to those because of their family history, it comes to those because of their spiritual destiny.

So, again, the caste system does exist... but, it exists *within* each and every Hindu. In fact, it exists within each and every human being, regardless of their faith. So, every Christian has a caste system. Every Muslim has a caste system. Every Jew has a caste system. Every Taoist and Buddhist has a caste system. Every person who aspires in some way for a deeper connection to Universal Consciousness will go through their own individual caste system as they evolve.

Keeping an updated Equinox Journal will help us more quickly ascend through our inner spiritual levels.

Faith is an Apple Tree – Man is The Gardner

Someone practicing with The Six Steps of Scientific Prayer will begin looking at our world religions like a gardener looks at an apple tree that is laden with apples. On an abundant and laden apple tree, all of its branches can have six or seven large apples coming off of one small branch. What does a gardener do when he sees an apple tree in this condition? First, he stands back and looks at it. He takes inspection of the situation because he knows that a lot of these apples – although ripe and juicy – might end up being unused. However, he will try to save as many as he can – and he will definitely look for the main branches that are able to harvest the best apples. He will also look for ways that light can shine throughout the whole tree. This light gives the tree its vitality, and will make it as healthy as possible.

When he begins trimming the branches, he focuses on three things; strength, health, and abundance. Granted, each gardener will have their own opinion on what the important smaller branches are, but most will agree what the main vital branches are. The smaller branches come from the larger branches, so the trunk and its main branches are more important to the tree's continued growth.

The gardener will first see several unruly extensions and twigs growing in all different directions; north, south, east, and west. But he doesn't cut only the northern and eastern growing branches... he trims a bit of them all. It is best for the tree to be pared down – that's what makes him an expert and what makes the tree reach its full potential. The remaining branches are those that have the best possibility to be a new source of Life as new shoots and buds begin to grow. A well-manicured tree gets its Life Energy from The Sun, The Earth, The Moon, and The Stars – all of which flow through it more efficiently because it has been so well cared for. Yes, you can choose not to trim an apple tree and leave it to its own devices. Yes, it will still bear fruit – even if you just pick apples from its northern branches. However, there is a difference between an apple tree that has been lovingly tended, watered, and pruned by an expert gardener and one that has been left to grow wild... or worse – wild and lop-sided.

Within each man and woman, Faith is their apple tree. Many say that their religion has it all. Followers of Judaism, Islam, Hinduism, and Christianity feel that their path contains everything they need. Their listening often shuts down when parts of another path might be different... or, even, similar to their own. Fear quickly comes into play, especially if it is a path that we have been at war with and have been taught to hate. This book shows us how the five world mantras are both different and complementary; Om, Amen, AUM, Tao, and Allah. Using them in pairs with renewed understanding can help us grow an inner manicured apple tree full of the abundance that comes from Universal Consciousness. Sometimes we have to put our hate and fears aside and turn to our hearts, compassion, understanding, and intellect for direction.

In our world, we are accustomed to trading goods, like products, raw materials, and commodities. But, we are not accustomed to trading spiritual ideas, divine concepts, and supportive scientific discoveries. The trading of goods and commodities has enriched us on our economic, materialistic and intellectual levels – otherwise, we would all still be living in caves. Think of how rich we have become from exchanging ideas. This interaction of ideas took us from the cave to the tent... and then from the tent to the cabin... and so on.

Consider too how rich we have become through the exchange of art and music. Through the exchange of food, spices, vegetables, and cultures. Having been opened to this, we have learned from people from other areas of the world. People who see the world in a different light – and even from the Earth that produces plants in different environments. As well... the people we have traded with have also learned from us and our ways. The interchange has been vice-versa. But still, trading has primarily remained fixed on the materialistic, financial, and intellectual levels. However, we've saved the best for last – as developing and enriching ourselves can and should also happen foremost on our spiritual levels.

The rest of this book is devoted to how we can actively induce spiritual exchange throughout the highest realms of our thoughts and hearts. We have countless examples here on Earth of how exchange leads to exponential growth. If, indeed, man is 2% matter and 98% spirit – then sparking this exponential growth on our highest realms will evoke Divine Inspiration and Transcendent Trade. Man is mostly spirit – not matter. We see this even in our DNA, which is 2% coded and 98% un-coded; in other words, our DNA 2% tangible and 98% intangible. Some scientists tend to call this intangible 98% of ourselves junk! Hence the term "Junk DNA". But, no, it is not junk. It is Pure Creative Intelligence. Why would God create junk at the atomic level of our cells?

If we see that this 98% realm of ourselves is spiritual, then we might come to think of it as an area worth exploring! An area where transcendence, Light, and pure joy reign. Where our thoughts and actions awaken the transmitter and receptor aspects of who we are. A new way to exchange in new realm of exchange produce new fertilizers for our inner apple tree.

With a paired mantra, that combines "The Eternal Field" with "The Cosmic Vibration", our inner apple tree can bring us as much light and wonderment as a Christmas tree.

Divinity and Transcendence are found in our Second Thoughts and Afterthoughts

Each of the five mantras have been practiced throughout the world for centuries… sometimes for millennium. Each one is impregnated with hidden power. Their power can take our thoughts into universal realms and eternal dimensions beyond this physical plane. The key to unlocking the power of "Amen", "AUM", "Tao", "Allah", and "Om" is knowledge, imagination, and an understanding of their root meanings. When we understand the root meaning of a word, our second thoughts and our afterthoughts are triggered.

We first have an initial thought and then we often have afterthoughts and second thoughts. Second thoughts are thoughts that analyze an idea or situation from a different point of view. Different points of view trigger our reconsideration, and can, thusly, turn a "Yes" to a "No" (Doubt) or a "No" to a "Yes" (Hope). Afterthoughts are thoughts that reinforce our initial thoughts. They add supportive information to a word or subject. They awaken our memories and experiences. Most commonly, our second thoughts trigger our fears. For instance, if someone asks you to do something next week and you say yes, at first. Then, after you think about it, you reconsider. You imagine the worst happening. You remember some bad experiences. Your fears are awakened. So, you make excuses – and you end up telling them no. That is the dark side of our second thoughts.

However, second thoughts and afterthoughts also have a positive side. A spiritually beneficial side that helps us to evolve. They can be used as a spiritual tool. Regarding the five world mantras, second thoughts and afterthoughts are essential in activating their power. For instance, when we say "Tao", our second thoughts will likely be "The Eternal Field", "The Lunar aspect of myself", "The Universal Mother supporting everything that is", and/or "The Divine Virtues". When we say "Allah", our afterthoughts will likely be "The First and The Last", "That without beginning… and without end", and/or "The phonetic palindrome". When we say "Amen", our second thoughts will likely be "God became The Word – and The Word became The Universe", "The Cosmic Sound", "The first

Universal body", and/or "The Solar aspect of myself"... etc. This shows how these following thought-ideas can help fulfill the thoughts surrounding any of the world mantras.

But unfortunately, most of us sit in our temples of worship, mechanically repeating these mantras without a better understanding of their meanings:

Christians repeat "Amen"
without giving it any second thoughts.

Muslims repeat "Allah"
without giving it any afterthoughts.

Buddhists and Hindus repeat "Om"
without giving it any second thoughts.

However... Locked inside all Five World Mantras is their immense power.

Getting Started! – Your Equinox Journal

Journals help us to see where we are and help us focus where we are going. Many types of journals exist to help a person discover their skills, values, and mission in life. They can also be used to help us look at our dreams, interests, and our goals. By reflecting on questions through writing, we can more easily uncover our passions and life purpose. When on a page, we can examine what we have achieved thus far in life.

By using the symbolism contained in The Earth's Four Seasons, we can not only see our strengths, our gifts, and our talents… but we can also see the cyclical advances in our spiritual evolution.

Starting Your Equinox Journal

One very important thing we can do before doing any spiritual exercises is preparing our own Equinox Journal. The Equinox Journal is a tool for our inner growth. A documented account of where we were, where we are, and where we are open to be. Every year contains two equinoxes and two solstices. One of them happens each season. An equinox is when night and day are equal in time (once in Spring and once in Fall). A solstice is either when the day is the longest (in Summer) or when the day is the shortest (in Winter). For this book, we call them all "Equinoxes".

There is one equinox for each season of the year – Spring, Summer, Fall, and Winter. These equinoxes are the four annual, spiritually dynamic times when the Earth, Sun, and Moon are in conjunction with a part of The Zodiac. These are alchemic moments for our evolving spirit. Each equinox corresponds to the cyclical journey we take over and over to evolve. This book has many exercises on Divine Science. Reading a new, spiritually oriented book likely means that we are coming out of a "Winter Equinox" and about to enter a "Spring Equinox". A spiritual book changes us and opens us to a new season. The Spring Equinox is dynamic. In the spring, new flower buds in our fields and meadows are starting to sprout. The air is changing. The Sun is shining down on us. We are in bloom. And… We are ready to receive new Light and new energy that will help us grow.

This book, "The Two Paths to God", is part of The Six Steps of Scientific Prayer series. These two paths are the first of the six steps. A book in this series will be devoted to learning about the four equinoxes and how installments in your own Equinox Journal can help you evolve. Not only that, your written installments can help you create a lot of beauty in your life. By recording your thoughts in a journal and then reviewing it another day, you can still spark "The Fire of Abundance" within you. Don't let this beautiful time pass without recording it and writing about where you are and how you feel today. You are likely in a "winter season" – a time full of wonder. You are hibernating. You are in a cocoon. Your tree branches are naked, as it is a time to look within. Though you may be in a caterpillar's chrysalis, you are also transforming into something very, very beautiful and free. So, capture, in written word, where you are. It will be a tool you can use for comparison and future reference.

When we chronicle our path in a journal, we keep some track of where we were, where we are, and how far we have come in our lives. Hopefully, this book will inspire you to practice some of the experiments and exercises in Divine Science it contains. Hopefully, it will enrich you in many ways. Inspiration and enrichment are elements of spiritual growth. So, before you begin reading further, STOP NOW and take a few moments to write down where you are. Date it and keep it somewhere safe. It is a vital element in your new spiritual treasure trove. A gift you give yourself, that will give back to you many times over.

A diary is something you write in every day. An Equinox Journal has periods between the written installments where there is growth because of your new spiritual habits. Four times a year, you look around at your life to capture what you see and what you have seen changed. It is a test to determine if your new spiritual habits are having positive effects on some of the important areas of your life. A good way to chronicle this is to add installments to your Equinox Journal every 3 months.

Preparing Your First Equinox Installment

The Equinox Journal is one of our most personal and powerful tools. It serves as a personal teacher, guide, mentor, evaluator, and assistant. With it... Life doesn't just pass us by - We take it by the horns! Because of our Equinox Journal, some of our moments in life become written and introspective "snapshots". A camera takes photographs of our body. A journal takes photographs of our thoughts.

The installments take us through the equinoxes of the four seasons; winter, spring, summer, and fall. As we go through all four equinoxes, many other of our inner realms get ignited - "The Fire of Abundance" being one. The Fire of Abundance gives us the ability to awaken and create affluence. Abundance is something we can all achieve. There are countless examples of people who knowingly or unknowingly triggered their own "Fire of Abundance": Winston Churchill, Nelson Mandela, and Karen Blixen… to name a few. In fact, these three also sparked it for millions of others. Throughout our human history, we have seen men and women who's fires were so abundant that they lit up the world.

So, begin today. Take 20-minutes to write down where you are and how you are feeling. Write today's date at the top of the page and save it as information to work with in your Equinox Journal later. In Truth, this page IS the beginning of your Equinox Journal. You might prefer to write an email to yourself, answering the questions listed below. Save your responses in a notebook or a new email folder. But remember to repeat this exercise every three months. Once you begin reading this book, you will see how your paired mantra and Divine Science have enriched you.

A.
Write in detail your current feelings regarding your:

- Finances
- Spirituality
- World Outlook
- Past
- Future
- Relationships

- Work
- Interests and Growth Projects
- Talents

B.
List 20 reasons why you are in a potentially advantageous position today.
(Reasons 17 to 20 are usually the best!).

C.
Write about what attracted you to this book. What did you hope to gain from reading it? Spirituality? Abundance? Knowledge?...

D.
To help you find what truly interests you, list your Top Five searches on the internet.
1.
2.
3.
4.
5.

Be general! In other words, instead of "recipes", say "food". Instead of "vacations" say "travel". Instead of "videos", say "music". Instead of "sex", say "intimacy" or "Love". This exercise helps you see what your truest interests are. We are all free to search anything on social media. What we spontaneously look for are signs of what resonates best with our needs now.

The Five World Mantras "Om", "Amen", "Allah", "Tao", and "AUM" The Words That Amplify Our Prayers

A big part of any religion is its mantra. Here we explore the mantras used by six of the world's most popular religions: "Om", "Allah", "AUM", "Tao", and "Amen". At its source, a mantra is used to enhance our communication with Universal Intelligence. By looking at these words and their root meanings more closely, we discover that they are all powerful keys into Eternal Transcendence, Pure Joy, and Universal Abundance.

What is a Mantra?

Mantras are Verbal Tools of Divinity that man uses to access Universal Consciousness. Before we can understand what a mantra is, we have to first examine what a word is...

What is a word?

The Five World Mantras have all been empowered by human thoughts and aspirations. We have done this in our highest and most intimate thoughts on and with Divine Consciousness. All five are among the rarest sounds with the ability to trigger immense power within and around us. When we think about it, the mind is full of thoughts. Our thoughts are a whirlpool of intentions, ideas, dreams, plans, and feelings. At times, very rare times in fact, a word springs out from this whirlpool and crosses our lips. In other words, not everything we think gets verbalized… and not everything we verbalize gets heard.

Words are rare.

Connected words, those that pass from thought to sound... to then being heard and understood, are even more rare. Mantras are spoken, sung, heard, and repeated in our places of worship. In the spiritual context that all of The Five World Mantras are used, we can see that they are among the most precious words humanity has ever empowered.

Words, thoughts, and the meaning we give to words have a great importance. All three are interconnected. Behind any word, there are ideas, images, feelings, memories, and/or meanings. For instance, if I were to tell you that "Barbara Kane" was a high school friend of mine, your mind would go blank for a second. Then it would immediately start to wander through its own thoughts and memories. As I continue to talk to you about Barbara Kane, your mind would try to create an image, a personality, and a body from the information I am giving it. Your mind processes her name, her likely ethnicity,

THE TWO PATHS TO GOD

that I knew her in high school, and that she was a friend. You would probably ask me questions to gain some missing information and fill the image of her you are creating. Your mind tries, but it still doesn't know who she is. So, it tries to make its own guess – a temporary portrait of Barbara to be able to return to if she is mentioned in a conversation again.

If I told a different person the exact same stories of Barbara Kane, their imagery of her would be totally different. Each person would build a different mental image of her from their own life experiences. The more I talk to you about Barbara, the more information you are given and the stronger your own temporary portrait of her becomes. You ask me even more questions to build up a stronger imagery and meaning of her in your mind. However, imagine if in the middle of our conversation Barbara, herself, were to suddenly walk in and sit at a table with us. Imagine if I were to say "This is the Barbara I was talking about!". If this were to happen, your whole image, impression, and thoughts of her would be instantly transformed. Your temporary portrait of her would vanish! That old impression would be quickly forgotten. Barbara's living, breathing reality is far more powerful than the various of temporary portraits you made of her. Once you meet her or see a picture of her, your whole perception changes. Barbara Kane has a "meaning" now. Her face, personality, style, hair color, voice, and maybe even her perfume are quickly being reprocessed in your mind from the groundwork you've already made from hearing my stories. Not only has the name Barbara Kane changed for you, but you have changed as well. Her reality has transformed you.

Art and music do this too, but in an indirect way. Both of these crafts are mainly visceral. Either our feelings, emotions, or thoughts are provoked through them. Imagine you hear a song you love on the radio. You love the singer's voice, the lyrics, and the melody. You hear this song all the time. Its story speaks volumes to you and reminds you of something or someone in your life. Soon, you find yourself wanting to buy the record. But, just like with Barbara Kane, once you buy the record and see the face of the artist who sings it or see him or her perform on television or the internet, you connect a real person to the emotions and images you have built in your imagination. Before seeing them, it was all visceral, emotional, and temporary. Your imagination was piqued.

It seems to be different when we speak of classical composers, sculpterers, and painters. That difference is because the meaning connected to the work is less evident than in a song with lyrics and a story. A composition, sculpture, or painting might evoke many emotions within us, but they do more so when there is a story attached. "The Mona Lisa" and The Sistine Chapel have a multitude of stories linked to them. If we know one of these attached stories, we enjoy looking at these masterpieces much more. When there is a story, there are words. When there are words, there is a meaning. When there is a meaning, art and music become very powerful conduits of Light.

Lastly, imagine, too, you are learning a new language. You are studying words that are foreign in their outer-construction, but familiar in their inner-meaning. As for these new words, the quicker we learn the meaning, the quicker we learn the language. If I tell you the Dutch word "Vrede", your mind would probably go blank. Again, it wanders and wonders through its own memory bank to try to put a meaning to this strange word. If you do not have a meaningful connection to that word, your mind goes blank. Your thoughts start searching and wandering. You quickly try to put meaning onto the word through the help of body language and vocal tone. This might help some, but it only takes you so far. You have to study the language to learn the meanings of its words.

Most people would not know that "Vrede" is the Dutch word for "Peace". Once you understand the meaning of this word, you then may try to remember it and might even try repeating it. Now that you understand its meaning, you will probably even verbalize it to experience it in a deeper and more physical way.

It is like meeting Barbara Kane for the first time. It is like seeing the singer on the CD cover of that song you've been hearing for the first time. After seeing the person in the flesh or in a photograph, there is now a more profound meaning of their names in your mind. Just as how learning a new language opens deeper levels of our mind. We now know who "Barbara Kane" is and what "Vrede" means. Hearing these words again, we sense we have changed because our knowledge has changed. It has grown. Both Barbara Kane and Vrede instantly give us an "Ah-ha!" moment when we re-encounter them. But, still… we can easily forget both if we don't often remind ourselves of Barbara or the meaning of Vrede. Ah-ha! moments resonate through us when we have connected a meaning to a word through repetition.

Examples like the ones above are quite common for everyone. We feel these joyous little Ah-ha! moments throughout our entire lives. However, not all words are the same. Some carry more potency. Some can take us to the deepest level of our being. Some can help us reach the highest echelons of our spirit. Some can take us to the edges of our galaxies and deep into the limitless realms of Divine Consciousness. The only thing we have to do is to have a better understanding their meanings.

A Mantra's Power is in its Root Meaning

Mantras are keys that our world religions use to remember God. Most of us have learned to meditate or pray with a mantra. But, their power is multi-functional. They can create abundance, joy, and World Peace. The added benefits of working with them every day is that they further open our third eye, we learn to focus our thoughts, and they awaken our inner Light.

By looking at their root definitions, we examine how they were originally defined by our ancient mystics. Some of us have sought out and contemplated these original definitions, but, for the most of us, they have been diluted, forgotten, changed, or homogenized. If a mantra does not evoke Light in our heart and intellect then we are probably thinking of it in a homogenized way. The last part of this book explores the many benefits in using two mantras or "Paired Mantras", and the power their mutual and complementary meanings awaken.

Mantras amplify our Thoughts

Before we think of what a mantra is, we should remember what a word is. A word is crystallized thought. As a thought solidifies more and more through the channels of our intentions, imagination, and desires, we often express that thought through a word. The source of our thoughts is the way our consciousness experiences the world. If we only see shit in the world, then the world will be a shitty place – and our words will reflect that. By the same token, when we see beauty in the world, our words will reflect that, as well. The biggest factor in this is habit. What we habitually tell ourselves and what we habitually think. In some extreme cases, we slowly go beyond our thoughts to where our mental health and physical appearance become reflections of what we see.

Words are our primary source of communication. They can be expressed in three different ways; the spoken word, the written word, and the gesture. Those who are deaf rely on the gesture over the spoken word. Words are a conduit of transformation. They are the most immediate ways we can change an action, a thought, or a feeling. Look at some of the ways we communicate. We communicate with each other, with ourselves, and with loved ones who have passed away. Beyond that, we communicate with plants, animals, and with God.

Mantras, too, are words. Mantras, too, are crystallized thought. Mantras, too, are used to communicate. However, mantras go to and come from a much deeper place in our consciousness than mere words. A word is crystallized thought, but a mantra is crystallized Divinity. A mantra builds bridges between our physical matter and our Universal Consciousness. A mantra is a link between The Tangible and The Intangible realms of our everyday reality.

As was mentioned in the introduction, the more we understand the meaning of a mantra, the more empowered it becomes. Mantras trigger the divine resonance we all have within us. Again, mantras are keys. They are keys in the form of a word. They unlock our resources of Love, abundance, and joy. They awaken our own transcendence and spiritual ecstasy.

In general, mantras come in different categories – The first are words and phrases inspired from by a Saint or an aspect of

God. Then there are words and phrases inspired from an ancient language, such as Sanskrit. But, just like with a word, for any mantra to work, it must be repeated with understanding. When a mantra is repeated with knowledge, love and faith soon follow. The five world mantras trigger both. It is our remembrance of God while repeating these words that allow us to emit the joy we feel

Words from ancient languages, such as Sanskrit, are used as mantras because it is felt that these languages were what we spoke when our societies were closest to God. We saw, lived, and viewed the universe in a different way than we do now. We thought and spoke in a different way than we do in our modern world now. These thoughts are still circulating in our collective consciousness, and we are all still able to able to tap into that collective library. During the times of their inspired inception, these mantras were born from a time when we were closer to Nature and to the wonders of Divinity. Sanskrit is one of the languages that reflected that.

Mantras amplify our Prayers

Later in the book, we will analyze the difference between these two prayers:
- "Thank you, God, for this food".
- "Thank you, God, for this food. Amen".

Both prayers could be said before a meal is eaten. However, the amplifying effect of Amen is only activated when we have a deep, far-reaching understanding of its meaning.

This book researches how all the five world mantras are "amplifiers". "Om", "Allah", "Tao", "Amen", and "AUM" amplify our thoughts and prayers in unique and specific ways.

When we more thoroughly understand their core definitions, our prayers are more empowered. The "Amen" amplifies the "Thank you, God, for this food". Our thoughts are spiritually charged even more when we remember that "Amen" reminds us of the bridge between Universal Consciousness and physical matter. The "Amen" connect us to The Divine Intelligence that created the apple seed... which grew the apple tree... that formed the apples... and inspired us to bake the Apple Pie we are about to put into our mouth. With "Amen", we are reminded of the Universal Intelligence that has created the potentiality and spiritual dynamics contained within that apple seed. The Divine Intelligence that inserts the same, yet uniquely different cosmic potential, into an apple seed, an orange seed, a pear seed, and a carrot seed. "Amen" reminds us of the bridge that EVERYTHING must pass through before becoming physical matter. And still... that is just when we use the "Amen"-mantra. "Tao", "Om", "Allah", and "AUM" elevate our thoughts and prayers in different, yet equally powerful, ways.

With the first prayer mentioned above, we are already showing God our gratitude for the meal we are about to eat. We are already evoking His blessing. We are already demonstrating that we have enough Spiritual Knowledge and experience to stop ourselves to perform this ritual before eating. The simple act of stopping ourselves to pray before eating helps activate our spiritual reserves and help us practice mind control. To the beginning Spiritualist, "Amen" will resonate the cells of the food and of their body. To the advanced Spiritualist, "Amen" will help them remember to see how this food came from The Eternal Field, through a mixture of Universal Intelligence and The Cosmic Sound, to be then manifested into the various food objects they now see on their plate.

But, what gives a mantra its power? The simple answer to that is "We do". Our state of focused Love and profound faith during our communications with God, has given mantras immense power. We live in a universe of thought. When we pray, meditate, or perform rituals, we are attempting to harmonize with the dynamic field within and around us. There are many times that we are not only attempting to harmonize with it, but we are also attempting to trigger abundance and blessings flowing from it into our lives. Billions of people, over thousands of years, who have been and still are using these mantras daily, have contributed to their power. In our ever-thinking universe, no thought is lost. The aspirations and faith evoked when spiritualists repeated them were meant for and sent to these five words. We have focused enormous power into a few concentrated words. Think of the miracles The Master Jesus created with "Amen" during his lifetime. And now think of the billions more people who have inspired "Amen" since his crucifixion.

Ultimately, the mantra becomes the meeting point where God and the aspirations of the person meet. Singing and chanting are beautifully inspired ways of repeating a mantra. Writing them out in long-hand funnel their alchemic elixir throughout our entire body. This interaction awakens the power you feel within. You are lifted to a higher place where the aspirations of the sender (us) meet The Divinity of the receiver (Universal Consciousness). The mantra is the cross-point.

The words "pocket watch", for example, does not trigger the divine frequency that "Hare Krishna" or "Jesus" does. No saint or group of believers have inspired the words "pocket watch". Yet, Krishna himself, and billions of Hindus, have empowered "Hare Krishna". Their Love, aspiration, and divine thought give meaning to this mantra. Remember that nothing is lost in our universe, and that everything is connected to the

Realm of Thought. Hindus have visualized, emotionalized, and verbalized Krishna's name. His life and image are celebrated in song and contemplated in meditation and prayer.

Our Divine aspiration is the essential key needed to empower a mantra. When we start to *WANT* to have a closer relationship to God and we start to *SEE* that bringing abundance and joy into our lives, then our Divine aspirations will increase significantly. In fact, ALL mantras can be traced to God. Even the words "pocket watch" can be traced to God and empowered, if we want them to be. However, countless souls have recognized that "Jesus" and "Hare Krishna", for example, were empowered with Divine Light. These spiritualists WANT a closer relationship with these examples of Living Divinity.

Mantras are channels to our one inner inexhaustible source. Allah, AUM, Tao, Om, and Amen are the highest mantras because they are inspired from God, and when we repeat them, we, in turn, think of God. Because they are inspired from God, they have an "involutionary flow", and because we think of God, they have an "evolutionary flow". Arguably, mankind has pumped its most heartfelt Love and deepest faith into all five of them. As we will discuss later in the book, The Star of David symbolically represents the cross-point between the flux of involution and the flux of evolution. With a better understanding of their root meanings, mantras put us directly into that flux.

The Power of Mantra Repetition

The practice of mantra repetition has existed for thousands of years in India. However, the word "mantra" came to the Western World through The Maharishi, the spiritual founder of Transcendental Meditation. Via him and the famous people who started practicing it, it spread throughout Europe, America, and The United Kingdom.

To begin working with a mantra, people are given one to regularly meditate on – Sometimes for two times ten minutes a day and sometimes for up to two hours per day. The mantra is a tool to enrich their connection to our Universal Consciousness. Mantras are empowered with thoughts and aspirations. If we believe the word to be holy, then we are filled with Light when we quietly concentrate on it. However, the true power of a mantra is expressed by the definitions and images we attach to it. Many mantras have definitions that are Universal and far-reaching. That is why it is good to not only meditate with a mantra in our thoughts, but to also study its many mystical meanings. In another book, we will go into the many mystical meanings of one of the world's most popular mantras "Om Namah Shivaya".

The five principal one-word mantras of the world – "Om", "Amen", "AUM", "Allah", and "Tao" - are all empowered mantras. The power of a mantra is most awakened from the knowledge and understanding of its root meaning. When its definition expands our thoughts, its power expands our hearts.

To get the full alchemic benefits of a mantra, it is best to repeat it with an image or definition in mind. Some spiritualists put a picture of their Spiritual Guide at the place they habitually practice their mantra repetition. Once you have an accompanying thought or image, repeat your mantra with love and faith to release its power. In Hinduism, and with its various Yogas, this practice of mantra repetition is called "Japa". Japa is often practiced with the image of a Guru in mind, but other powerful images can also be used. True Masters would rather you focus on God and not on them.

When we repeat or chant an empowered word or phrase several things happen simultaneously within. Light, healing, and improved mind-control are triggered. Mantras are used not only in Hinduism and Yoga, but throughout all religions. They are an immediate way to focus our thoughts on our own Divinity. For instance, japa can be seen in Buddhism, Christianity, and Islam. If you were to ask a Buddhist meditating on "Om" in a temple, a Baptist singing the song "Amen" in a church, and a Muslim chanting "Allah" from the minaret of a mosque to describe what they feel, their descriptions would be interchangeable. "Joy!" would probably be the most common word. "Love!"... "Transcendence!"... "My heart fills with Light!"... would probably also be on their lists. The repetition of a mantra with Love and aspiration is japa.

When we practice japa, we trigger joy. When conscious thought and the definition of the word are added to our japa, we trigger transcendence. We also discipline our mind and connect to the inexhaustible source of our Universal Self. We purify and touch our own Divinity. "Conscious Japa" is an easy way to fill our spiritual reserves and bring instant Light into our auras. Japa brings us health, youth, and vitality. It is an elixir and a highly-potent drug that is more addictive than anything synthetic or grown. Because it is Pure Thought, at a time our thoughts and imagination are harmonized higher, does it become so intoxicating. Through japa, every cell of our being is invigorated and rejuvenated. Our body is truly baptized within and our cells begin to sing with pure Love and happiness. Japa is pure because, through our repetitive devotion and thought, we connect to God within. Japa is pure because we harmonize our conscious mind with The Universal Mind in The Eternal Realm of Divine Thought.

Long-term, daily japa practice will evoke alchemy within us. It is unavoidable, as we are changing our thoughts

– so we are changing our lives. The more alchemic we are, the more universal we are. Inspired thought and situations come to us to help manifest our desires. With japa, we instantaneously ascend to a loftier plane. We feel spontaneous light enter our body. We awaken kriyas and diffuse any negative forces that have entered our energy field. With mantras and japa we develop a place within ourselves we can come to at any time and recharge. Practicing japa before we sleep takes this divine energy into our unconscious, subconscious, and superconscious minds. We enlighten not only our physical bodies, but also our ethereal and astral bodies during our sleep. When we awaken and practice japa for a few minutes the next morning, the light that was reverberating through our bodies through the night can help re-energize us throughout the day.

Locating Our Inner Prayer Mechanism

Does Talking in our Sleep reveal an Inner Bridge?

If we are spiritualists who pray, one of the most fundamental questions we can ask ourselves is "Why do we pray?". When we look at this practice in depth, we first come to see that the reason we even feel we can pray is because we know at some deep level that we are inherently connected to Divine Intelligence. In other words, we instinctively know that we are children of God who are born with the ability to communicate directly with Universal Intelligence. Through intense and faith-directed thought, we can send our personal wishes, ideas, and desires deep into The Cosmic Mind.

When we pray, we normally ask God for something that will benefit our lives or the life of a loved one. However, our belief in the power of prayer is so strong that we believe that our innate power to ask God for his blessings extends past ourselves and our loved ones. So unlimited is our individual capacity to communicate with God, that we feel we can pray for a friend's cancer-stricken mother who we have never even met. We are often asked to pray for a variety of things that have nothing to do with us personally. Our individual power of prayer is even strong enough to pray for Peace in the entire world. A spiritualist believes in the far-reaching power of prayer. We believe that our imagination, combined with our aspiration, faith, and words, are effective enough to initiate God's favor. We believe that our individual connection to God is strong enough to be heard and to receive the result we are looking for.

But, what proof do we have that this connection exists within us? What evidence to we have that an inner prayer mechanism is there? A bridge between this physical world and our individual connection to Universal Consciousness.

Scientifically, one area we can look to is the realm of REM-sleep (Rapid Eye Movement). In our daily lives, we go from the awake state to the sleep state to the deep-sleep (or REM-sleep) state. If not for this daily cycle, we would have a lot of severe psychological and health problems. Countless studies have proven this. This daily cycle takes us into different levels of our own mind: the conscious state, the unconscious state, and the super-conscious state. Scientifically, we can measure our brain waves going from Beta-waves into Alpha waves as we go from the conscious to the unconscious states. In our super-conscious state, our REM-sleep, our mind is transmitting Delta waves. We are also transmitting Delta waves when we are meditating. Meditation is when we are inducing a merge between our individual mind with The Universal Mind. Delta waves are a scientific measurement showing our brain activity in this deep state - whether dreaming or meditating. However, there is something else that happens when we are in this state that may indicate that we have an inner prayer mechanism.

When we are in REM, there is a strange phenomenon that has happened to us all when we are in this Delta-transmitting deep-sleep – We begin talking. Think about it for a moment, "Have you ever talked in your sleep?". Even babies talk in their sleep. When we do this, words and sounds travel from thoughts and images in our super-conscious and subconscious worlds down into our physical and audio worlds. This means that there is a deep mechanism within us, from infancy, where words can pass through from our super-conscious mind down into our physical reality. They go from Delta through Alpha down into Beta.

When we are dreaming, thoughts and images don't just stay in this higher state of consciousness. The most prominent experiences pass, via that prayer mechanism we're born with, down through our thoughts and feelings to form words. It is also possible that even in times we "talk to ourselves" that we are using this prayer mechanism, and that our brains are in a fleeting Delta-wave state. Even In our Alpha and Beta wave states we can still connect to this inner pipeline. In any event, there are various signs, beyond meditation and prayer, where we can see that we regularly communicate with the many higher states within us. Even if we are not spiritualists, we all instinctively commune-icate with the higher dimensions of our existence that are beyond this physical plane; Feelings, perceptions, insights, and hunches are not of this physical world.

We were all born with this inner pipeline, so it is natural that we find ourselves spontaneously interacting with it. It is unavoidable, as it is a part of what makes us human. It is what gives life force to Life. When it is active, we are "alive". The question is, "What do we do with this pipeline into The Universal Consciousness? Do we neglect it or do we turn it into a cylinder of golden Light?". This pipeline is the mechanism we use to communicate back and forth between ourselves and our subtler states - namely, our subconscious and our superconscious. Beyond that, our cylinder of golden Light could be our prayer pipeline between our True Self and Cosmic Intelligence.

Yes, prayer works! But, not all prayers are answered in the way WE think they should be answered. So, what was faulty… the question, the answer, or the interpretation? When we don't get what we pray for, we often get somewhat angry or frustrated. The fact of having even prayed for a blessing softens the disappointment. But still, we are confused as to why our prayer wasn't answered at all or in a way we were convinced would better our existence. We know for sure that our hearts and our thoughts were engaged – So, what did we do wrong? A possible answer is we haven't prayed, we've begged. We've approached God in a state of need or lack. That is why if the prayer seems unanswered, we're disappointed that we weren't heard. We've pleaded for something and we didn't get it. To avoid this, spiritual adepts advise us to pray with detachment for the results. When we are detached in prayer, it leads us to either the answered prayer or the unanswered prayer. With both results, lessons are learned. Praying with detachment is a good way to pray because it tempers our expectations. It puts our ego and self-importance to the side.

Yet, there is a third way to approach prayer and praying…

The third way to pray is from the point of Universal Abundance and Grace. It is diametrically opposite to praying from a point of need and lack. As children of God, we were born with abundance and grace - just for being born a human being here on Planet Earth. Not only abundance and grace, but a MULTITUDE of other Divine utensils are within "The Spiritual Toolbox" we all possess. As such, we can come back to these inherent states before we begin to pray.

When we routinely remember our inherent Divinity and Universal Abundance, our actions, thoughts, and our lives become prayer. We are no longer in a state of need. When we routinely focus on The Universal Abundance we truly are, we then attract the joy, abundance, and Light we pray for. When we develop new Divine thoughts as a daily habit, meditation and prayer become tools we choose to use, rather than tools we have to use to practice our faith. As we consciously place our true abundance and grace into the forefront of our habitual daily thoughts, the roads and bridges between ourselves and Universal Intelligence get built and maintained. A perpetual form of meditation and prayer will begin to exist in our awakened, sleep, and deep sleep states. We no longer live in a state of answered and unanswered prayers, rather we see our lives fill with "unasked-for answered prayers". In other words, we see more and more abundance and joy filling our lives. Serendipity becomes our normal state.

This book is partly about helping us achieve a State of Serendipity, where we use The Five World Mantras to open our thoughts, so that joyous and fruitful occurrences can routinely happen in our lives. "Un-Requested Answered Prayers" will be able to fill our lives. But what is really happening is that by opening your thoughts, The Universe fills your many reserves and reservoirs with The Light from your renewed spiritual knowledge and habitual focus on the five pathways mankind has built into Eternal Abundance.

The Universal Consciousness is inherently dynamic, so aspects such as transcendence, grace, and serendipity naturally spring forth from it. Dynamic divinity is part of the intelligence it truly contains. Abundance and joy are the states it awakens within us. The two paths to God – "The Eternal Field" and "The Cosmic Vibration" – are the realms that bring us into this transcendent state. Mantras are the keys that lead our thoughts into these realms. Through prayer, we attempt to unlock blessings from Universal Consciousness. We use our thoughts and mantras to combine with our imagination and aspirations. However, most of us don't think of the deeper powers of prayer beyond what we have been taught in churches, mosques, and synagogues. We don't live a life of Universal Prayer in our thoughts and actions. We use prayer only in a time of dire need. We don't live a life of prayer as a preparation for the times we do communicate with God. This book helps us to routinely put our thoughts into that realm of Eternity. Then, we are always well-prepared before we start praying.

"The Eternal Field" and "The Cosmic Vibration" are two keys to that dynamic, Universal realm. Most religious teachers tell us that there is only one key – THEIRS! However, this book explores the possibility that there are TWO keys into that realm. Our prayers are empowered and that realm is unlocked when those two keys work as one.

When we think about it, we normally need two keys to get into our homes, our businesses, our apartments, and our places of work. Even our cars need two keys – one for the door and one for the ignition. The multi-key concept is not a new practice. If we look at the chambers in the Pyramids of Giza, The Aztec Temples, or the Tombs of Ancient Chinese Emperors, there have always been a number of keys needed to unlock these chambers and secret rooms. This book explores the possibility that there is more than one key needed to unlock some of the deepest chambers of Universal Consciousness.

The Eternal Field Mantras – Tao & Allah

At first glance, Taoism and Islam seem to be two distinct and vastly different faiths. It is true that these religions originate from different parts of the world and are practiced in different ways. However, there are many spiritual elements that they have in common; The way their mantras ("Allah" and "Tao") take our thoughts to The Eternal Field, how their calendars and festivals are calculated by the moon, and how each of these faiths awaken our "Inner Moon". These two faiths complement The Solar aspects that both exist within all human beings. A human being is both Lunar and Solar. Looking at these religions from this angle, we can see how Islam has more in common with Taoism than it does with Christianity or Judaism, and how Taoism has more in common with Islam than it does with Buddhism or Hinduism. They each can help awaken The Eternal Field within us.

The Eternal Field is The Source of "Tao" and "Allah"

Stop for a few moments and look at all the things around you...

Wherever you are, whoever you are, and whatever objects you have around you have come from the SAME source. Even if what you are looking at in this moment is a cactus in the middle of a desert – It all came from the same source. Every grain of sand, every pink cactus flower, and every thorn came from The One Source of Creation.

Looking deeper, you will see that even you came from that same realm of existence. Everything around you, including you, was created or born from that ONE dynamic, universal source. There were limitless possibilities for that chair you are sitting on and of that person you finally came to be. Who you have come to be at this moment and the form and design of that chair were the strongest thought forms during the creation of both. When an architect sits down with a young couple to design their new house, it is the strongest combination of their thoughts that end up in the blueprint. And even with a blueprint, things change. Thoughts change things. It is possible that when we are conceived, our souls act as the architect, our parents act as the young couple, and God acts as the change-agent.

Even though we all come from the same source, ourselves, the chair, the zebra, the cactus, and the Empire State Building are all temporary. If we have come INTO existence, this means we came FROM a much deeper realm. We came from somewhere. Before we came through the portals of a physical womb, we came through the portals of a Universal Womb. Once we are born here on this physical plane, we have a beginning and we have an end. Everything has a beginning and will have an end. Even the Earth, The Sun, and The Stars have all had a beginning and will have an end. Yet, by contrast, the one dynamic, universal source we come from is eternal – it has had no beginning and will have no end.

One huge grace of being a human being is that we have a mind that can conceptualize that one thing that has no beginning and no end. It cannot even be called a "thing", because a thing implies birth. It is better to think of it as a limitless realm of dynamic and transcendent thought – or as "Pure Creative Consciousness" or an "Eternal Field". It is a place where we all emerge from and will all merge back into. The term "The Universal Source of Life" applies to it in every imaginable meaning.

Taoism and Islam recognize and revere this Eternal Field that is within and around us. This reverence is inextricably part of the inherent definitions of "The Tao" and "Allah". Ancient Taoists and Islamic Mystics used two different ways to lead our thoughts to the same realm of Eternity and Pure Potentiality. Other faiths too recognized this eternal field we all come from, but did so in writing, theory, and spiritual discourse. However, "Allah" in Islam and "Tao" in Taoism are one-word mantras that can take our thoughts directly to this eternally dynamic limitlessness as we pray or meditate.

The Holy Koran describes Allah as "The Eternal that has no beginning and The Everlasting that has no end" (57 :3). It also describes Allah as "The First and The Last" (112 :2). "Allah" has also been translated to mean "The undying". Try to name something that has not had a beginning and will not have an end. The mere fact that it exists has brought it onto the Wheels of Birth and Death. Only "Allah", Divine consciousness, is unborn, and so it is undying. Allah is The Eternal. The Everlasting. Allah stands apart, yet permeates, everything we see in this material world.

This same description of Divine Consciousness is found in Taoism. In the Tao Te Ching – The book of Taoism – The "Tao" is described as "The Eternal Field behind the 10,000 things". "Eternal", meaning "beyond birth and death". "Field", meaning "realm". And "10,000 things" meaning "man, woman, plant, Earth, Sun, Stars, etc...". You probably won't need to think of ten thousand things to find your thoughts swimming in Divine Consciousness. Try writing even a list of one thousand things to see if you can feel tremors from The Eternal Field bubbling within yourself. Like "Allah", "Tao" takes us past the materialism of what we are and what we see to what is divine, what is eternal, and what is dynamic about who we are. We are taken to the same field of Divine Consciousness through these two words by our renewed understanding of their root definitions. So powerful are Allah and Tao, they have the ability to induce a transcendent, meditative state with our eyes open.

A mantra's true power comes from its ability to induce transcendence. Transcendence is experienced and described in many ways - "Filled with The Holy Ghost", "Spiritual Ecstasy", and "Flying!" to name a few. But what is common in a transcendent state is that our cells are vibrating at a higher than normal frequency. Our thoughts pulsate with Light and our inner vision opens when we are in this state. Our hearts and chakras expand, and our ability to receive and transmit Divine Thought is enhanced. In other words, from this state is a good place to pray.

Using an empowered mantra is like climbing high up your own spiritual tower or climbing to the top of a mountain. The air is fresher and our view is farther than from when we are at the ground floor or at the base of the mountain. With Allah and Tao, we ascend by remembering that these mantras lead our thoughts into the beginning-less and endless field of Divine Consciousness. From their root definitions, we see that they were both conceived to bring us to this exalted state.

Allah and Tao are reminders of what is within and around us. Because this Eternal Field is invisible, it is easy to forget. With a mantra, however, we remember. With its definition, we understand. And with our habit and repetition, our feelings transcend.

Allah and Tao are pure because they take our thoughts to the dynamic unborn within. We repeat and remember them to trigger a pure and dynamic state. The same state that resonates with the dynamic source from whence all life began and will return. In this book, neither "Allah" nor "Tao", nor

"Om", "Amen", nor "AUM", are about converting anyone to another religion or faith. Believers and non-believers are quick to point out today's radicalism found in a few extreme cases of some spiritual paths. However, just as much or even MORE radicalism is found in politics and sports. Allah and Tao are about bringing our thoughts back to the one realm of our existence that is dynamic, transcendent, and abundant. Human thoughts empowered these mantras. The divinity we felt during our prayers, rituals, and meditation were induced by our Love, faith, and harmony. "Tao" and "Allah" are two keys to The Universe and its Universal Abundance awaiting us within.

Tao and Allah are Lunar – They awaken "The Moon" within

In the second and third section of this book, we will discuss how these two mantras awaken our inner Lunar aspects. In many of the exercises and experiments in Divine Science and Multiplicative Joy, we will practice with this Lunar aspect within ourselves. But, for now, realize that in both Taoism and Islam, their calendars are based on the cycles of The Moon, their celebrations (Ramadan and Chinese New Year) are based on the cycles of The Moon, and that they both describe Divine Intelligence as a Dynamic, Eternal, Unborn and Undying realm within and around us.

**Definitions of The Eternal Field
outside of Islam and Taoism**

God described as an Eternal Field is not exclusive to Taoism and Islam. For example, in Judaism, Rabbis have repeatedly insisted that God is not a "concrete being". They go on to say that God does not have a tangible form, occupying a specific magnitude in space. "Such a being would be part of the Universe, not its master". In The Talmud, or Holy Jewish Scripture, God is "The Place", or the ground of creation. The epithets of The Talmud say that The Universe exists in Him - not He in the Universe. In the words of the Midrash, "The Holy One, blessed be He, is the place of His universe, but His universe is not His place."

Other religions and spiritual scripture also describe God in terms of a limitless, Eternal Field:

The Vedas (In Hinduism) say that God is "body-less" and "whose image cannot be made". God is The Paramathma, The Unlimited which is not a He or a She - it is a state of consciousness.

In Hinduism, several places in The Bhagavad Gita also describe God as The Supreme, infinite, all-encompassing, all-pervasive (6.30-31, 9.4). Omnipotent, beyond action (13.29-31). The beginningless and the endless (13.12). The Source of All (10.4). Indweller in human beings (8.4, 8.9, 10.11, 10.20). The sustaining Life Force (7.5). Teacher (11.43). Illuminating the entire field (13.33)/ The Absolute, ineffable, un-manifest, inconceivable, transcendent, unchanging, Infinite spirit (7.13, 7.24, 7.29) The womb of God from which finite, created beings come forth (14.3-4, 14.27).

Undoubtedly, there are many other sources where God is described by ancient mystics as an Eternal Field of Pure Consciousness. However, "Allah" and "Tao" condense these descriptions into one-word.

The dual uniqueness of "Allah"

"Allah" is a deep, profoundly enlightening, and mind-expanding mantra. Knowing its meaning can first take our thoughts to the edges of our galaxies and beyond the manifestation of Time - And then simultaneously activate an inner resonance within us from its palindromic aspect. These two inherent dualities of "Allah" combine to evoke an immense amount of Light within us as we repeat it.

If your path up until now has been to use "Allah" in your prayers and rituals, ask yourself what "Allah" means to you? Does it mean "The Great One"? Does it mean "God"? Or do you simply interpret it to mean "Everything", without considering what it deeply could mean at its origin? Saying and thinking that "Allah" means "Everything" is too vague. Too general. Too nonchalant and, sometimes, too off-handed. Our mind works better with a more focused idea.

Saying "Allah is everything" is true. It sounds impressive, but it is imprecise. "Allah" deserves more precision. "Allah" blossoms within us the more we study its meaning and multi-leveled aspects.

Yes, it can open our vision somewhat, but our human mind operates more powerfully when it can focus on something more specific. Specificity is the overall theory behind the various yoga practices in Hinduism; Since God is so vast, it is better for us to focus on one specific aspect of him like Love, devotion, work, thought, etc… By giving our mind a few divine and far-reaching acts, it expands more than trying to encompass the Universe all at once. Specific thoughts and actions also give us more defined knowledge than vague, non-specific knowledge. We can see many examples of how giving our mind specific thoughts and actions works in many areas of our lives – milk, for example. A cow's utter has several teats. Yet, the farmer only has two hands to squeeze out the milk. But with repetition, the farmer can fill his bucket.

THE TWO PATHS TO GOD

Specific thoughts that take us to either higher or deeper realms can expand our minds and fill us with Light. For the mind, specific and defined is better than general and vague. Specific and defined broaden our vision and insight. Saying "Allah means everything!" is not specific and defined. So, the problem then becomes "What one or two specific thoughts can we give to 'Allah' to connect us to The Universal whole?".

When we examine "Allah" more closely, two of its root definitions reveal themselves. Firstly, listen to yourself slowly saying "Allah" a few times – "Aaaaaaah....Laaah". Try saying it twelve times with the definition "That without beginning and without end" in your thoughts. Try saying it twelve times in two parts – with "Aaaaaah" meaning "without the beginning..." and "Laaah" meaning "without the end". Your imagination helps when you say it in two parts, because your inner eye looks into Eternity twice. When you combine repetition, imagination, and definition, a mantra's meaning becomes more powerful as you consciously listen to yourself say the word – this technique applies to the other four world mantras as well. But, with "Allah" and its palindromic aspect, your inner-vision faces Eternity twice. Once with "Aaaaah"/"That without beginning..." and then with "Laaaah"/"Than without end". "Aaaaah... Laaaah". "Allah".

"Aaaah..." in "Allah" is the same "Ah" in "Amen" and "AUM". When someone is in "awe", their thoughts are open. It is a sound showing our receptiveness to Light. To be "awe-stricken" means that we are in a feeling of wonder and amazement. We are in an inspired state of being. Three of the five world mantras begin with "Aaaah...". They can put us directly into this state when we repeat them. However, "Allah" is unique. With it, we say "Ah" twice.

By consciously practicing "Allah", we can trigger an immense amount of inner-light. For Muslims, God, Universal Consciousness, and The Eternal Divine Mind can all be descriptions of "Allah". It is this mantra that is incorporated into Islamic spiritual practice, ritual, and prayer. It is the word used to amplify our communications with God. From Allah, all things are born. "Allah is The First and The Last". The eternal and dynamic source of all that is.

If to you "Allah" is specific, then your prayers are more powerful than having a vague concept of it. Your inner-vision and imagination can see "Allah" and "Tao" behind a plant, your neighbor, The Sun, The Stars, and yourself. If something is made up of molecules and atoms, then it has had a beginning and will have an end – only "The Tao" or "Allah" does not. Allah is The Eternal, The Endless, and The Everlasting realm of existence. Tao is the non-beginning/un-ending realm of Pure Potentiality BEFORE it fragments into the multitude of things we see, hear, taste, smell and touch. With some slight, yet immensely beautiful and thought-provoking differences, Allah = Tao and Tao = Allah.

All five mantras studied in this book are unique. The first part of Allah's uniqueness comes from its definition - One, from it being a phonetic palindrome and two, from it taking our thoughts to a realm beyond birth and death. There are these two inherent TWO aspects of Truth contained within it. As we practice with it, our mind learns to quickly focus on both of its eternal aspects in one short word. Again… our Third eye looks into Eternity TWICE; we see the eternity before the dawn of creation and we see eternity beyond the end of destruction. We come to see and feel an omnipresent realm of Light and abundance. At this point, you, yourself, become a tool of transcendence. You become this all from having a more profound and knowledgeable use of "Allah".

Imams have described Allah as being "Alone, with no place, no sound, no Light, and no darkness". In other words, beyond the materialistic world we see, hear, touch, smell and taste with our five senses. Even though it is intangible, our thoughts can still be lead to The Eternal Field. As it is impossible to describe the indescribable, when we ponder and meditate on empowered mantras, they can take our thoughts past the manifested façade and into the dynamic abundance of The Universe. It is easy to get caught up in the hustle and bustle of our busy lives and forget that before us... before our world... before this universe there was and still is an invisible field of pure, transcendent, and divine potentiality - "Allah". This field in is an incessant and cyclic motion of creation, sustainment, and destruction - "The Tao". Again, we all emerge from and will merge back into it - "Divine Consciousness".

Imams have said that Allah is beyond the atom. Scientists would agree, as our faxes, cellphones, televisions, radios, and computers are all only able to communicate with each other because we can send waves across this field. This not only makes Allah and The Tao spiritual... but, also useful. A Muslim calls it Allah. A Taoist calls it The Tao. And a scientist calls it The Ether. We use it all the time! And incredibly... it never gets our messages mixed up! – Human error notwithstanding. Yet still, in matters of Divine Consciousness, our scientific discoveries and practical uses of the ether are only the tip of the iceberg.

One of the beautiful aspects of the "Allah" mantra is that it itself contains a spiritual duality. Not only because repeating it implies "The first and the last", but also because it is a word that starts and ends with a vowel. The "h" at the end of "Allah" is an aid to help us say it correctly. Otherwise, without it, some people would be saying "All-eh" or "All-ay". "Amen" and "Om", for example, are spoken in various ways. Yet, thanks to the "h", "Allah" is said in one way.

Vowels are open-ended. "Allah" starts and ends with an open-ended vowel. It is more than just any vowel. It is the vowel "Alpha", the first letter of the alphabet. When ancient mystics created the alphabet, the first letter always pertained to our connection to The Universe. Alpha takes our thoughts to the source of creation. Again, when we chant, repeat, or hear "Allah", with our new understanding of its inner duality, our thoughts can go beyond the façade of this material world… to merge with the source of creation twice – That Divine and Eternal realm that has existed beyond the beginning of our Universe and will still exist after the end of it.

Another way we can sink our thoughts into this field of dynamic creation is to ask ourselves two simple questions. The first one is "What was before that?". With this question, we can contemplate the beginning of humanity, our Earth, our Sun, and even our Star Constellations… each time asking ourselves "Well, what was before that?". Scientists contemplate Darwin's Theory of Evolution saying that we were fish that crawled out of the sea… but "What was before that?". Astronomers contemplate the birth of The Sun…. But "What was before that?". This first question leads our thoughts to The Universal Intelligence that created this huge and immensely hot fireball in the sky that not only gives us light, but also electricity, magnetism, vitality, and warmth. If that Universal Intelligence was able to create The Sun, then that same Universal Intelligence was also able to create me. Scientists and Atheists contemplate The Big

Bang... but "What was before that?". Even before this theoretical Big Bang created the entire Universe - with its trillions of stars and zillions of planets and moons - there had to be an even more super-powerful, super-abundant, and super-transcendent creative Universal Intelligence to KNOWINGLY light the spark! Just to create this one planet Earth we live on, with its Nature, weather, gravity, regulated days, seasons, and rotation, there has to be a mind-bogglingly HUGE super-intelligent force that is operating within and around us. With the question "What was before that?", we look into The Un-Born Eternity behind us.

The second question we can ask ourselves is... "What is after that?". This is another way we can bring our thoughts into the same Eternal Field. By contemplating the limited amount of time we each have in life, we can ask ourselves "What is after that?". Going further, we may even start contemplating the end of mankind and of Life on Earth, the end of our Earth, of our Sun, and of our Star Constellations, each time asking ourselves "But, what is after that?". We talk of Armageddon... The Sun burning out and engulfing the entire Solar System... and Black Holes absorbing our entire galaxy - "But, what is after that?". "After all that happens... Is there something still remains?" "If a Black Hole is going to absorb all the Life of the Universe into it... what will be left? What remains?". Many atheists and scientists will say "Nothing". However, the power of that Black Hole came from something, the Life it absorbed will be going somewhere, and it generated its power somehow. Should we all get sucked into a Black Hole (that no astronomer has ever seen), there will still be The Universal Intelligence that created its immense force. With the question "What is after that?", we look into The Un-Dying Eternity in front of us.

This second question takes our thoughts in the opposite direction of the first question. We look at eternity on both sides of the coin. With "Allah", our internal vision looks beyond both the beginning of Life ("What was before that?") and beyond the end of Life ("What remains after that?"). In these two ways, we come to the same one eternal, dynamic, and underlying Universal Intelligence. "Allah", and its built-in dual definition, submerges our mind into the scope of what that Eternal and spiritually dynamic field could be conceptualized as being.

Another thing to consider is that The Koran describes Allah as "The First and The Last"... but what is "The Middle"? In short, WE are "The Middle". Everything we see, everything we are, and every-manifested-thing around us - The Earth, The Sun, and all of the Stars - encompasses "The Middle". The visible spectrum of Life is definitely "The Middle". By living in this dynamic cycle of materializing and un-materializing, of birth-living-dying-birth-living-dying, this "Wheel of Life", we find ourselves in "The Middle". Everything in the Universe is a crystallized manifestation of divine thought... This Universe we are in is "The Middle". Allah, however, is "The first and the last".

In conjunction with the two "Aahs" of "Allah", the two "LL's" represent "The Middle". To enjoy the Earth, the Stars, and all the beauty within and around us, we use our five senses to connect to The Middle. We are caught up in it, entangled in it, and are in the midst of the all-important Middle...but, luckily, through thought can we take our minds out of its entrapment and into The True Source.

One of the most prominent, yet overlooked, aspects of Allah is that it is a phonetic palindrome. Palindromes are words that can be said or written exactly the same when backwards or forwards. Ancient mystics used them in rituals to trigger Light. They intensified what was being practiced. Allah's palindromic aspect ties into its dual definition of God as "without beginning and without end". No higher palindrome exists that gives the empowered resonating effect that Allah does. It is a palindrome whose root meaning triggers our second thoughts and after-thoughts in numerous exalted ways. The "h" in Allah ensures we say it correctly. The girl's name "Ava", for example, is a written palindrome, but is not a phonetic palindrome. When we say Ava, we say "Ay-Vah". But, when we say it backwards, it sounds like "Ah-Vay". When it is both a written and phonetic palindrome, we say "Ah-Vah". Remembering its root meaning in combination with its correct pronunciation gives this mantra a tremendous effect.

Allah is the highest phonetic palindrome

Of the five world mantras - "Om", "Amen", "AUM", "Tao", and "Allah" - "Allah" has a unique and rare quality within its verbalization. The other four mantras are different, and just as powerful, keys to unlocking Universal Consciousness, but it is "Allah" that is the only phonetic palindrome. The other four mantras connect us, in their numerous and dynamic ways, to our same Universal Source. However, "Allah" incorporates a palindromic factor that is found beyond its root definition.

Certain phonetic palindromes are thought to awaken both the divinity existing within ourselves and the supernatural existing within Nature. Their mirror-like quality gives them an extra potency beyond writing them down or what their literal meanings define them to be. Palindromes have been used in China, India, and Arabia for rituals, incantations, and astrology. They were thought to protect people from danger and illness. Allah's symmetric and palindromic aspect perfectly fits with its dual definition of God as the beginning-less and the endless.

Even though many Muslims express doubts about the science of astrology, they are, in fact, practicing an alternate form of it. In Islam, an overwhelmingly majority of the main techniques take into account The Moon, Time, and the direction north. Muslims are not only highly aware of The Sun, The Earth, and The Stars, these celestial bodies are incorporated into their daily practices. For example, during their five daily prayers, The Hajj, and Ramadan is this especially true. During any of these events, a Muslim aligns him or herself with The Earth's north pole and The Stars. In astrology, we examine the celestial influences that the day, time, and month of our birth has on our life and personality. Taking it further, we can then examine how our sign of The Zodiac influences our day to day life. But, it is all intellectual and food for thought. An astrologer can tell us if there is an approaching celestial change, so that we can use that knowledge to benefit ourselves. If we don't know about this change, then it will just pass or it will have its unbeknownst effect on us. The highest action we can take to any approaching celestial change is a spiritual one. So, instead of conceptualizing astrology and The Zodiac, a Muslim is acting a large part of it out. It is both a spiritual and physical form of astrology.

The other, interior, or meta-physical, form of astrology aligns us to The Earth, The Moon, and The Stars through The Zodiac. Many Christians and Jews are very conscious of this inner form of astrology. Most Christians, for instance, know their astrological sign, their ascendant astrological sign, and what attributes are strongly associated with them. There is a whole esoteric science that proves how the time, date, and place of our birth affects our personalities, our God-given talents, and our lives. Both of these interior and exterior forms of astrology complement each other. One is physical and one is meta-physical. We all benefit from astrology by becoming more intellectually knowledgeable of our inner alignment with The Stars, while at the same time practicing some form of physically connection to them. The third step of Scientific Prayer is a physical and spiritual technique that connects us to the Sun, the Moon, and a number of our planets through the aid our right hand.

The Zodiac can be seen like a filter with two sides. The Christian and The Jew see the Zodiac filter from underneath, where the influence of all of our celestial bodies have made and are making a powerful imprint on our daily lives. The Muslim sees the filter from above. They focus on their connection to Allah. After all… He is the One that controls the Sun, the Moon, and all twelve Star Constellations of the Zodiac. In other words, regarding our relationship to The Horoscope, we can imagine The Universe as a "Cosmic Coffee Machine"; Where God is the coffee machine itself. His intelligence, Love, Light, and cosmic power is the water being poured into the coffee apparatus. The Stars of The Zodiac is the coffee filter, filled with nutrients and stimulants. Human actions, personalities, talents, fate, etc… is the brewed coffee that falls into the coffee cup (The human being). And Divine Thought is the element of heat that gives a dramatic influence upon the water, the coffee filter, and the coffee itself. It is good to practice our paired mantra from two levels of thought – as the coffee and, by transcending above the coffee filter, as pure and transcendent water.

Here are some thoughts of how Imams have defined the word "Allah":

"There is nothing like Him and He has the attribute of Hearing and Seeing". (The Qur'an, in Surat ash-Shura, ayah 11). This ayah separates Allah of resembling anything in creation. The Imam goes on to say that Allah exists without a place, because the one who exists in a place would, by nature, be composed of atoms, i.e., he would be a body, occupying a space, and Allah is beyond occupying spaces.

"Allah existed eternally and there was nothing else." Al-Bukhariyy, al-Bayhaqiyy and Ibn al*Jarud related that the Messenger of Allah, sallallahu alayhi wa sallam. This hadith implies that Allah was alone in al-'azal, (the status of existence without a beginning,) i.e., before creating any part of creation. There was nothing with Him: no place, no space, no sky, no light, and no darkness. Allah, the Exalted, does not change. Hence, it is impossible that after having been existing without a place, He would become a "place", because this is a development, and development is a sign of needing others. The one who needs others is not God.

"Allah existed eternally and there was no place, and He now is as He was, i.e., without a place." Imam Abu Mansur al-Baghdadiyy related in his book, Al-Farqu Bayn al*Firaq, that Imam Aliyy, the fourth of the caliphs.

"Allah existed eternally and there was no place. He existed before creating the creation. He existed, and there was no place, creation, or thing; and He is the Creator of everything." Imam Abu Hanifah, an authority of as-Salaf, wrote in his book Al-Fiqh al Absat.

In closing, one final thing to consider are the far-reaching influences that Allah has had on our collective thought – how thinking of God as something beyond this façade of creation has helped us in other areas. Mathematics is one of those such areas. The biggest example being is that we can thank Muslims for introducing "the zero" into our numeric system. It is possible that the habitual practice of focusing on The Absoluteness of God among mystic Imams inspired them to concretely introduce the zero into the Arabic numerical system. "Om", "Tao", and "Allah" take our thoughts directly to this beginningless/endless realm. However, "Om" incorporates the vibratory sound of both creation and the absolute. And with "Tao", we get there through logic, emotion, and observation. But, with "Allah", our thoughts are a taken to the dynamic absoluteness of God by putting aside everything that has been or ever will be created. It is as if everything that is manifested is a number, but Allah is the zero - The Absolute. Allah is the eternal, dynamic field from which everything is born.

Zero was first thought of by The Babylonians, The Mayans, and many Indian mystics 4,000 years ago, but was only spoken of. By 773 A.D., the concept of zero was also known in China and the Middle East, according to Nils-Bertil Wallin of Yale Global. But when the concept of zero reached Baghdad, it quickly became part of the Arabic numerical system. This society had a long history of focusing on the Absoluteness of God in their spirituality, so it could be that they were well prepared to accept the absoluteness of zero into their mathematics. Up until then, people counted "one, two, three...". After that, people counted "ZERO... one, two, three...". They began from The Absolute, and then started counting the manifested things. Counting, itself, became a form of prayer and remembrance. It became its own unique numeric system. Clearly, Islamic mystics considered zero, and the "O" they designed for it, an important enough concept to change their entire numeric system in order to incorporate it. What is often forgotten is that the "O" is symbolic for The Absolute. The Yin/Yang symbol represents The masculine energy, The feminine energy, and The Absolute.

A Persian mathematician, Mohammed ibn-Musa al-Khowarizmi, suggested that a little circle should be used in calculations if no number appeared in the tens place. The Arabs called this circle "sifr," or "empty." Zero was crucial to al-Khowarizmi, who used it to invent algebra in the ninth century. Al-Khowarizmi also developed quick methods for multiplying and dividing numbers, which are known as algorithms — a form of mathematics based on his name. - http://www.livescience.com/27853-who-invented-zero.html

Tao, The Virtuous Mother of The 10,000 Things

"Allah" is not the only mantra that takes our thoughts to God as an Eternal Field. "Tao" takes us to the same realm of Eternity, but in a number of various and unique ways. In "The Tao Te Ching", the first book on Taoism written by its founder Lao Tzu, our thoughts are taken to this realm via God as "The Eternal Field behind the 10,000 things", God as "The Universal Mother", and God as "The Divine Virtues".

The Tao Te Ching is divided into different chapters. Here are some excerpts of how Lao Tzu describes The Tao:

Chapter 1)   The Tao is The Mother of the ten thousand things.
Chapter 4)   An empty vessel. It is used but never filled.
             The unfathomable source of the 10,000 things.
             Hidden deep, but an ever-present mystery.
             "I do not know from where it comes".

Chapter 14)   Stand before it and there is no beginning.
Follow it and there is no end.
Stay with the ancient Tao - Move with the present.

Chapter 16)   Being at one with The Tao is eternal.
Although the body dies, The Tao will never pass away.

Chapter 20)   I am nourished by the great Mother.

Chapter 21)   The Tao is elusive and intangible.

Chapter 25)   Mysteriously formed before Heaven and Earth in the silence and the void.
Standing alone and unchanging. The Mother of the 10,000 things.

Chapter 32)   The Tao is undefined.

Chapter 34)   It nourishes the 10,000 things and yet it is not their Lord. It has no aim.
The Tao cannot be seen, cannot be heard, and cannot be exhausted.

Chapter 41)   Hidden and without name. Nourishes and brings everything to fulfillment.

Chapter 42)   Tao begot one. One begot two.
Two begot three. Three begot the 10,000 things.

Chapter 51)   All things arise from Tao.

Chapter 52)   The beginning of the Universe is The Mother of all things.

Chapter 60)   Approach the Universe with Tao and evil will have no power.

Chapter 62)   Tao is the source of the 10,000 things. The treasure of the good man and the refuge of the bad.

In Taoism, God is thought of differently than in Christianity or Judaism. For the Taoist, "God" is not a jealous and vengeful person ready to send us to Hell for our sins – but, rather, an eternally creative, incessantly dynamic, transcendent intelligence that is existing within and around us. The Tao Te Ching describes "The Tao" as the dynamic universal source behind "The ten thousand things". Should we start making a list of ten thousand things, none of would get very far before realizing this. Ten thousand seems a small, attainable number... until we start making a list. Like "Allah", the "Tao" can take our thoughts into the beginning-less and endless realm of all existence. We are taken past the façade of this material world and into the dynamic source of Divine Consciousness itself.

Of the five mantras, "The Tao" is the one that most overtly references the qualities of a relatable person; namely, a Mother. It is interesting that Lao Tzu chose our sentiments of a Mother as a pathway to God. Every mother aspires to have a number of divine qualities between them and their children – both in the way that the mother relates to her child, and in the way that she hopes her child will relate to her. Even the mothers who are perceived as "cold-hearted" want their child to be independent.

Motherhood goes beyond religion. A Jewish, Christian, Muslim, and Hindu mother all strive for the same maternal qualities. As soon as a woman knows she's pregnant, she becomes a mother. Possibly, even before she knows… when she suspects. In that instant, all kinds of maternal instincts immediately kick in. Her thoughts start to tap into the feminine aspects of The Father/Mother God. More and more maternal instincts get activated as time and experiences pass. Even if she becomes 100 years old and her "child" is 80 years old, she will still feel maternal towards them. Once these instincts are activated, they remain with her throughout her life - All because she gave birth to a new human being, and by remembering herself going through one of the ultimate divine transformations.

Some of the qualities a mother strives to be for her child are listed below. They are either what she wants to be for her child, what she wants to teach to her child, or what she hopes the child will see in her:

Caring	Relatable	Not overbearing	Fearless
Always available	Good	Thoughtful	Peaceful
Supports dreams	Unconditional Love	Heals	Accepting
Affectionate	Role model	Never neglects	Comforts
Constant Love	Gives birth	Generous	Balanced
Joyful	Trustworthy	Patient	Kind
Strong	Forgives	Wise	Humble
Quiet	Silent	Self-sacrificing	Brings order
Sets rules	Treats individually	Supports her child's path	Helpful
Progressive	Listens		Encourages
Intuitive	Understanding	Consistent	Delegates
Spontaneous	Receptive	Sees the big picture	Truthful
Involved in our lives	Creative	Aspiring	Open
		One step ahead	

By reading this list, we see that everything that a mother wants to be for her children, God is for us.

Adoptive mothers reach the same point. Even though the mother did not undergo the biological process, the spiritual process still takes place and becomes just as strong. When an adoptive parent raises a child, there is a gradual conscious and unconscious assimilation of maternal ideas and knowledge. More than that, there is also the Love she feels for her child that helps accelerate her to the point where all of her maternal instincts are triggered. Biological differences may present themselves at times, but her awakened divine maternal aspirations will, by then, overwhelm her thoughts and actions.

Even though Lao Tzu never talks overtly about Love, he alludes to it through our thoughts of a mother's qualities. By saying that The Universal Mother is the nourishing source of everyone and everything, he awakens more than Love in our hearts. He opens our vision to where we transcend past the façade of this manifested universe. Our thoughts become ALIVE with The Universal Love we can tap into at will. Our mothers were our first examples in life. Memories of her, combined with our aspirations towards oneness with God can evoke an immense amount of Light within. One good exercise to do is to sit down for some time and describe twenty of your Mother's best qualities. Items 17 through 20 will likely be her most divine ones.

Towards the end of "The Tao Te Ching", its tone changes as you are reading it. In General, Lao Tzu takes us from seeing God as "The Universal Mother", to seeing God as "The Eternal Field behind the 10,000 things", to finally talking about reaching oneness with God through "The Divine Virtues". Other spiritual guides, like Omraam Mikaël Aivanov, tell us in their books of the five divine virtues: Justice, Truth, Love, Kindness, and Wisdom. These five form a pentagram, or five-pointed star – A powerful symbol of perfection that we can use to further amplify our prayers. "The Pentagram of Virtues" and "The Pentagram of Akasha" are the two main components of the 4th step of Scientific Prayer. These are two simple techniques we can do to activate our inner resources before we pray. They help bring our thoughts to its highest state of Universal Oneness.

In The Tao Te Ching, before Lao Tzu starts writing about Virtues, he prepares our thoughts about the ascending nature of The Five Virtues in its 38th chapter:

Chapter 38)   When Tao is lost there is goodness. When goodness is lost there is kindness. When kindness is lost there is justice. When justice is lost there is ritual.

He also alludes to the important role of Virtues in the latter chapters of The Tao Te Ching:

Chapter 39)   *Lao Tzu compares Virtue to clarity, firmness, strength, fullness, growth, and leadership.*

Chapter 41)   The Highest Virtue seems empty. A wealth of Virtue seems inadequate.
The strength of Virtue seems frail. Real Virtue seems unreal.

Chapter 49)   Virtue is goodness. Virtue is faithfulness.

Chapter 51)   All things arise from Tao. They are nourished by Virtue. Thus, the ten thousand things all respect Tao and honor Virtue. Respect of Tao and honor of Virtue are not demanded, but they are in the nature of things. Guiding without interfering, this is Primal Virtue.

Chapter 54)   Cultivate Virtue in yourself, and Virtue will be real.

Chapter 55)   He who is filled with Virtue is like a newborn child.

Chapter 59)   If there is a good store of Virtue, then nothing is impossible.

Chapter 60)   *Lao Tzu talks about how a sage can protect himself from evil with the Tao and how Virtue will refresh both the sage and the evil doer.*

Chapter 65)   Rulers who try to use cleverness cheat the country. Those who rule without cleverness

	are a blessing to the land. Understanding these (alternatives) is Primal Virtue. Primal Virtue is deep and far. It leads all things back toward the great oneness.
Chapter 68)	The Virtue of not striving has been known as the ultimate unity with heaven.
Chapter 79)	A man of Virtue performs his part, but a man without Virtue requires others to fulfill their obligations.

In this sacred book, a lot of attention is put into this word. But, what, in fact are Virtues? We often talk about principles, laws, virtues, and morals very "loosely" – but, what, in fact, are they? Regarding our Virtues, where is their place in our lives – and why did a Saint, such as Lao Tzu, devote so much time in his teachings to them?

One thing we have to first define for ourselves is that…

Virtues are different than principles.
Virtues are different than morals.
Virtues are different than laws.

In our various world societies, our principles beget our morals and our morals beget our laws.

In our spirituality, our principles beget our morals, our morals beget our virtues, and our virtues are what resonate with The Universal Laws. For example, no world government has a law that enforces kindness, however, every human has a virtue for it – and it is this Virtue of Kindness that resonates with our higher, Universal Laws. Karma, one expression of Divine Justice, is another Virtue that resonates with our Universal Laws.

As for all four terms, they are defined in our dictionaries as:

Principles	A fundamental source or basis of something. The foundation for a systemof belief, behavior, or for a chain of reasoning. A scientific theorem that has numerous special applications across a wide field.
Morals	Concerned with the principles of right and wrong behavior. High principles are used for proper conduct. Morals are also a lesson that can be derived from a story.
Virtues	Behavior showing the highest moral standards. The good result that comes from something. Moral excellence, goodness, righteousness.
Laws	Regulate actions. A rule defining correct procedure or behavior. A fact, deduced from observation, to the effect that a particular, natural or scientific phenomenon always occurs if certain conditions are present. The body of divine commandments as expressed in religious texts.

Like Taoists, we can combine "The Eternal Field" with "The Divine Virtues" within their thoughts and actions. We can give all four of these terms a place, and see how they are divinely interconnected:

> *We extract our morals of right and wrong out of the vast number of our principles. Our highest and most righteous morals are our virtues – Justice, Truth, Love, Kindness, and Wisdom. It is this tiny group of virtues that resonate with The Universal Laws.*
> – 19 June, 2017. Joliette - Marseille, France

Xavier Clayton

The Cosmic Sound Mantras – Amen, Om, & Aum

At first glance, Christianity, Judaism, Buddhism, and Hinduism seem to be four distinct and vastly different faiths. It is true that these religions originate from different parts of the world and are practiced in different ways. However, there are many spiritual elements that they have in common; The way their mantras ("Amen", "Om", and "AUM") take our thoughts to The Cosmic Sound that exists within every manifested thing, how their calendars and festivals are calculated all or partly by a Solar calendar, and how each of these faiths awaken our "Inner Sun". These two faiths complement The Lunar aspects that both exist within all human beings. A human being is both Lunar and Solar. Looking at these religions from this angle, we can see how Buddhism and Hinduism have more in common with Christianity and Judaism than it does with Taoism, and how Christianity and Judaism have more in common with Buddhism and Hinduism than it does with Islam. All four of these faiths can help awaken The Cosmic Sound existing within every atom of ourselves, and connect us to that One Cosmic Vibration resonating in every molecule of our Universe.

"Conches-ness" and The Power of Sound

Many of us are familiar with the circular seashells known as conches. It is often said that when you place your ear next to a conch, you can hear the ocean. This phenomenon, whether real or not, shouldn't surprise us. Conches come from the ocean and are often found washed up on our beaches. Other times, deep-sea divers go into the ocean and come back with a conch they found there. The circular shapes within, as well as the seashell's geometric form, contribute to the sound we are hearing, or imagine we are hearing. Yet, we do hear something that sounds very similar to the waves of the ocean.

In some ways, an atom can be compared to a conch. If we could put our ear next to an atom, we would hear The Ocean of Consciousness… or, as another way of looking at it, The Ocean of "Conches-ness". Scientists and spiritualists have already confirmed that there is a vibratory field permeating all atoms and molecules in existence. This vibratory field connects us all. Many of our newest scientific discoveries depend on this universal and interconnected vibratory realm in order for them to work. If it weren't there, the Internet, the radio, cellular phones, and our television sets would be of no use.

All physical matter is made up of cells, molecules, and atoms. For example, our body is made of cells. Cells are made of molecules. Molecules are made of atoms. And atoms… are made up of Divine Intelligence. Logically, they have to be. Atoms are in incessant action. A continuous action between its nucleus and its electron. What other force, other than Divine Intelligence, would keep an electron spinning around the nucleus of an atom at The Speed of Light? What other force could incessantly do this for the infinite number of electrons, spinning around the infinite number of nuclei, in the infinite number of molecules, within the infinite number of cells, throughout our infinitely vast Universe?

In our Universe, the two most powerful forces are The Speed of Light and The Speed of Sound. Today, God is very often described as Light. Even ancient mystics would describe or compare God to Light. So too have The Masters Buddha, Jesus, and Krishna been described in terms of Light. And no matter what spiritual path we are on, we all want to reach enlightenment. When we think of Light, we ascend. When we think of darkness, we descend. Light is a beautiful road towards our oneness with Universal Intelligence. However,

Science is beginning to see that Sound is a force as powerful or more powerful than Light. A spiritualist knows that with "Om", "AUM", and "Amen", we can come to the same oneness and realization of God through Sound as we do with Light.

Of our five senses (seeing, touching, tasting, smelling, and hearing), sound (hearing) is among the senses that are nearly impossible to suppress. It can be argued that sound is much more variable than light. The Earth makes a variety of sounds. Nature, animals, inanimate objects, and of course man, all make a variety of sounds. Even the sky makes numerous sounds with its wind and thunder. We can find a wide array of sounds within the very small human audio spectrum of things we hear. Dogs and birds can hear in an even wider spectrum than we do. To a spiritualist, the sounds of "Om", "AUM", and "Amen" extend to the edges of our galaxies. Sounds we may not hear – But, we definitely feel.

Scientists throughout the world have recently been making new discoveries involving sound. Sound has the power to influence atoms. And therefore, atoms influence molecules. And then molecules influence objects – both animate and inanimate. Sound will make the molecules of a liquid or object resonate in unison. Already today, treatments involving sound waves are used on some cancer patients. Some of the many most recent discoveries involving sounds are:

1. Sound can modify DNA.
   This discovery was made in 2011 by the Russian biophysicist Pjotr Garjajev.
   By using only sound and light, his team of scientists changed frog embryos to salamander embryos. In other words, sound and light changed one life form into a completely different life form.

2. Sound can levitate objects.
   In 2015, a team of Spanish and English scientists levitated small objects into the air. Water droplets, coffee grains, Styrofoam, and toothpicks were some of the objects levitated. They did this with only the use of sound. These scientists theorize that if sound is amplified high enough, larger objects could also be levitated.

3. Sound can create light.
   When water is excited by sound, short bursts of light are emitted. This technique is called "Sonoluminescence". Doing this also creates an intense amount of energy. Theoretically, sound could be a new energy source to light our homes and power our vehicles.

4. Sound moves faster than light.
   In 2007, scientists used experiments to demonstrate that "sound pulses" can travel faster than The Speed of Light. As for "sound waves", they showed that the velocities of audio waves can become infinite. In other words, we can leave "messages" in the vibratory field of our Universe that will remain there forever. We can communicate with other life forms on distant planets by the use of sound.

5. Sound can kill viruses.
   In 2008, scientists mathematically determined that the frequencies of simple viruses could be de-activated. Within this study, scientists showed that there is a "resonant frequency" existing in our Universe. Every object, molecule, and atom naturally resonates with this one eternal vibration. Human beings also resonate with this one vibration. If mathematically correct,

science could de-activate viruses by using discordance or dissonance. This could be a whole new way that our medical community could cure an Ill-ness or a dis-ease.

6. Sound can boil water.
The inventor, Peter Davey, created a sound device that boils water. As we have seen with light and DNA experiments, sound waves can excite molecules and atoms. For water to be boiled, it has to reach 100°C. In this experiment, Davey boiled water in seconds by only the use of sound. This was a physical demonstration of sound's physical ability to change atoms and molecules.

*GAIA, "Six Secret Powers of Sound". 23 December, 2016.

Through sound, we can find a new and undiscovered path into Universal Intelligence. "Om", "Amen", and "AUM" can take our thoughts through the kaleidoscope of sounds we hear every day, directly into the Divine Source from whence they all originate. In these chaotic, multi-sound metropolises we live in, these three mantras can pinpoint our thoughts and aspirations into a field that exists beyond the clutter.

As for the link between "Om", "Amen", and "AUM", all three are related. All three are similar. They are all cosmic mantras that harmonize our thoughts with The Universal Sound. They form a trinity, but are, in fact, one. It can be useful to metaphorically think of them as one tool – like a hammer. A hammer is really three tools in one. One part of it is used to pound in nails (The head). Another part of it is used to pull out nails (The 'V'). And a third part of it is used to tear off tree bark or dig a small hole (The tongs). All three of the techniques we use a hammer for are easy to learn. As with "The Three Cosmic

Mantras of Universal Sound", every aspect of a tool depends on your intentions, your needs, and practice.

Oneness with The Universal Vibration takes us beyond The Ego

One thing that religions teach us is to see the world as an illusion. "The world does not exist". "All manifested things are an illusion". "Everything is illusive". "The only things that exist are The ego and The Self"... etc. The basis of this teaching is to show us that there are two things operating in The Universe – The Real Limitless Eternal Consciousness and its unreal manifestations. We are reminded not to get entangled in our everyday lives, that are filled with objects and people that will not lead us to anything anywhere as deeply fulfilling as Divine Consciousness does. We are taught to overcome our own egos that do get lost and entangled in its own self-importance, greed, lust, and attachments.

Upon hearing this advice, many spiritualists try to see the world as a façade. That the apple you are eating, the body you inhabit, and the world you live in is somehow unreal. When questioned about this, even yogis find it hard to deny that the chair they are sitting on is somehow not there.

The intended lesson of this practice is to get us to see that everything emerges from and is supported by The Eternal Field. It is to bring our thoughts to Non-Duality – where there is no ego and there is no self. There is only the one dynamic field of Pure Consciousness within and around us.

First of all, the ego will always be there – enlightenment or no enlightenment. If you've incarnated into a body, it will come with an ego. It's part of the package. The ego helps keep us alive. The ego helps protect us and connects us to our sixth sense. The ego inspires us and helps us improve the situations in our lives. The ego connects us to our intuition. In the 1950's, when the telephone was popularly in use, people would call a telephone operator and tell her what number they wanted to reach. She would be sitting at a large console with cables and phone lines. At her switchboard, she would listen to your desire and then instantly connect your call with who you wanted to reach.

"Good morning, E.G.O. Telephone service, can I help you?".
"Yes, I'm trying to reach Mr. Arro Gant at #555-1234".
"Please hold, I'll connect you".

Whether you wanted to reach Mr. Arro Gant, Ms. Hyan Mighty, or Mr. Sel Fish, really wasn't her concern. Her concern was to connect you to what your Mind wanted among the vast number of different options on her telephone console. That was her job, and she was busy enough with that.

The ego is a lot like our own inner telephone operator. We all have numbers that we habitually call. Lines that we habitually connect with. When we need an "answer" to a problem or a situation, we usually call up these same numbers. But, with this inner service, there are no busy signals. There are no wrong numbers. We will always get instantly connected to the party we are trying to reach. But, it is on us if we want to call "downtown" or if we want to call "uptown".

So, even though we will always have an ego, what the problem is, is that we have learned to habitually use it to call on our lower senses. Even though we have an ego, we can still teach it to call on kindness. We can teach it to call on selflessness. It can learn to tap into love. It can connect to Truth. And it can be used to reach Universal Consciousness.

The problem with overcoming the ego and the "façade" of the materialized Universe, is that it takes a lot of effort. It can trigger frustration and confusion. "Is this apple I am holding in my hand real or not?". However, studying the Universe from the aspect of The Cosmic Sound takes us past this ego frustration. In this frame of thought, we instead say "This apple in my hand is real because every atom and molecule within it resonates with The Cosmic Sound that emerged from The Eternal Field... Just like I resonate with The Cosmic Sound and every star in The Universe resonates with The Cosmic Sound... and that we all have come from The Eternal Field". In this latter way of looking at an apple, the ego is taken out of the equation and we are instantly placed in a higher state of mind.

The origins of "Amen", "Om", and "AUM"

The mantra "Amen" is widely used within and beyond the Christian faith. In Judaism, Amen is said for blessings and benedictions. In Christianity, Amen is said at the end of prayers and songs. In Islam, Amen is said at the opening of the first Islamic prayer - the Al-Fatiha. Clearly, our mystic ancestors gave it a huge and far-reaching importance. For it to be able to cross the "barriers" of three faiths, to where it is used in blessings, prayers, and song, its permeating benediction has to have been recognized for at least 2,000 years. But, how do we think of it today? Is the way our ancient mystics thought of "Amen" the same as we think of it in our modern times?

At best, "Amen" today is thought to mean "so be it"... "truly"... or "verily". More often, it is said as a sort of agreement or affirmation – "Amen to that!". At worst, it is subconsciously thought to mean "The End", as it is said at the end of prayers, the end of songs, and at the end of a Biblical reading. We also hear it said at the end of sermons and masses, which further helps lead us into thinking that "Amen" means – or at least feels like - "The End". But, as Christians, we should ask ourselves… How could Jesus Christ, who repeated "Amen" so often, have performed miracles with it if it meant "Verily"? Those who were near him have written of how he spontaneously used it within his inspired teachings and blessings – How could he have done all this and thought that Amen meant "The End"?

We should remember where this word came from, and how it has spread throughout our World Christianity. "Amen" came from Jesus Christ himself – from his very own lips. It was the prominent and often repeated utterance he spontaneously made throughout the day. And because of this Divine habit that Jesus Christ was known to have had, the Catholic Church adopted it and incorporated it into its prayers and rituals.

We should also remember that the environment Jesus lived in was centuries before The Bible was written. Overwhelmingly, most of the stories and parables we read in it now did not yet exist or were of minor importance to him in his lifetime. The raising of Lazarus, the changing of water into wine, The Sermon on The Mount, his feeding of 5000 people with a few loaves and fishes, The Last Supper, and his Crucifixion were all happening to him "In Real Time" – and the one thread throughout it all, was that he was in the continuous habit of repeating "Amen". Through his own words and example, we know that was important to him was his naked relationship to Divine Consciousness. And we know that the spiritual tool he used to either confirm, amplify, or teach others of their own naked relationship with God… was the word "Amen".

From stories in the Bible and the Gospels, we deduce that "Amen" was a word not commonly heard before in that region. It was a new word that permeated the atmosphere around Jesus, and triggered Light and joy within people who heard him say it. Throughout the world, many spiritualists say mantras that fill their body and the atmosphere around them with Light. The habit of doing this is an elixir. It awakens Pure Joy within every cell of our being. For example, saying "Amen", with an enlightened knowledge of its meaning, is like taking a sip from The Fountain of Youth. The word ITSELF is an elixir. You get drunk on its ecstasy and power. Your thoughts immediately transcend this physical world to take you into the sublime realm of Divine Quintessence. This habit starts to take place on its own once Transcendent Joy has awakened within you, and you begin practicing the spiritual techniques that are right for you. No one orders a yogi or a yogini to lovingly repeat their mantra. They begin spontaneously saying words like "Namasté", "Om Namah Shivaya", "Sai Ram", "Hare Krishna", and the like. This also happens on its own when the person is meditating, chanting, or the many other techniques that they are taught in an ashram. The most important element to triggering sustained and abundant joy is practice; something that The Master Christ subtly demonstrated to his disciples.

The fact that words can trigger Divine Light is seen throughout all faiths. Christian Evangelicals repeat "Hallelujah!" or "Praise Jesus!" with a deep amount of Love and faith. Greetings like "Shalom" or "Salam Allekum / Allekum Salam" also spark Pure Joy and Light within us and our vicinity. But, for a spiritualist, what is indispensable with any mantra is that its root definition takes our thoughts into the realm of Divine Consciousness. It is the starting point of our spiritual trajectory. However, when a Master Teacher, like Jesus Christ, utters a mantra you can BE SURE that there is something entirely different going on in his or her mind than in a yogi's mind! The Master is more evolved, more practiced, and more knowledgeable. It is like comparing a child who is just learning how to count to a PhD professor in Mathematics. The numbers are the same, but the possibilities that the professor can do with them are a stark difference to what the child can do! The child gets a lot of happiness and pride when he or she can use their fingers to count to ten. Their self-esteem rises and they get a lot of encouragement and Love from their parents. But the Mathematics professor is a master in algebra, calculus, statistics, and geometry! There is no comparison. So, to say that when Jesus spontaneously said, as he often did, "Amen" that he meant "truly" or "so be it", that is probably not recognizing the depths of his thoughts. Rather, it is showing our own limitations to the thoughts he must have had as a Spiritual Master. If all he meant was "verily", "truly", or "The End", then how could he have performed his Transfiguration? If his thought behind "Amen" was merely "So be it", then how could he have been and still be The Prince of Peace?

Stories of disciples close to Jesus also tell us that he would say "Amen" to affirm his own utterances. Meaning that Jesus would say something of great Truth and then he would say "Amen" after it. This was more than a habit of his, when Truth and "Amen" went hand in hand – this was a revealing of his True Self. A revelation of Truth, paired with a subsequent "Amen", were an outer exposure of his Inner Nature.

We can never know exactly what Jesus Christ thought, but by examining his habits, his words, and the results of his actions, we can get some indication of his possible motives and intentions. As for his habit of spontaneously saying "Amen", we can assume a number of basic things…

His teachings of Truth sprang from a deeply inspired place – and from that same place sprang also "Amen".

Truth and "Amen" both came from his connection to a realm of Light, Joy, and Transcendence he embodied.

As he often indicated, this is a place we can feel when we ourselves become more transcendent through spiritual practices, like prayer, baptism, and Faith.

When The Truth he had just said resonated with those around him, the vicinity's atmosphere changed to a more exalted state.

When he saw that what he was saying to those who were with him was being deeply understood, saying "Amen" while his disciples were in this momentarily transfixed state was giving them a very high blessing.

Again, The Bible says that "In the beginning, God became The Word... *and then...* The Word became everything in the Universe". This sentence, in fact, describes two steps. With the first step, God condenses himself into a word. When we think about what a word is, we can say that a word is a combination of sound, thought, and vibration. The word that The Bible describes is one that filled the entire Universe with these combined three aspects. With the second step, that word, sound, thought, and vibration expresses itself into becoming everything that is manifested or created in our Universe. The first part of this sentence is about contraction. The second part is about expression. But, both steps originate from a Universal Whole. How the Word contracts and expresses describes many of the actions taking place in vibrational realm that permeates all atoms. Thought is the central factor in this. The root meaning of a mantra combines thought and vibration.

Even though he never wrote down any of his teachings, there are several accounts of people who lived with The Master Christ during his lifetime. His use of "Amen" is often mentioned - how he used it and when he used it. It was something that he had the habit of saying many times throughout the day, especially when he was giving his sermons. In other religions, this habit is also seen. For instance, many Hindu yogis and Gurus have the same habit of spontaneously repeating "Rama" or "Om Namah Shivaya". Buddhist monks have the same habit with "Nam myoho renge kyo" (meaning, "I am determined to manifest my Buddha Nature"). Like these other mantras, Amen is FULL of Light. Amen awakens inner-light. Amen evokes transcendence and Pure Joy within and around us.

In Hinduism, we learn about The Akasha. This is the realm of existence that is seen as the very first creation of God. The Universal Primordial Source that Divine Intelligence created before all else. From the Akasha spring – in successive order – the five elements of Ether, Air, Fire, Water, and Earth. All five of these elements resonate with Sound (known as "Shabda"). The Akasha itself is the endless, un-manifested, Eternal Space. Some refer to it as "The upper sky". The Ether, Air, Fire, Water, and Earth are part of the limited, manifested, material space. It is referred to as "The lower sky". Techniques like The Pentacle of Akasha unite the upper sky and the lower sky into harmonic oneness.

For this book, The Akasha and Amen refer to the same manifestation to first emerge from The Eternal Void. The first thing that God created, and that is still here, is a primordial

Divine Realm – the first endlessly dynamic creation from whence everything else in the Universe originate. It is "The Word" that John 1:1 in The Bible talks about. Saying "Amen" out loud awakens sound, thought, energy, and Divinity. It is also a technique that brings the upper sky and the five elements of the lower sky together. Amen is the bridge that connects Universal Consciousness and physical matter.

Let us remember that The Master Jesus did not go around saying "Jesus" to amplify his thoughts, discourses, and prayers. What he said - repeatedly - was "Amen". So, Amen must have meant a great deal to him. It must have had a great many exalted meanings for him. It had to have connected him in many ways to "God, The Father" that he often reminded us of. He did this throughout his teachings, and even at the end of "The Lord's Prayer" he gave to the world. Even there, we come into his thoughts of divine reverence when it says "For thine is the kingdom, the power, and the glory forever and ever, Amen".

Scientists theorize now that the creation of the Universe was 14 billion years before the birth of Christ. It is not known if the people living in the era that Christ did would have concepts of billions of years before their time as the beginning of the Universe. But, what is more probable, is that they probably looked around at their world and asked themselves 'From where did this all begin?'... and "How did this all start?". After much elimination and several layers of deduction, we can come to either two choices that were the first to emerge from the Eternal Void – Light or Sound. Of these two candidates, Light would probably have been eliminated because if something is to emerge then there involves thought and movement. The Universe emerged from Pure Thought and, from this universal and multi-dimensional action, it had to have created Sound before Light.

Quantum Scientists and Nuclear Physicists can use their knowledge about the creative energy of Cosmic Thought to tell us a lot about the mantra Amen. In The Bible, John 1:1 starts with "In the beginning...God became The Word". It then goes on to say that "The Word" then became "Everything in The Universe". For whoever wrote this passage, that word had to contain the same Divine power as God himself. It does not say "God became The Universe". Rather; it theorizes that The Universal Mind's first and purest step in manifesting all that we see and hear was to form itself into a Word. And as this was the first word, it formed the basis for all other words. All words are a combination of vibration, thought, and energy. They often also contain an intention and an idea. The primordial word contained all of these elements and more.

There is a Biblical passage that says "We are to pray in accordance to The Word". For emphasis, short-sighted Evangelical Ministers will put their hand on The Bible when they talk about or reference this passage to their congregations. It is easy to misguide people into thinking that it means The Bible itself when these ministers say "We are to pray in accordance to The Word". It is to keep their followers in control. But, The Bible does not say that "We are to pray in accordance to The Word*s*". It does not say "We are to pray in accordance to the parables you read in this book". It does not even say "We are to pray in accordance to Jesus Christ". It simply says that we are to pray in accordance to "The Word". When zealots reference The Bible as "The Word", they forget that the people in The Bible did not have a Bible. There are no stories about people reading The Bible in The Bible. Not even The Master

Christ had a Bible... but, what he did have was The Word. The problem is... what Word does The Bible mean?

In truth, The Universal Word that The Bible is talking about goes beyond any one religion. The Word that John 1:1 references is older than The Bible. It is older than even The Manusmriti or The Vedas – 4,000 years is nothing in comparison to the birth of the entire Cosmos. The stories we read in The Bible are around 2,000 years old. The birth of The Universe is estimated to be around 14,000,000,000 (14 billion) years old.

> The Word is not The Bible.
> The Word is beyond a written page.
> The Word is a creative, dynamic, and intelligent force, born from The Eternal Consciousness, to create this vibrant, multi-dimensional Universe we live in.

What John 1:1 truly describes is Divine Metamorphosis. It is something beyond Divine Creation, as it shows how everyone and everything come from One Dynamic Source. To create this multi-dimensional Universe, as John 1:1 is describing, God first transformed himself into a word-vibration-thought-idea-energy-intention-sound, and that Divine Primordial Word is what has morphed itself into every atom and molecule throughout the millions of galaxies that we already know exist. That Word combines spirituality, The Universe, and science into one. It is far more and far beyond the parables in The Bible.

Today, we get caught up in the many stories and metaphors of The Bible, The Gospels, The Nag Hamadi, and other Christian scriptures. We study the symbolism of Christ's Life and crucifixion. We take communion as representations of his body and his blood. However, we forget one important thing. During his own lifetime, The Master Jesus himself did not study The Bible. He did not spend his time cutting ribbons. He walked the walk and talked the talk, because he was a living example of The Divine Virtues. He never inaugurated a new church, because he was a Temple of Light wherever he went – and showed us how to be Temples of Light in our own lives. From what we know about him, all he needed to perform the miracles he did and channel the Truth he said was his conscious connection to God and his use of "Amen". As for Amen, this was his most perceivable tool – and he used it liberally during the last 3 years of him actively bringing God's Light and Truth into our world.

Jesus never said "Amen" to affirm something someone else said. These days, if you agree with something someone has said, you say "Amen!" or "Amen to that!". Even our Evangelical preachers say, "Can I get an Amen?". But, the moment of fleeting joy this awakens in the pews when they respond "AMEN!", but The Master Jesus did not use it in this way. To him, "Amen" went hand in hand with Divine Truth, Universal Laws, and Cosmic Inspiration. It was never tied to guilt, shame, blame, or chitchat. It resonates a The Higher Truth, and is a key to opening your mind and to evolving your Soul. The Master Jesus never said it off-handedly. He knew its power is to awaken your consciousness and to enlighten your being. For him, spiritual knowledge and Divine transcendence were always used together. "Amen" brings them both into one word.

After his crucifixion, where The Master Jesus transmuted from a physical body into a "Body of Light", the usage of

"Amen" was adopted by the church and incorporated into its rituals, prayers, songs, and masses. During our Catholic communions, we affirm the transmutation of Christ when we say, "This is the blood of Christ", "This is the body of Christ", and then we drink and eat these symbolic examples of how we too are transforming. Even in The Gospels, "Amen" or "Amen and Amen", are used to introduce the solemn statements Jesus spoke. "Amen" is a key that opens our minds to receive these solemn, universal teachings of Light.

Today, "Amen" is not only heard in churches and chapels, but also in mosques and synagogues. In Islam, it is heard at the beginning of a prayer or rite. In Christianity and Judaism, it is heard at the end of a prayer or rite. When used at the beginning of a prayer, Amen prepares our mind to receive Light and understanding. When used at the end of a prayer, Amen helps to internalize and establish the knowledge and Light we have just received. Unfortunately, because it is used at the of a prayer, most Christians have attached the meaning "The End" to it. It is because Christians are not exposed to "Amen" used in other ways, in other rituals, at other points in the prayer, or in other temples of worship. If, for instance, we saw how "Amen" is used at the beginning of a prayer like in mosques ("Amin"), then that would challenge our thoughts of it meaning "The End".

Jesus did not go around saying "Jesus" when he spoke Universal Truths. He neither said "Father" nor "God" to affirm his words in the minds of others. Again, what he said was "Amen" – and he said it often. Jesus, the Son of God, who said "The Father and I are one" and "I am The Life, The Truth, and The Way" can be the ultimate example of how to use that mantra and its alchemic power. It is a word that embodies the essence of transformative energy. Of how everyone, every being, and every manifested thing in our Universe has transformed from Universal Consciousness into physical matter.

So, again, it is very unlikely that when Jesus uttered "Amen" he meant "so be it", as it is thought to mean today. "So be it" is open to many interpretations from "It's out of my hands"… to "Forget about it. I have nothing to do with it"… to "It's God's way". There is not much divine enrichment that we can learn from "So be it". A Spiritual Master, like Jesus, who uttered this word so often, and at times that were so highly auspicious, would only utter a word that was FULL of universal power and Divine Quintessence. How could it be anything less?

Another aspect of "Amen" that we can examine is, when we read John 1:1 is that this sentence tells us that "Amen" is a bridge. A unique pathway between Universal Consciousness and physical matter that we can resonate with during our "Conscious Prayers".

The passage Matthew 24:35 has come to be translated as: "Heaven and Earth shall pass away, but my words shall not pass away". Even here, the word "words" can not be taken to mean "The Bible". In fact, if this is the translation we are reading, then it was misinterpreted by the person who translated it and, unfortunately, by those who read it. The original text is: "The Heaven and The Earth shall pass away. However, The Words OF ME no not shall pass away". This passage, in fact, is to show God's limitless intelligence. In many ways, it is also to remind us of His grace – and to awaken our gratitude and joy. God is eternal. God is dynamic. He became The Word that created this Universe. Because of His limitlessness, He could have become ANY Word to create a Universe – But,

He became The Word that creates and sustains every molecule in what He chose to become ours. When a passage evokes thought, Light, and mind expansion, then we can see its True meaning.

Luke 21:33 (The Lord endureth forever) and 1 Peter 1:25 (The Word of God will remain forever) can only resonate with John 1:1 (God became The Word... and The Word became The Universe) and Matthew 24:35 (My Words shall not pass away) when we see that The Word is not a book, but rather a Universal Realm of Cosmic, Intelligent, and Divine Vibratory Thought.

"When we see God as a Divine Mother, then Amen is The Womb – The portal through which all physical matter incubates, develops, and passes through before becoming matter"

When we look at experiments with Light and the experiments done with Quantum Theory, scientists tell us that thought is the main component behind both. A spoken word is a thought in the form of a sound. A word is crystallized thought. Spoken words are temporary. Written words are longer term. And memories come and go.

Before we could write, we spoke words to obtain our needs. "Mama!", "Milk", "Ball", and "No!" are some words we used to obtain our needs before we could write. A word is a thought that we hear. A word has immense power! Take a walk through any town or city. Consider the skyscrapers. What built these towns were written words, spoken words, thoughts, and drawings. Quantum Science and John 1:1 in the Bible both say that a thought, a vibration, is the source of the atom. Again, "Amen" is the middle step between Universal Consciousness and physical matter:

Physical Matter	Cells	Molecules	Atoms	**Word**	Desire	Intention	Thought	Universal Intelligence
Material Objects				AMEN				Universal Consciousness
The Tangible				**Word**				God, The Intangible
Cosmic Sound				**Mantras**				**Eternal Field**
Matter				**Word**				**Spirit**

THE TWO PATHS TO GOD

There are many undocumented years of Jesus's life. For the lost years he travelled, some assume he evolved into the master he was and is. India is often mentioned as a place Jesus visited during these lost decades. India has long been a place of spiritual awakening for many Saints, Sadhus and Gurus. The Ganges river and The Himalaya mountains are both found in India. Two places where intense rituals and spiritual aspirations have been practiced for millennium. The search for spiritual knowledge, in all its religious forms, is respected and practiced in India… even to this day. Sanskrit is one of the languages of India. It is considered one of the oldest languages in the world, as well as one of the most sacred, having syllables and an alphabet that are thought to resonate at the highest and most divine frequencies within the human body. This is why many chants, mantras, and songs use Sanskrit.

When we look at the origins of "Om", we see similarities between it and "Amen". "Om" is an ancient Sanskrit "word" that was first felt by Rishis as they meditated. When they did this, it was more about the essence of Om than the chanting of it. Rishis knew that Truth was not to be found or experienced in this material, physical, outer world. Truth is to be experienced on a realm within ourselves. Before meditation was called meditation, Rishis knew where and how to look for Truth. In other words, they found that by looking silently within themselves they could experience an inner peace and joy that came forth. This happened while they were meditating and eventually even while they were not meditating. Truth in this meaning is not something you hear someone say and then agree with. But rather, Truth is a realm of abundance and Light deep within your own soul. You come closer and closer to this realm as your mind quietens through the regular practice of meditation.

Fortunately for us, the first people that practiced this art, The Rishis, discovered that there was a word ("Om") that resonated with that inner limitless realm of Truth. Saying this word and focusing on it took us to that timeless realm. This is another example of where the experience of Truth and the utterance of a divinely inspired word go hand in hand. Jesus teaching Truth and then saying "Amen" can be directly compared to Rishis meditating on Truth and then discovering "Om".

"Om" is a mantra often used in prayers, affirmations and meditations. Buddhists, Hindus, and Yogis are known to use mantra repetition (or japa) with this powerful and mystical word. Ancient Rishis discovered this cosmic sound that exists in everything in The Universe.

Matter is made up of cells, molecules and atoms. All atoms are made up of a nucleus with an electron spinning around it at the speed of light. Both "Amen" and "AUM" are connected to "Om". Amen, like the Akasha, takes our thoughts to the first creation of God – which was a sound vibration. AUM reminds us that cosmic vibration exists on our 3 levels of thought: the conscious, subconscious and superconscious realms. Om reminds us of the cosmic vibration created by the electron spinning around the nucleus that all manifested material is created from. Quantum Science confirms that there is one universal vibration existing in all matter.

Many of us can see how Om exists in matter... but what we might forget that it also exists in other realms around us. For instance, Om also exists in gravity. Om exists in electricity. Om exists in magnetism. It exists in Light and in The Electromagnetic Light Spectrum. Om exists in radiation. And it exists in chemical reactions. Why? Because all of these are manifested vibrational phenomena that are happening on this physical plane. Everything that is a part of our physical experience of Life has Om inhabiting within it.

"Amen", "Om", and "AUM" are all related. They all spring from the inner experience of Divine Light. In Churches and Ashrams, we often hear "Amen" and "Om". But when we look back from where and who they came from, we see that it was from an expression of Pure Joy and Spiritual Knowledge. Eventually, as the experience was shared, these words started to spread and people started chanting them or repeating them to get the same experience.

In ashrams and temples, "Om" is either repeated by itself over and over or in combination with a longer Sanskrit mantra like "Om Namah Shivaya", "Om Guru Om", or "Om Shanti". "Om" is the operative word in the vast majority of Buddhist, Hindu, or Yoga chants. In Sikhism, as well, Guru Nanak spoke of how 'Om'/'Oang' being the primordial sound of the Universe. In his travels throughout the world, he spoke of how it echoes undyingly within and throughout everyone and everything. Through spiritual practices, like prayer and meditation, it is heard and felt by those who tune into the frequency of Cosmic Transcendence. Sikhism says that eventually, even without spiritual practice – by just a one-pointed focus, developed through years of practice – a person himself will come to completely resonate with this Universal and all-pervading vibratory sound.

When we study Buddhism and "The Four Noble Truths", a Buddhist is taught that because of desire all Life is suffering. To overcome this desire, he or she must follow The Eight-fold path, where they focus their minds on Right views, Right conduct, Right livelihood, Right speech, etc… to reach Nirvana. It is similar to how Christians follow The Ten Commandments in order to reach Heaven. Between The Eight-fold Path and Nirvana, we find Zen. Zen is a realm above our desires where we can consciously focus minds, as we slowly reach the Nirvana state of well-being. There is Zen-breathing, Zen-eating, Zen-meditation, Zen gardens, Zen-gardening, and Zen-chanting, to name a few. It's all about calming the mind and placing it above our desires in the midst of all of our activities on The Eight-fold Path.

This is all very good! However, Universal Consciousness is not only the Zen of Peace and Tranquility. It is also limitless abundance and incessant activity, to say the least. Zen Buddhism helps their followers develop mind control. It is helping the mind and body experience a divine state of being throughout their daily activities that they are really practicing. A Buddhist can relate to a Christian saying "Lead us not into temptation, but deliver us from Evil". Buddhists are constantly focusing their thoughts on the realm of Zen above temptation and Evil. But, if we only see Peace and Tranquility in this realm, then we are missing the MANY other aspects that God is.

At the temple, Buddhist monks work in function of their own spiritual growth. They work in the garden, in the kitchens, and work to keep the temple clean. But, like in other religions, monks don't work in the Western sense of the word, because they see the desire for money it triggers as un-clean and impure. To many of them, work awakens attachments, and this goes against The Four Noble Truths. If it is work outside of the temple, then it has the danger of triggering our suffering. But, since everyone – even monks – are born with a physical body that needs to be fed, monks choose to beg rather than work. Starving monks walk the sweltering streets of Asia with their hands out – and whatever they get in their hands that day is what they will eat… even if it's just one grain of rice. Your starvation, thirst, and that grain of rice are to teach you to keep your thoughts above your desires and your focus fixed on Zen. The non-Buddhists and the non-monk Buddhists in the cities are very aware of this Buddhist tradition and will often help the starving monk to bring Good Karma on themselves. However, there is still desire within both the monk and the person helping him or her. For the receiver, the desires are often money or food. For the giver, the desires are often blessings and "good karma".

Desire is part of Life. Plants, insects, and animals all have desire. Universal Consciousness even gave The Earth a "desire" to rotate on its axis every 24 hours and revolve around The Sun every 365 days. Without sexual desire and the desire for procreation, Nature would not exist. So, for a Buddhist to break beyond the inherent desire of our Earth would be quite a feat.

What can be transformed are our thoughts. Seeing the abundance, activity, and WORK inherently contained within both The Zen and Nirvana realms of existence, seems to be something very Non-Buddhist. But, the ability to stop, observe our actions, and then place our thoughts on the Zen above our activities strengthens the mind. Using our ability to consciously place our thought on Zen as a realm of Light empowers our actions. The light of Zen we awaken within us helps us quickly evolve to Nirvana. The mantra "Om" encompasses the word "Zen" into a tiny corner of its Universal meaning. Zen can evoke Light and lead our thoughts into the Universal Om. It is possible to see beauty and Transcendence contained within Zen and Nirvana while giving up the guilt from desires that will always be there.

In churches and chapels, there are many inspired hymns and songs. However, "Amen" like with "Om", "Allah", and

"AUM" are songs and chants of only one word. Even "Hallelujah!" has more words – "In Excelsius Deo". When "Amen" is sung by itself, as the only word, we feel a unique power from it. This should tell us that there is a special rejuvenating force in the word "Amen" itself. Even if we have never studied its meaning, we feel joy and Light just by listening to people sing that one word. This alone should make us think how highly inspired the word "Amen" is. No Pop song could get by with just one word. There are a few versions of people singing "Amen" as the only lyric and people never get tired of it. Why? Because "Amen" has the power to awaken ALL of the molecules in our body when in the environment it is heard. Like a flintstone, Amen is a verbal expression of the sparks of Inner Light being spontaneously ignited. When we hear, sing, or chant "Amen" or "Om", it cleanses our spirits. It revives us. Our environment is transformed because we ourselves become instruments of Light and transformation. Long after we have stopped singing these words, that Light lingers in the room and beyond. There is a transcendent and purifying aspect to the chanting and singing "Amen", "Om", and "AUM". And this aspect becomes more powerfully acute when our own thoughts of it are on it's true, omniscient meaning as The Cosmic Sound of The Universe.

The first thing we can recognize when we look at these three mantras is that they all have different syllables. "Om" has one syllable. "Amen" has two syllables. And "AUM" has three syllables. All three direct our thoughts to God as The Universal Sound, or cosmic vibration. Each exists within every molecule and atom. Of the five mantras discussed in this book, "AUM" is the only one with three syllables. This makes it extremely unique.

Three is a powerful number that is not only found throughout all of the religions, but also in many other areas like astrology, geometry, and music. In our zodiac, the 12 signs are divided into four equilateral triangles; fire signs (Aries/Leo/Sagittarius), water signs (Cancer/Scorpio/Pisces), air signs (Gemini/Libra/Aquarius), and earth signs (Taurus/Virgo/Capricorn). In geometry, an equilateral triangle is the strongest geometric shape. And in music, all songs are made up of chords and a basic chord is made up of three notes.

As for "AUM", this mantra encapsulates a Trinity when you say it. This gives it a power that can take our thoughts not only deep into The Universal Sound, but also into and throughout the many Trinities that exists within and around us. To say "AUM" correctly, we need to say each of its letters individually "A"… "U"… "M". "Aaaaah…Oooo…Mmmmm".

The three syllables of "A-U-M" penetrate into our three states of consciousness; The conscious state (awake), the unconscious state (sleep), and the superconscious state (deep-sleep and our "a-ha" inspired thoughts). The subconscious can be seen as a combination of our unconscious and superconscious states. It can inspire us directly from our super consciousness when we are awake, and it can also inspire us in our sleep state. When we suddenly get an inspired thought to a problem we've had or when we wake from a dream with a new idea or a solution to a problem, our subconscious has been working with either our unconscious or superconscious. Our sub-conscious mind works with all three levels of thought.

In Judaism, "AUM" is widely studied and used. In the Kabbalah, A stands for "Shin", U stand for "Aleph", and M stands for "Mem". "Shin" is translated to mean "Sharp" or "Fire". "Aleph" is translated to mean "Ox". "Mem" is translated to mean "Water" or "Transformation". Taken together, we can arrange the letters of AUM into:

Xavier Clayton

Sharp – Fire (SHIN – "A")
Ox (ALEPH – "U")
Water – Transformation (MEM – "M")

When we examine the first letter "A" (or "Shin"), we see that this letter symbolizes fire. In Hebrew calligraphy, the way it is written confirms its relationship to fire, as there are three flames depicted when it is drawn. Shin is one of the most important letters in The Hebrew alphabet. The Mezuzah, which is found next to the entrance of Jewish homes, contains the letter Shin and its three inner flames. These flames form and inner trinity within the trinity of "AUM". In the Jewish faith, there is the habit of kissing this plate or ornament as you leave or enter a home. It is a protection for the family. Both "Allah" and "AUM" have a profound inner-dimensional aspect to their mantras. Allah's phonetic, mirror-like palindrome takes our thoughts to its meaning as "The beginning-less and the endless". The three flames depicted when the letter "Shin" is written connect our thoughts to the triplicate power of "AUM".

When we examine the second letter "U" (or "Aleph"), we see that it symbolizes the Ox. The Ox has always been a reference to man's sexual energy. For instance, in the Christmas Nativity scene, the donkey and the ox are some of the figures surrounding The Infant Jesus. The five-pointed Star, the manger, The Three Wise Men, Mary, Joseph, and all the shepherds bowing towards the Infant Christ each represent an aspect of ourselves. The Christmas Nativity scene is full of symbolism. The donkey symbolizes our lower nature, the ox symbolizes our sexual energy, and the newborn Jesus symbolizes our Transcendent Universal Light. Finding ways to transmute our lower nature into our higher nature and our sexual energy into spiritual energy have always been two of the goals in all religions.

When we examine the third letter "M" (or "Mem"), we see that it symbolizes water. Water is symbolic for transformation. It is part of the four primordial elements; Earth, Fire, Water, and Air. In many faiths, water is used as an alchemic tool of metamorphosis and spiritual purity. Baptism in Christianity, washing of the feet (known as "Wudu") in Islam, and The Holy Ganges in Hinduism are a few examples of where the cleansing power of water is used in rituals. On this physical plane, water itself is mysterious and transformative, as it can transform from a liquid to a vapor (steam) to a solid (ice). Since a major characteristic of water is alchemic, it is a transformative tool to help us evolve and aid us in our spiritual growth. Water is the opposite of fire and we see both contained within AUM.

There are many different letters in the Hebrew alphabet. As with "Shin", "Aleph" and "Mem", each letter has both a mystic and symbolic meaning. Each letter is a symbol or letter that represents something outside of ourselves and a sound or thought that evokes something inside of ourselves. It can be compared to Chinese Calligraphy, where each stroke has a symbolic meaning – yet, when they are put together, they have a combined higher meaning, or even tell a story or create an image. When Hebrew letters are put together to form a word, the different letters form something greater than they do individually. We also see this in many other languages, like Arabic and Sanskrit.

As "AUM" is a word used for spiritual enrichment, we can be sure that these letters were not haphazardly put together and that there are several deeper dimensions to it. It is a mystical word that was meant to be used in our prayers and meditations. Using it to direct our thoughts to God as The Cosmic Vibration is just one of its many facets. However, we can go further than that to see some of the other possibilities contained within this word of wonder, knowledge, and Light.

When we closely examine "A-U-M" and the definitions of its individual letters, we can see that there are two possible inner meanings contained within it. The order of the letters is the first thing we should recognize. Any other configuration would still have the same letters but not the same order. "UAM" or "MUA", for example, would still give us the same letters, but not the same overall meaning. We gain knowledge and Light not only from the individual letters, but also from the overall order and configuration of these letters. The order of the letters that we are speaking is also something to bear in mind as each of its three syllables crosses our lips.

Sexual energy is a powerful force existing within and around us. Finding ways to harness and transform it has always been a primary objective for many spiritualists. As for most of our religious leaders, they just tell us to suppress it. But some spiritualists have found ways to transmute it into something full of Light. Their goal is to use it for something that enhances their evolution.

As we are repeating "A-U-M" ("Fire-Ox-Water"), one meaning of it could be that "this mantra is a way of BURNING our SEXUAL ENERGY in order to TRANSFORM". The fact that "Fire" and "Water" are at the opposite ends of this word is relevant. This polarity can lead us to a second possible meaning of "A-U-M". "To overcome our SEXUAL ENERGY, we transcend the realm of duality (FIRE and WATER) to reach Universal Oneness (The Cosmic Sound)".

We can also work with AUM and its Trinity of letters to bring Light into three connected realms of our various realities. For example, we all know that we have a conscious state (waking state), an unconscious state (sleep state), and a superconscious state ("Eureka!" and "Aha!" moments beyond our conscious mind that spontaneously send us ideas and solutions to our problems). As we repeat "A-U-M" throughout the day or before falling asleep, we can consciously focus on these three realms and bring Light not only into our physical bodies, but also into our unconscious and superconscious (REM-dream) states.

Again, the equilateral triangle (or The Trinity) is the strongest geometric shape. It contains a triplicity of power, as all three sides have equal force and equal influence. There are many trinities within and around us. "AUM" is the perfect tool to use in conjunction with any trinity. Below is a list of some of the most common spiritual triplets:

A "Shin"	U "Aleph"	M "Mem"
Our body of Sound	Our body of Vibration	Our body of Light
Our Causal body (Soul)	Our Astral body (Spirit)	Our Physical body (Matter)
Our super conscious state	Our unconscious/ dream state	Our conscious state
Brahma	Vishnu	Shiva
Masculine	Union/Love	Feminine
Yin	Absolute	Yang
Father	The Holy Spirit	Son
The Will of God	The Love of God	The Conscience/Mind of God
Fire	Air	Water
Our will	Our sensation	Our intellect
Our Causal body*	Our Buddhic body*	Our Atmic body*
Our Mental body**	Our Astral body **	Our Physical body**

*These are our three higher bodies.
**These are our three lower bodies.

"AUM" has also been referred to mean "The Hidden", "The concealed", "The True Witness", "The Truth", or "The Hidden God". When something is hidden it is concealed behind a façade. There is a veil, an exterior front blocking us from seeing the truth hidden behind it. It is the Truth we want to see not the façade. As spiritualists and scientists, we all look for the deeper truth we have in the world around us. If we can see it, touch it, hear it, taste it, or smell it, it is not the Divine Truth we are looking to discover and incorporate into our daily lives – It is the veil. The façade. To discover the truth behind the façade, we have to use another sense – our sixth sense. This is the sense that connects us to our Universality. It is a conglomerate of our sublime senses that open the pathways to our higher senses – like ESP. The sixth sense is varied, abundant, and is centered in the realm of thought.

As when we pray or meditate, we use thought or no-thought ("emptiness") to help us experience our own divinity. In the Bible, there are important passages that take our minds to the dawn of creation: "In the beginning was the Word and the Word was with God and the Word was God. Amen" (John 1:1) and "These things that saith Amen, the faithful and true witness, the beginning of the creation of God" (Revelation 3:14). It says these *things* that *saith* Amen… not these people that saith Amen or these righteous or these faithful that saith Amen. Can we interpret that to mean that everything speaks this cosmic vibratory sound? Every molecule and every atom?

Revelations 3:14 combines well with John 1:1;

"In the beginning was the Word, and the Word was with God, and the Word was God. He was in the beginning with God; all things were made through him, and without him was not anything made that was made. In him was life, and the life was the light of men. Amen".

Other religions also mention the power of God as a word or cosmic vibration. For instance, in Hinduism, God says "I will deliver this Word so that she will produce and bring into being all this world". (Tandya Maha Brahmana 20.14.2). To spiritualists throughout the ages, this light and this life we have within us is directly connected – through the mantras "Om", "AUM", and "Amen" - to the dawn of creation, and how a word has dynamically created not only us, but everything in our Universe.

Mystics not only advise us to look for Truth, but to look for it beyond our materialistic world. The joy we get from anything material is triggered from that material thing. Material things age. They rust. They die out. And they lose that initial sparkle they had when we first saw them. When we find joy in Universal Consciousness, it never fades because we always find renewed inspiration everywhere we look. This morning, it was realizing the beauty of the flowers on my windowsill opening to the morning Sun. This afternoon, it was looking at a pigeon in flight, and realizing that I, too, have wings from my inner Caduceus. Tonight, it was receiving a heartfelt "Thank you" email from my one Buddhist friend for having sent her 3 days ago a text message that read "Hi Karen, I wish you a Joyful Elephant Day festival today!". All of these little events have filled my day with immense joy and transcendence. Yesterday was a different set of my own spiritually private events, and tomorrow I know there will be a new set of inspired things I will see and encounter. A new car or a new house does not fill me at this type of sustained level of deep rejuvenation.

"The Truth will set you free", as is said in the Bible (John 8:32). Actually, this passage says much more than that in the lines before and after this verse:

John 8:31	"So, He said to the Jews who had believed Him, "If you continue in My word, you are truly My disciples.
John 8:32	"Then you will know the truth, and the truth will set you free."
John 8:33	"We are Abraham's descendants," they answered. "We have never been slaves to anyone. How can You say we will be set free?

Different people may have their own interpretations to these three verses, but what can be read from them is... If we are spiritualists ("Abraham's descendants"/ "Jews who believe in Him")... we can use Amen or AUM ("My Word") in our habitual practice ("continue in My word")... to know Divine Truth ("you are truly My disciples"). If we just look with our eyes, then we will fail to see that this is The Truth that is beyond our materialistic world ("We have never been slaves to anyone")... yet it gives us the true freedom from a deeper dimension ("You will know the truth, and the truth will set you free"). Those who practice this technique ascend to a much higher plateau of human existence ("you are truly My disciples"). This Godly advice was given to The Hebrews who were unaware of the immense power of The Word ("How can you say we will be set free?").

**Om, Amen, and AUM are Solar –
They awaken "The Sun" within**

In the second and third section of this book, we will discuss how these three mantras awaken our inner Solar aspects. In many of the exercises and experiments in Divine Science and Multiplicative Joy, we will practice with our "Inner Sun". But, for now, realize that in Christianity, Judaism, Buddhism, and Hinduism, their calendars are wholly or primarily based on the cycles of The Sun, their celebrations (Christmas, Easter, Hanukkah, and The Festival of Lights) are based on the cycles of The Sun, and that they both describe Divine Intelligence as a Word, a Sound (or Sounds), or a Cosmic Vibration that exists within us, around us, and throughout every atom in our Universe.

What is the difference between "Om" and "AUM"?

In a very subtle way, "Om" and "AUM" sound similar. Many people who are beginning the practice of meditation wonder what the correct way is of pronouncing these extremely popular mantras. Even people who are yoga teachers tell their students that they are the same. Students are told the correct ways to hold their lips, how to stand or sit when practicing them as japa, and on which parts of their bodies to concentrate on when saying them. But that still doesn't satisfy our interest in what their differences are or why there are two words for what seems to be the same thing.

In fact, they are both the same, in that they both lead our thoughts to the same one omniscient realm of our Universe. But, they lead us there in two very unique ways and can be used for two very different techniques.

The power of "Om" and the power of "AUM" lie in their syllables. The first has one syllable and the second has three syllables. Counting the syllables of any word connects our thoughts to the inner vibrations of that word. Try it with your own name – the number os its syllables and the sound each of its syllables makes.

Of these two mantras, "Om" is the oldest, as it has one syllable. Saying "Om" during meditation or chanting brings a cosmic, all-encompassing effect into our thoughts. We harmonize with Universal Oneness. "AUM", on the other hand, has three syllables, so it came after "Om". Techniques where a trinity is involved are best used with "AUM". When we want to focus on three individual aspects of some part of ourselves, "AUM" helps our thoughts to probe them more deeply. "AUM" has a inner, dimensionally deep-searching aspect to it. Some Trinities that "AUM" is perfect for are:

- Awake state, Sleep state, Deep-sleep state
- Brahma (The Creator), Vishnu (The Preserver), Shiva (The Destroyer)
- Our Past, Present, Future
- Universal Consciousness, The Word, Physical Matter
- The Three Passions: Sex, Love, Romance
- Our Red Chakra (Root), Our Green Chakra (Heart), Our Violet Chakra (Crown)

"Om" takes our thoughts to the one, cosmic, all-pervading realm that exists throughout the Universe. At the deepest level, all things resonate with one vibration. Further than that, both every material and non-material thing resonates at the deepest level with that one same vibration. A star and a dandelion resonate at one universal vibration. A human being and a waterfall resonate at one universal vibration. And too, a thought and The Sun resonate at one universal vibration. That one universal vibration is the same - Om.

"The Universe" is translated as meaning "One Song" – (Uni = One / Verse = Song). Like a song, "Om" leads our thoughts into harmony, rhythm, and vibration. Synchronization is also evoked when we think of Om in The Uni-Verse.

"AUM" might be easier thought of as one word with three dimensions – "A"- "U"- "M". As we say each syllable, our thoughts activate a Trinity. This is in contrast with "Om", where our thoughts are to one whole. Both "Om" and "AUM" evoke immense power and Light within us. Depending on what we intend to do during our meditation or prayer, will dictate which would be more suitable. Just like when a handyman considers if he is going to use a hammer to pound nails or pull bark off of a tree. They are both part of the same tool. Together, both are in resonance.

When we remember that "Amen" is also related to "Om" and "AUM", we can take the hammer metaphor even further. The tongs of the hammer ("Amen") remind us of the pathway that all Life has taken from Universal Consciousness into physical matter. "Om", "AUM", and "Amen" are one tool. They vibrate our cells differently. They are three different ways to start our inner tuning fork harmonizing with Cosmic Resonance. Practicing with all three helps develop a strong mind. They are three totally different techniques used for totally different aspects of ourselves… but, they all are part of one and the same tool.

So, what is the difference between "Om" and "AUM"? The difference is in what we plan to do during our meditation or prayer. The difference is in our own needs and intentions.

Like a Hammer… Om, AUM, and Amen are three tools in one

One way we can consider these three Solar mantras is how they are pronounced. "Om", "Amen", and "AUM" all have a different number of syllables. This is a subtle way we can use each one as a different tool. A hammer is a good metaphoric tool to have in mind when we think of them. A hammer is three tools in one; the hammerhead, the tongs, and the "V". Depending on what we want to use it for, we can either pound nails into wood, pull them out, or dig a small hole. Yet at the same time, these three techniques are different aspects of one and the same tool.

Like the hammerhead, Cosmic Vibration has three known tools to it. We can concentrate on The Cosmic Vibration as one syllable ("Om")… two syllables ("Amen")… and three syllables ("AUM"). It is good to take a few days to meditate on all three vibrations contained in this Trinity – From one syllable to two syllables to three syllables… then from three syllables to two syllables to one syllable. When we do this, we feel our own Divinity in three unique ways. "Om" brings our thoughts to the one cosmic sound that vibrates in every atom throughout our Universe. "Amen" is the link between Universal Consciousness and physical matter. And "AUM" takes our thoughts to the three states of our own consciousness; The conscious, unconscious, and superconscious. As we go through this exercise, our vibration changes. As our thoughts change, the cells of our body change. These different thoughts are like putting different colored filters over the same Light. In other words, the filter changes, but the white light Source is always the same.

We do not know if our ancestors had the scientific proof to put an exact date on the birth of the Universe. Many of their theories have been lost to fire or are still buried, waiting to be excavated. Even now, with our modern scientific knowledge and techniques, we cannot put an exact date on the birth of

The Universe. We have theories of it having begun "billions of years ago", but no specific moment that we can actually calculate. That moment is a mystery. It is something theoretically and immeasurably vague. It's not even really a moment, it is thought to be, rather, more like a phase. Yet, still… there had to be a moment when that very first atom that emerged from The Universal Consciousness. In that one moment, with that very first atom, not only did the Universe start, but also Time began.

By their scriptures and documents, what we see is that our mystic ancestors deeply pondered that moment – The beginning of The Universe. Even without modern machinery, they theorized and conceptualized it. Questions we ask ourselves like, "Why was man born?" and "Why was The Universe created?" can lead us back to that point of universal inception.

Today, even though we can't yet put the exact second on it, many of us still do ponder the beginning of Life. As for the answers our ancient mystics came up with and wrote about, this pondering brought them to theorize that the universe condensed itself into a sound. That before something becomes physical matter, it was first vibrational energy. A thought, a word, a desire, and an intention are intense forms of this vibrational energy. To these ancient mystics, condensed sound was in the form of a word that then expressed itself, and continues to express itself, into the innumerable creations and manifestations within and around us today. That expression comes from an inexhaustible source that is manifesting itself in an unlimited number of ways. For some of our ancient Christian mystics, the operational word that drives this whole universal system is "Amen". It is the pathway that took that first atom from Universal Consciousness into physical matter when it finally emerged. "Amen" is the word that unfolds Life through its processing mechanisms. It channels Life to and from the intangible field of Divine Consciousness.

Still, most Christians have forgotten that this word is the first vibratory-sound that ever existed. It connects us to the cosmic field, resonating within everyone and everything. It is the first thing Divine Intelligence ever manifested. Obviously, God created "Amen" with the intention of manifested everything we see and hear. It is God's first utterance from the Dark Matter of pure potentiality. Unfortunately, we skim over that passage in Genesis and never stop to examine or deeply think about it's meaning. Religions have developed spiritual habits that focus more on rituals than on reason. Today, we ritually repeat "Amen", but it is never allowed to resonate within us from the meaning of it we have read about in John 1:1. During service or mass, "Amen" is said and then we quickly move onto the next item in the program. The potential power of "Amen" is lost because our minds are quickly brought to the next thing on the agenda. People want to get back to their homes. After years of sitting in church hearing "Amen" and then a hymn, a sermon, or the reading of the Bible directly after… how can we help but not think that "Amen" means "Ok, that's the end of this. Now we'll go onto the next thing"? How far can "Amen" take you with the thought of "The End" in your mind?

> *"Amen" is the cosmic vibratory field that everything and everyone passes through when coming into existence.*
> *"Amen" unfolds Life through its processing mechanisms. It channels Life to and from the intangible field of Divine Consciousness.*
> *"Amen" is the bridge between Universal Consciousness and physical matter.*

Another thing to reconsider is when we cross ourselves while repeating "The Father, The Son, and The Holy Spirit. Amen". When we speak or read, we often take a "beat" in our thoughts and in our speaking. Often the punctuation in these beats refers to a comma – as they do when we read "The Father, The Son, and The Holy Spirit". But, what does the beat we take between "The Holy Spirit" and "Amen" mean? Imagining that there is a "period" between the words "Holy Spirit" and the word "Amen" can also lead us to think that Amen means "The End". The words are true, but the punctuation that is used between them can be challenged. Who says that there is a period between "Holy Spirit" and "Amen"?... It could be a comma. It could be a dash. Or, best of all, it could even be an arrow! "The Father, The Son, and The Holy Spirit Amen". This would make The Holy Spirit and Amen the same. As it is said in other parts of The Bible, The Holy Spirit is Amen. When we are filled with The Holy Spirit, we are filled with Amen. "The Holy Spirit is God's power in action, his active force" (Micah 3:8, Luke 1:35).

Amen is powerful. But, its power is only activated by the thoughts we have of it. As with the other four mantras, it can amplify our thoughts and aspirations.

For a moment, examine the difference between these two prayers...

The first prayer: "Thank you, God, for this food"
The second prayer: "Thank you, God, for this food, Amen".

Why do we add the "Amen"? In both, we are already speaking directly to God and showing him our gratitude. In both, we are already saying it before we take a meal into our body. In both, we are triggering Light and Universal resonance between God, ourselves, and the food – especially, if we cross ourselves at the end of saying it. But, what does the "Amen" add? One answer could be that with the "Amen", we amplify the other words, their meanings, our gratitude, and our thoughts. In John 1:1, we remember that, through a Word, God created this food... and he created us. For the same reason, many Muslims say "Bismillah" before eating – which is to give gratitude to God for a meal. However, with Amen, it can put our thoughts into the transition our food went through to go from Divine Consciousness into the physical matter we see on our plate.

If churches and synagogues were to devote some time every week to reading John 1:1 and then repeating "Amen" or "AUM", it would awaken a spiritual nectar within everyone who heard or repeated it. As with anything, we grow through new understanding and awakened knowledge. Growth not only affects the individual, but also everyone in that individual's personal life. The spiritual nectar would renew their understanding, and Light would spread within, from, and around that person.

Om, AUM, and Amen resonate with everything that exists. They are three tools we can use to harmonize with Nature and with The Universe. If we are to believe our scriptures, God started The Universe from a single word. He first made a vibratory field before making his physical matter. Our world would not be the same without that Cosmic Resonance. Scientists can testify to this, as the internet, television, cell phones, and the radio can only operate because there is this Universal Vibration existing within and around us. So, that came first. Everything that came after "Amen/Om/AUM" was built from this cosmic vibrational sound. This vibration is the most fundamental element of ourselves and of everything we see. And so, when we allow ourselves to feel "Om/AUM/Amen" and remember its meaning... then WE resonate with it and with everything that exists. Remembering its meaning gives it a moment to sink deep into our conscious and subconscious minds. Repeating it never gets boring, as it is the material from which every atom and molecule are made.

The Synergy between Quantum Science and "AMEN"

Take a moment to examine your own thoughts and habits regarding your spiritual growth. If your habit up until now was to repeat "Amen", ask yourself what "Amen" means to you? Does it mean "The End" or "Truly"? Does is mean "So be it"? Does it mean "Verily"? Or does it mean anything at all? Obviously, it was and is a very important and highly spiritual word you've learned and have incorporated into your spiritual practice. However, did someone ever explain it to you? Did they tell you of its origins? Why is it a word that should be so central to your spiritual life, that you have been strongly advised to use it during your prayers and communications with God? So central is this word, that it is used many times during the open rituals at your temple of worship. A word you hope will amplify your thoughts and aspirations. How could a word we hope to signify all that mean "The End" and make us feel… "Ok, this part is over. Next!"?

However, if Amen means to you what the Bible has written about it being the beginning of our Universe and its existence in every manifested thing… then your prayers become more intensified when you say or sing it. This happens when your Third eye and imagination can see "Amen" in your garden flowers, "Om" in your next-door neighbor, and "AUM" in The Stars. Your prayers are amplified when you can see all three of these mantras in everything around you... and in yourself. If it is made up of molecules and atoms, it contains "Amen" at its essence and it is automatically connected to that one Universal Vibratory Field. Amen is the pathway between Universal Consciousness and physical matter. It does not mean "The End" – If anything, it means "The Middle". Once you start seeing "Amen" in everything you see, then you yourself become a tool of transcendence. All from having a more profound and knowledgeable use of this mantra.

In John 1:1, it does not say "God created The Universe". It reads "God created THE WORD and then The Word became everything else in The Universe". "The Word" is the often overlooked vibrational step between God and this Universe he created. Spiritualists, and even spiritual teachers, forget it. However, our scientists do look at that step. They work with it. They have created new technologies and many beneficial products from looking at that inter-connected middle-step of divine and abundant Cosmic Resonance.

In the field of Quantum Theory, Scientists today are catching up with what was written thousands of years ago in The Bible, The Upanishads, The Talmud, and The Bhagavad Gita.

Quantum Science tells us that there is a definite vibrational field of thought behind the atom. In their experiments, atoms can unpredictably move and even appear simultaneously as two atoms at different places in our physical world. We are all part of that one field. The scientist, him or herself, is a factor in their own quantum experiments. Because of their own thoughts, intentions, and expectations, the scientist can greatly change or alter the outcome of their results. This again shows that the scientist is a part of the Universal Mind he or she is studying. Similarly, it would be hard for an aquatic scientist to be busily studying the effects of still water, working inside of a swimming pool.

Repeating "Amen" with knowledge of its root meaning is Quantum Science in practice.

Repeating "Om" with knowledge of its root meaning is Quantum Science in practice.

Repeating "AUM" with knowledge of its root meaning is Quantum Science in practice.

All three mantras take our thoughts to The Cosmic Vibration permeating every atom that manifests.

Spiritualists have always told us that our Universe was formed from Thought. Every manifested thing comes from Universal Thought. But, where do thoughts come from? Our individual thoughts come from The Universal Thought. Outside of human free will, most of our experience with The Universe is predictable. Throw a ball up into the air – Will it stay suspended there or will it immediately drop back down? Gaze up at the Moon tonight – Will there be six moons in its place tomorrow? Feel your heartbeat for one minute – Is it pumping with a regular beat? Why are the stars of Orion in the same order today as they were when the Egyptians built the pyramids? The fact there are Universal Laws tells us that there is Universal Thought. To keep anything in order and balance, there needs to be thought and intention.

In our immediate surroundings, we can see that all of the objects around us came from thoughts; That table, that painting, that house... all came from thoughts. Someone was inspired to design them, sketch their ideas of them, pitch them, discuss them, and work on them. Words are one of the main ways that man brings things into this world. Words inspire thoughts and actions. A word can express a desire, a need, or an idea. A word is, as it has always been, the beginning of creation.

But what about The Earth, The Sun, The Moon, and The Stars... Are they from thoughts? In short, Yes! Look around you again... There are, in fact, only two things you see – Things that man has made and things that God has made. We already know that God created this Universe from a Word. The Word that is the bridge between Universal Consciousness and physical matter.

In our Universe, we can see numerous signs of universal thought behind celestial activity; The Earth's 24-hour rotation and 365-day revolution around The Sun. The circulating Red Spot of Jupiter. The influence of our moon on our tides and emotions. Sunspots. The rings of Saturn. The influence of The Zodiac on our personalities and psyches. And the fact that Mercury is the only planet in our Solar System that does not revolve are some pretty big reasons that demonstrate the perpetual and incessant thought and intention in our Universe. Thoughts beyond our control that keep our galaxies in balance. Comparing this to ourselves, thoughts and intentions give birth to the words we use to manifest creation.

Looking again at John 1:1, what Word is it talking about? That word cannot be "Jesus" or "Abraham" because they were born 2000+ years ago. Yet, The Universe is thought to be between 12 and 14 billion years old. To compare, that would be 2,000 vs 14,000,000,000 years. The word in this verse cannot even be "God", because it says that "God became The Word". God condensed himself into the form of a word. It doesn't say "God is The Word". This verse describes the intermediate step that takes place when anything is created.

We probably will never be able to precisely calculate when the first atom emerged from Universal Consciousness. It seems that our ancient mystics did not approach it that way either. What they did do was they pondered it. We can never measure the birth of the first atom (there were no stopwatches when it happened) – But, we can have ideas and theories about how it emerged. The important thing is how we *conceptualize* the birth of The Universe, and how its beginning can in some way help us to spiritually evolve.

People who knew The Master Jesus wrote of his habit of saying "Amen". To them, when you thought of Jesus, one of the things you thought of was "Amen". For the people who knew him, it must have been an important enough characteristic of him for them to mention it. Amen and Jesus became spiritually intermingled. They both evoked Inner-Light. When we look further in The Bible we find in Revelation 3:14, that Jesus is referred to as, "the Amen, the faithful and true witness, the beginning of God's creation." The whole passage reads as "And unto the angel of the church of the Laodiceans write; These things saith the Amen, the faithful and true witness, the beginning of the creation of God". Even by The Master Jesus's own words and actions, he is not "The Amen". He did not have the habit of repeating his own name. What linked him to Universal Consciousness was "Amen". He resonated with its cosmic power. He became a lightning rod for its transcendent energy. We see signs of his destiny in the few stories we have of his early life, but he made the steps to eventually walk the walk and talk the talk he did in his later years. From his own lips, he said "I and My Father are one". Amen is eternal and dynamic. Through it, The Master Jesus became, and is now, eternal and dynamic. We too have access to this mantra of abundance, glory, and Universal Quintessence.

Amen takes us into The Eternal Void. "Amen" is "the beginning of God's creation". "The Amen" is "The faithful", "the sacred believer", "The true witness", and "the omnipresent observer". Jesus Christ and Amen became inextricably linked – however, the former was once tangible, and the latter was, is, and will forever be intangible. When a Teacher of his status repeatedly utters a mantra, at times that are sacred to himself and the blessing of others, it is likely that his thoughts are full of Light and grace – and that the divinely connected thoughts of this master are able to empower everything in his surroundings. We, too, can evoke this Light by remembering Amen as a cosmic bridge. That Light is concentrated when together we remember it in our Churches, all of which are Temples of The Sun. Churches are some of humanity's most important Sun Temples where grace, glory, and abundance can thrive and be sent out to many parts of the world. God, our Universal Consciousness, reminded us "Whenever two or three of you gather in my name, I am there" (Matthew 18:20). What more confirmation can you get from The Word that built The Universe?

Solar Mantras And Lunar Mantras

From here on Earth, our two most prominent celestial bodies are The Sun and The Moon. They were born with The Earth and are inseparable from Life here on it. Throughout the year, The Sun or The Moon is linked to a mantra's corresponding religion, its calendar, and how that religion calculates its festivals and rituals. Because of this celestial link, our churches, Buddhist temples, Hindu shrines, and synagogues can be seen as "Temples of The Sun" and our Mosques and Taoist shrines can be seen as "Temples of The Moon".

"The Cosmic Sound" and "The Eternal Field" are the two Universal Constants. They are the two paths that lead our thoughts to Oneness with The Universal Mind. Our Five World Mantras are keys that help us unlock these two exalted, higher resonances. They open the pathways that let us experience Universal Consciousness in two different, yet inter-connected, ways. Both paths are limitless, incessant, and eternally dynamic.

Xavier Clayton

The Sun And The Moon

Our relationship to The Earth is different than our relationship to The Stars

From time primordial, we have looked in wonder and curiosity at our Sun and Moon. The Stars, Constellations, and The Eclipse have also captured our fascination. We look up to these heavenly bodies from down here on Earth. With Earth, we have a hands-on, direct relationship with our beautiful planet. We can smell its flowers, hear its oceans, and walk through its forests. We can see and experience the beauty and nourishment it gives us. Yet, with The Sun, The Moon, and Stars, there is not a hands-on relationship. These all awaken our imagination and spiritual aspirations.

With the Sun, The Moon, the Stars, and Eclipses, we have an as strong and as direct relationship with them as we do with Earth – but, the relationship is distant and abstract. Our relationship to The Earth can also be spiritual and abstract. With them all, we cannot control or influence The Earth, The Stars, The Sun or The Moon. They are really out of our hands. All we can do is observe their influence within and around us. However, contemplation of these celestial bodies helps inspire universal relationships and cosmic connections. With the Earth, we build a relationship to it through our five senses. With The Celestial Bodies, we build a relationship to them through thought and intuition – our sixth sense.

It can be argued that the Sun and the Moon are our two most influential celestial bodies. Even in our religions they both play a big part. They are used in mystic metaphors, in descriptions of God or one of his aspects, as the basis of our calendars, and are found in the symbolic décor of our places of worship. If we are coming together in faith and use Om, AUM, or Amen to amplify our prayers, we in a Temple of the Sun. If we are coming together in faith and use Tao or Allah to amplify our prayers, we are in a Temple of the Moon. By our calendars and how religious celebrations are calculated, we can see this very clearly. Ramadan and The Chinese New Year are calculated by The Moon. Christmas, Easter, Hanukkah, and The Festival of Lights are either wholly calculated by The Sun or strongly calculated by The Sun.

The goal of this chapter is to explore some of the cosmic influences both the Sun and the Moon have on our spiritual life. As humans, we have esoteric aspects of each of them. But, with knowledge and practice, we can learn to bring our solar aspects and our lunar aspects in alignment to form an inner eclipse.

The spiritual role and cosmic influence of our Sun, our Moon, and the Eclipse

From here on Earth, The Sun is an ever-constant heavenly object, while The Moon is an ever-changing heavenly object. The Sun is invariable and fixed. The Moon variable fluctuating, as it passes through its various monthly stages from Full Moon to New Moon, and back again. Both are important to life here on Earth.

Some may argue that sunspots make the Sun also an ever-changing celestial body. However, sunspots are different than moon cycles. Sunspots are temporary, unpredictable, and can appear in sizes as big as The Earth. They differ in magnetism and temperature. Unless they are immensely huge, they are invisible to the naked eye. For all intents and purposes, they don't change The Sun's overwhelming influence on Life here on our planet. The Earth protects us from the solar flares they might create. As far as we can see, they don't change Life in our Solar System. If they did, for the few days that they appear, we would see drastic shifts in the orbits of at least the two closest planets to the Sun – Mercury and Venus. But, we don't. So, in general, to us here on Earth and to our neighboring planets, The Sun is the fixed, ever-constant, Life-giving, focal point of our Solar System.

The Sun gives us light, vitality, electricity, magnetism, and warmth. The Moon plays an influence on our moods, bird migration, birth rate, Earth's revolution on its axis, and The Earth's metal ore. The fluctuating characteristic of the Moon accords well with the ebb and flow characteristic of our ocean tides. For that matter, our moods, bird migration, and birth rates also have an ebb and flow characteristic. Ancient scientists and spiritual adepts saw the importance of both of these celestial bodies. They incorporated the cycles of the Moon and our Earth's cycles around the Sun into the way we calculate Time. Because of this, the one thing that they developed, and that we still use today, is the calendar.

Nearly every religion and civilization has its own unique calendar. They can look quite different than our western Monday through Sunday/ January through December ones. But one thing behind them all is that they are based on either The Sun or The Moon. The relation between The Sun, The Moon, and The Earth form a Trinity. Time on Earth is based on the cycles and interconnections between these three. A calendar based on the rotation of Jupiter and its moons, or Venus that has no moon, would look totally different than any of ours.

Here on Earth, calendars are Solar, Lunar, or Luni-Solar. Festivals or important religious events (for example, Ramadan, Easter, and The Festival of Lights) are calculated by The Sun, The Moon, or a combination of both. As we are all spiritual beings, we need both The Sun and The Moon for our existence.

If we had no Moon, our climate, our tides, our gravity, and the Earth's axis would go TOTALLY out of whack! We humans and animals would go out of whack, as well – seeing how the Moon has an influence on our moods and tendencies! For instance, many studies have shown that crime rates, sexual activity, and car accidents are higher during a full moon. A full moon is when the maximum amount of light is shining down on The Earth at night. Why is this extra light instrumental enough to influence our actions so drastically?

Scientists and spiritualists are still studying the effects that The Moon has on us and on our Earth. The scientist does this in his laboratory, with his telescopes and machinery – Looking out. The spiritualist does this in his meditation, with his insight and perception – Looking in. Having no Moon would mean that the physics in our physical world would instantly go into havoc. Our Earth with no Moon could, at the very least, mean we would ALL be emotional basket cases floating in air on our gravity-free planet in a random and unpredictably spinning world full of constant hurricanes and tornados. The Moon keeps us and our world in balance. The Moon is vital to our existence! It is a blessing to the Life we all enjoy!

Regarding the Sun, it is obvious that if we had no Sun, we would have no Light – but, we would also have no electricity, no magnetism, and no food. There would be no vitality, as no Sun would mean no Life. No Life means no flowers, no plants, and no trees. Without them, there would be no insects, no fish, and no animals. And without those, there would be no humankind. We would live in darkness, and we would not even be able to see our Moon. If there were no Sun, our Earth would be a huge, cold, ice-covered, pitch-dark, life-less rock.

To palm readers, acupuncturists, massage therapists, and spiritual adepts, the Sun and the Moon are not only found in our skies - they are also both part of the many "Solar Systems" that exists in our own body. To an esoteric healer certain points on our ears, hands, feet, and retina correspond to our major planets, Moon, and Sun. On our hand, for example, our ring finger corresponds to the Sun and the side of our hand under our pinky finger corresponds to the Moon. Our ears, feet, and retina also have points on them that correspond to a planet, the Sun, or our Moon. The attributes of the corresponding celestial body are included with its point. Even to Astrologers, each of us has a unique "Solar System" that we were born with to help us learn and grow spiritually. Some of the attributes of The Sun are abundance, Divinity, romance, and enlightenment. Some of The Moon's attributes are wisdom, knowledge gained from past lives, and reason. The Venus, Jupiter, Saturn, Mercury, and Mars points have unique characteristics that we can focus on to help us during our spiritual evolvement.

How Calendars Can Help Us Evolve

Lunar Calendars and Solar Calendars

Regarding the two paths to God, where we see God as "The Eternal Field" and God as "The Cosmic Vibration", many interesting things come to light when we add the aspects of the Moon and the Sun. Again, calendars were created from mystic observations of our Sun and Moon in relation to the Earth. They are to help us spiritually connect to the Cosmos through the observation of Time. They are religiously based because they were born from mysticism. Throughout all religions, The Sun is always masculine and The Moon is always feminine. Calendars are spiritual timetables. Even the names of the days and months often have an astrological, mystical, or symbolic meaning.

Calendars can be divided into lunar calendars, solar calendars, and lunar-solar calendars (often called Luni-Solar calendars). Islam and Taoism use lunar calendars. Christians, Buddhists, Hindus, and Jews use solar or Luni-Solar calendars.

In Islam, we repeat "Allah". In Taoism, we repeat "Tao". Both mantras direct our thoughts to God as "The Eternal Field" – "The first and the last" – "That that has no beginning and has no end". Our thoughts are directed to the limitless, unborn, undying, eternal realm of Universal Consciousness. But what is spiritually coincidental, is that both Islam and Taoism are the only religions that use a Lunar Calendar. In other words, to calculate Ramadan, Aid El Kebir, or any Islamic festival, Imams observe The Moon. In Taoism, The Chinese New Year, All Souls Festival, The Dragon Boat Festival, etc… are also all only calculated in accordance to the cycles of the Moon.

On the other hand, Christianity, Judaism, Hinduism, and Buddhism, direct our thoughts to God as "The Cosmic Sound". The cosmic vibration that is within every atom in our Universe – from every cell I can see through a microscope to every star I see through a telescope. "Amen", "AUM", and "Om" take our thoughts to this Cosmic Sound-Vibration within ourselves and within every-thing.

LUNAR CALENDARS	LUNI-SOLAR CALENDARS	SOLAR CALENDARS
Islam	Hinduism	Christianity
Taoism	Buddhism	
	Judaism	

In regards to the spiritual timetables that we call calendars, Christianity, Judaism, Hinduism, and Buddhism have their festivals calculated totally by The Sun or in a strong correlation to The Sun. In other words, by a solar calendar or a Luni-Solar calendar. The Gregorian calendar, for example, is completely based on the cycles that The Earth makes around The Sun. That is why Christmas is always on December 25th. It can be on a Wednesday, a Friday, or a Tuesday. Because of the way The Gregorian calendar is calculated, Christmas stays on December 25th because we have fixed that date to a calendar that is based on The Earth's revolutions around The Sun.

When holidays are calculated by a Luni-Solar calendar, like Hanukkah, Easter, and The Festival of Lights… it is because these calendars have lunar months and solar years. That is why Easter and Hanukkah, for instance, can occur on different days… even different weeks and different months. Sometimes Easter is in March and sometimes it is in April. The biggest difference between Luni-Solar calendars and lunar or solar calendar are the Leap Years. By incorporating the cycles of The Moon, the rotation of our planet, and the revolution of The Earth around The Sun, Leap Years re-adjust the slight changes and miscalculations that occur in Time every day.

What helps us evolve is being spiritually aware that both The Moon and The Sun are vital to us all. We might be romantically aware of The Moon and physically aware of The Sun, but awareness of their influence on our spirits will hasten our growth and connection to The Universe. They become our passageways to the galaxies.

We are all Lunar and Solar.
We are all Human Luni-Solar Beings.

Beyond race, religion, gender, and sexuality, every human being is both Lunar and Solar. Beyond wealth, education, culture, or intelligence, every human being has both The Sun and the Moon within. These celestial aspects reveal themselves in many different ways: Abundance/Wisdom, Masculine side/Feminine side, Heart/Intellect, Yin/Yang, and Amen/Allah. They express themselves within us as "The Cosmic Vibration" and "The Eternal Field". The one positive aspect of the many Religious Wars during The Age of Religion is that they have directed our thoughts to both of these aspects found in our faith. It has exposed us to the inherent diversity of Universal Consciousness. Spiritual diversity induces inner strength. Religious diversity induces outer abundance.

Practicing with one of the twelve paired mantras, such as "Tao-AUM" or "Om-Allah", brings both aspects of The Sun and The Moon in alignment – Both in our thoughts and in our being. Paired mantras create an inner eclipse that resonates with ourselves as Luni-Solar beings. Practicing with these paired mantras awakens our connection to The Universal Mind. The more we practice, the higher we rise above both the Sun and the Moon… to find that we have landed in the Stars!

The Temples Of The Sun And The Temples Of The Moon

Spiritual Temples help magnify our Lunar and Solar selves

Our Sun and our Moon are our two most prominent celestial bodies. They rule our skies and at times come together to form an eclipse. Metaphysically, The Sun is masculine and The Moon is feminine. The Sun is the father and The Moon is the mother. Both share our day. For 12 hours, The Sun rules our day, and for 12 hours, The Moon rules the night. The Sun is constant, and influences our life, growth, and vitality. The

Moon is ever-changing, and influences our moods, emotions, and tendencies.

When we build a place of worship, it is to connect to the divinity within and around us. The temple itself works like a magnifying glass to enhance our connection to either The Sun or The Moon. The temple's mantra, calendar, and the way its spiritual celebrations are calculated reinforce this either lunar or solar link. In many ways, the overall influences of both The Sun and The Moon are involved in all spiritual temples. In prayer and rituals, we use both strength and contemplation. We use both the heart and the intellect. We use both Love and Thought. Whether we are using our solar or our lunar aspects, both require us to look to the sky… into The Heavens. It is in The Heavens we become a master of our future. By working with both our solar and our lunar aspects, we transcend above them to materialize our desires. The only way we can see either The Sun or The Moon by looking down here at The Earth is by looking into a reflection.

When we look at our temples of worship from the perspective of its mantra and its calendar, we can see that Catholic Churches, Jewish Synagogues, Hindu shrines, and Buddhist sanctuaries are Temples of The Sun. In other words, their calendars and celebrations are calculated completely or primarily by The Sun; Christmas, Easter, Hanukkah, The Festival of Lights, etc… By the same token, we can also see that Mosques and Taoist Shrines are Temples of The Moon. Their calendars and celebrations are calculated completely by The Moon; Ramadan, The Chinese New Year, El Aid, etc… This is what we see when we look at our Religious Temples from a celestial perspective. But, ultimately, when we look within ourselves, we see that as human beings – for both men and women – we are Temples of both The Sun AND The Moon. Man is a Luni-Solar Temple. In our spirits, we have both the qualities of The Moon and the qualities of The Sun. Through knowledge and spiritual practice, this book, and its exercises in Divine Science, proposes that the purpose of human life is to bring these two qualities in alignment. By learning how to do align our Inner Sun and our Inner Moon, we can consciously create an Inner Eclipse to magnify our thoughts, prayers, and actions.

Creating Light in our Modern World

In Europe and America, we talk of "Islamic Terrorism" and "The Islamitization of The West". In the East, we talk of "Zionist dominance" and "Christian or Jewish occupation". Reports from both the occidental and the oriental media say that we will have a problem with "terrorism" or "occupation" for decades to come.

In The West, we say "We have to stop these people from coming and invading us! – Look at what they've done in other countries!".

In The East, we say "We have to stop these people from coming and invading us! – Look at what they've done in other countries!".

By saying this, we are creating a glass ceiling for ourselves. We are telling ourselves and our children that because of someone else's faith and presence we will either live in fear forever or unless that other person and their faith are eradicated. We tell ourselves this but, simultaneously, our world societies are getting more and more mixed. We don't look for ways to transcend our fear to see that behind this world spiritual integration we now find ourselves in, that there may be some higher purpose.

We have power over our own thoughts and can choose to use the presence of a person from a different religion than our own to awaken moments of spiritual transcendence. Instead of seeing another person's religion as a sign of hate or fear, we can choose to remember that there are two complementary and intertwined paths to God. One path is solar and the other path is lunar. One path leads our thoughts to "The Eternal Field" and the other path leads our thoughts to "The Cosmic Sound".

"Tao" and "Allah" are the complementary, intertwined mantras of "AUM", "Amen", and "Om". "Om", "AUM" and "Amen" are the complementary, intertwined mantras of "Tao" and "Allah". In other words, if you are a child of The Eternal Field, you can be inspired by children of The Cosmic Vibration – and vice versa. If your faith is inspired by The Sun, you can choose to use your thoughts to be empowered by spiritualists of The Moon – and vice versa. There is no fear when we speak in terms of our Sun and our Moon, as we all know, love, and need both. Life is full of moments. We can consciously fill many of these moments with Light and transcendence, instead of with hate and fear. When we realize what our primary spiritual influence has been thus far in Life, we can take our newfound knowledge about other faiths to help ourselves evolve in this multi-cultural world we now live in.

Our news outlets and politicians are so fixated by war, world destruction, and nuclear bombs that they are rarely use their global influence to open our thoughts up to other possibilities, views, or spiritual solutions. Our thoughts are habitually directed towards darkness. Politicians and The Media can help change our world by habitually directing our thoughts and imagination more and more towards Light. This is not meant to ignore the destruction we see around us, but rather to look for the reasons behind the destruction and help find spiritual solutions to solve it. People, countries, and situations get tagged with labels of fear and hate – and we, the viewers and constituents, get passively brainwashed as a result. For many, this perpetuation of fear has gone on for years – from our childhood, into our adolescence, into our adulthood, and then up into our old age. And because of this perpetuation of fear, if we don't find a spiritual way to transcend it, it will stay with us until the day we die! What a wasted Life. How many wasted years of living with constant hate and fear!

There must be better and more productive ways to use the short time we have here on Earth and many of the prominent thoughts that fill our days. Conscious Luni-Solar thought is a simple way to reverse this perpetuation of fear and easily open ourselves to bringing more light into the world. Again, using some of the keys we already have, we can evoke multiplicative joy – a joy that not only fills our own spiritual reserves with beauty and light, but the reserves of others around us, as well. Our religious celebrations are some of the events we can use to open our world to Collective Transcendence.

Every religion has various celebrations throughout the year. For example, Hanukkah, El Aid, and The Festival of Lights are religious celebrations where numerous people come together in spiritual joy. At religious times, such as The Chinese New Year, Christmas, and Easter, there are large segments of our world's population who are spiritually open to Universal Joy. At these religious times and celebrations, not only are people "open" here in our physical world, but there are also many pathways that are open into our collective consciousness. These times, which are all calculated by The Sun and/or Moon, are very auspicious. They are favorable times when many of us are receptive to Universal Abundance. Gift-giving during these celebrations is symbolic of that. Furthermore, when we congregate and pray at these times, we augment these transcendent openings. During these celebratory periods, the possibilities for multiplicative joy, at levels within ourselves and within our collective consciousness, are heightened. Each of us has the opportunity to transform our individual joy into unlimited Universal Joy. Any religious celebration, where there is a large group of people remembering God in some way, will give us the conditions to access his cosmic mind.

Religious celebrations can be seen on different levels – and utilized on several more; They can be seen as a time where spiritualists come together in remembrance and joy, and also when Divine thoughts are able to be utilized to spread Light and transcendence in the world. Regardless if it is from our own religion or not, they are spiritual openings that humanity consciously makes into Divine Consciousness. They are portals of opportunities where man uses rituals and remembrance to spiritually evolve.

Each of these auspicious days can carry a significant spiritual meaning with it. For example, Halloween (31 October) and All Saints Day (1 November) is a time where we can consciously purge our darker forces and habits, and replace them with our Higher, Divine Entities and Universal Light. For this reason, midnight on Halloween is the most mystical time during this particular 2-day celebration.

Religious holidays can also be used between faiths. In other words, just because it's Christmas doesn't mean that it is only for Christians. Hanukkah, Ramadan, and The Festival of Lights are world-wide celebrations that can and are used to transmit light beyond the Jewish, Muslim, Hindu and

Buddhist faiths. To do this, there is a simple way to consciously turn our individual joy into multiplicative joy. It just takes compassion, thought, and a little bit of planning. One beautiful and effective way to multiply Divine Joy in the world is to simply send a note, a gift, an email, or a text message to our friends and family members who are celebrating a particular religious event that is NOT of our own. The ripple-effects of this are amazing! When a thoughtful, joyous, and unexpected message from a friend or family member is sent to another God-loving person, it starts a lot of the wheels in our spiritual realm turning. However, if the messenger is of a different faith that the receiver, those wheels happily go into overdrive! The most remote corners of our gratitude and thankfulness are aroused. Light within both persons is sparked and multiplicative joy is triggered.

A public Facebook, Twitter, or Instagram post of a religious celebration to friends on your own profile is also one way to create multiplicative joy. Many of your friends and family members will see it, and will then be inspired to pass it forward. Remember that, religious celebrations, intended to help large groups of people re-connect with their Divine Self, are only seen amongst human beings.

Here are some important celebrations of various religions we can use to create and spread our own Network of Light across the world:

Christians	Christmas and Easter.
Jewish	Hanukkah and Passover.
Muslim	El Aid and Ramadan.
Buddhist	Buddhist New Year and The Elephant Festival.
Hindu	The Festival of Lights and Shiva Ratri.
Taoist	Chinese New Year and The Dragon Boat Festival.

Sending and receiving a "Happy El Aid!" or a "I wish you a wonderous Elephant Festival!" message, for example, creates instant joy. The capacities of ourselves as both transmitters and receptors are activated. If we are the sender of the message, empathy is awaked within us from a position of strength – because what we have done is something we have consciously chosen and planned to do. It is not an awakened empathy from seeing sadness in the world, pity, or because of something that has pulled at our heart strings. It is an empathy created from a conscious Divine Choice.

Imagine, for instance, we are a Christian and a Zen Buddhist wishes us a "Happy Easter!" – That builds a Network of Light. If we are the Christian, the rituals we perform during that religious celebration will be even more pronounced. By remembering how The Zen Buddhist's spontaneous and heartfelt message has touched us, it will take our thoughts beyond the confines of our religion into the true universal meaning of the religious event itself. This works between any two spiritualists for any religious celebration – where the messenger's religion is not of the receiver's. The act of thoughtfulness touches the hearts of both and a Network of Light is created between them. The more and more that that Network is empowered, the quicker and more likely it becomes a bridge. When these bridges start to crisscross within our multi-cultural communities and our wide variety of friends, then we will be able to create a Divine Network of Light throughout the entire world.

For this exercise, birthdays don't count. Saying "Happy Birthday!" to your friend, cousin, or associate is a nice way to express joy between you and them – but it doesn't add as much energy to that Divine Network of Light, as the remembrance of their religious celebration does. "Happy Birthday!", although wonderful, focuses on one person. A few people might celebrate it with them and share a lot of joy, but sharing joy and light during a world-wide religious event is quite different. Birthdays of Saints, like Jesus Christ, Mahatma Gandhi, and Sri Satya Sai Baba, are some exceptions to this. These Spiritual Guides have inspired countless people towards their Divine Reunification. World-wide celebrations of their birthdays are also ways to recharge The Network of Light between us. But, for most of us, our birthdays won't trigger that same global stimulation. For one, most of us expect, or at least hope, to get a message from someone who remembered it. And when we do, we are extremely happy and flattered. So, whether it happens or not, there was some expectation there. But when we get a "Happy Easter!" or a "Happy Shiva Ratri!" from a person who has never practiced our faith, it is unexpected. It surprises us in even more ways than a "Happy Birthday!", as it was something we did not even consider hoping for. Their compassion and consideration are what help to instantly build a bridge of joy between us. These are what awaken transcendent light within us both – and will make us want to reciprocate. Saying "Happy Birthday!" to a friend says you recognize them as a person. But, saying "Happy Chinese New Year!" or "I wish you a Joyous Passover!" to a client, friend, or colleague shows that you recognize and respect them as a spiritual being.

National Holidays don't count either. Most national holidays are, in some way or another, linked to a war. Wars and conflicts remind us of our fears. This exercise works best with any religious holiday or celebration – many of which are thousands of years old. Billions of spiritualists have put their thoughts, love, and aspirations into each one of them.

They have become spiritual openings into The Eternal Realm. They are all both unique and exceptional. We can consciously use them to spread Light throughout our world. All of these mystical times help remind us of our True Selves as spiritual beings – all of whom are working towards our oneness with Divine Consciousness.

One of the meditative exercises in The Divine Science section of this book helps take our thoughts and imagination back to our time from the womb to our infancy. Before we could even speak or even knew we were male, female, black, white, Latino, or Asian – we experienced Life as spiritual beings. Our "world" was nothing but sight, Light, sound, feeling, and wonder. Before we even started teething, the reasons we cried, felt hunger, pain, love, and joy were from spiritual experiences. When a baby cannot see its mother, it starts to cry. Its mother has been linked to Love. When mother is out of sight, to the baby, all that she represents is gone. That is a spiritual experience. We were all born spiritual beings in a physical body. And… we still are! Yes… our religions, spiritual guides, and spiritual books can help us to remember who and what we are at our core being – but, we can do a lot of the work ourselves with thought, empathy, and selfless acts of kindness. The exercise above is one of the ways we can do this by using our religious celebrations as tools. If, individually, each of us remains defiantly fixated on our one religious path, we will stay segregated and a glass ceiling will remain above our heads for decades. But when we begin to remember ourselves and others as Divine Beings, then we will integrate. This exercise creates a Spiritual Infrastructure – A Divine Network of Light. When we are able to inspire joy in others, that glass ceiling will be shattered into a million pieces.

THE TWO PATHS TO GOD

Christianity, Islam, And Judaism Are Three Pieces Of The Same Heart

The mystic, poetic, and symbolic bonds in Judaism, Islam, and Christianity

When we think about why we have created religions, how we use them, and what purpose they ultimately serve, we come to the conclusion that they all are to help us build a more intimate connection to Divine Consciousness. They are to help the spiritualist create a cosmic relationship with The One omniscient, Universal God. The One God who has dominion over every atom in The Universe... because He created every atom in The Universe. Knowing this helps us to realize our ideas and aspirations, our healing and purification, and our spiritual knowledge and prayers.

Since all of our prayers are directed towards the same Supreme Godhead, all religious thought and divine knowledge coexist together on several progressively higher planes. Down here on our physical plane, we often have an inkling of their higher co-existence. For example, the many times we have heard or read a Universal Truth coming from another religion. We hear a phrase of deep mystic power that sparks our spiritual intellect and, at first, think that it is coming from our own faith... until we know that it is something that was inspired from a different religious path. The words inspire the deeply similar feelings we have had when studying our own path. These words rang true because they were inspired from Truth. It is we who segregate it, in spite of it all coming from God.

The fact that God has generously and compassionately spread Truth to a variety of mystics throughout human history shows that there is a connection to him – above our own thoughts – on a higher, universal level. Logically, He must want that. When a wealthy father shares his fortune with his five sons, we all think that that is normal. He loves them all, and wants them all to be abundant and happy. When we hear of a story like of a generous and wealthy father, we try to put ourselves in their shoes and begin to imagine how we would feel if we were either the father or one of the sons. Comparing both, when we put ourselves in the position of the father, it is infinitely more powerful to our mind, our heart, and our spirit than it is when we put ourselves in the position of one of the sons. As a son, we feel grateful and blessed. As the father, we are not only conscious of our actions and Love, but we are also generous with our knowledge, experience, and wealth. If a wealthy human father is this way, then it is logically possible that our Universal Heavenly Father is the same way.

A mystic is an inspired and conscious spiritualist who actively take steps towards his or her Divine inheritance. A mystic is aware of his or her dynamic connection to The Kingdom of Heaven. Mystics have been Christian, Muslim, Jewish, Hindu, Taoist, Buddhist, and even scientists. Many of the ancient ones helped to inspire the world religions we practice today. Again, since their inspired thoughts came from The One Supreme God, what we practice today cannot help but be inter-connected on many ascending levels. One of the clearest demonstrations of this is when we look at three of the world's greatest religions, and how they are linked by their sacred books, region, stories, and origins. These three practices are known as Judaism, Islam, and Christianity.

The Prophet Abraham is considered to be the father of all three of these faiths. Because of that, they are known as The Abrahamic Religions. Like tributaries, they all lead back to him as their source. A Muslim, a Christian, and a Jew are descendants of the same father. Some spiritualists even connect Hinduism to The Prophet Abraham, when we consider that "Brahma and Saraswati" could, in fact, be "Abraham and Sarah".

As for Christianity, Islam, and Judaism, we can study these faiths to see how their origins and teachings have not only always interacted and intermingled, but have also helped to bring about profound and major changes in each of their conceptions. Important and influential Christians are found in Mohammed's life. Important and influential Jews are found in Jesus's life. And, Ishmael is an important and influential Muslim found in Isaac and Jacob's life. Interactions between the three Abrahamic lines of thought were all-important turning-points for the mystics who founded these faiths. This divine crisscrossing has shaped the ways we practice these religions today. It has also shaped our thoughts into three distinct arteries that lead us all back to the same Supreme Heart. Furthermore, we can look to the practices of Christian followers, Muslim followers, and Jewish followers to see the resulting differences in how they approach the same God.

The most defining parameter of a religion is not how it is practiced, but, rather, what we understand to be the motivating reasons behind the rites we are performing. Our thoughts, not our actions, are what help us to more quickly evolve. In other words, the thoughts we have while performing the ritual are what constitute its effectiveness. When we examine many of the prominent spiritual practices throughout our faiths, we can see that there some common threads in our thoughts during actions we perform; from being spiritually cleansed in The Holy Ganges... to lighting a Hanukkah candle... to meditating with a mantra... to The Holy Month of Ramadan... to a Baptism in a church... our first intention always is to purify our mind and body. Purification prepares us for prayer. It is beautiful the many ways that human beings have developed techniques to spiritually purify. When conscious thought is then added to our prayers, any of these methods help our minds develop a closer relationship with God.

Yes, globally, all of these methods are ultimately to purify the body and mind, as a way to better enhance our communications with Divine Consciousness. However, because of the religion and the tendencies it contains, the underlying trend of its techniques often vary from faith to faith. For example, if we examine the three major faiths of Judaism, Islam, and Christianity, we can see how their unique trends differ. What we can see is that an overwhelming majority of Jewish rituals and practices are mystic. An overwhelming majority of Islamic rituals and practices are poetic. And an overwhelming majority of Christian rituals and practices are symbolic. The inherent spiritual tendencies of all three confirms this. When we look into their teachings and practices, we can generally say that Christianity is a "Symbolic path to God". Islam is a "Poetic path to God". And Judaism is a "Mystical path to God". Together, they contain three central approaches to the one same Source of Creation. They are three different paths to the One Universal God. They are three pieces of the same Heart.

Christianity is Symbolic

Of the three, it is easiest to see that Christianity is a symbolic path to God when we look at our churches, saints, relics, icons, paintings, and the many depictions regarding the life of Jesus Christ. There is symbolism throughout them all. The cross itself is a symbol. The Last Supper and Nativity Scene have many symbolisms. Statues and relics of saints can symbolize fertility, faith, protection, etc. The white dove symbolizes peace. The halo is a symbol of enlightenment. The Sacred Heart is a symbol of our inner connection to God. Both Heaven and Hell can be considered symbols. Icons are abundant in the Catholic faith, and the saint depicted often holds a symbolic wheel, globe, lily, scepter, etc. Also, in the icon, the depicted saint's fingers are placed in a certain way which symbolize aspects of our inner world and particular celestial bodies in our Solar System.

Catholic rituals are also full of symbolism. For example, when a priest gives communion, all of the aspects - including the bread, wine, and cup - are symbolic. It is even said during the mass that the bread represents "The body of Christ" and that the wine represents "The blood of Christ". In Protestant churches, when we are baptized, the water symbolizes a cleansing and purification of our hearts, mind, and soul. A baptism is to symbolize the "washing away of our sins".

We should remember that many of the first Christians did not read. So, symbolism was – and still is – a powerful and effective way to trigger remembrance and Divine Thought. When a follower is taught of something's symbolic meaning, from then on, the symbolism is always there – even when the priest or the pastor is not.

The symbolism in Christianity also reaches into The Bible itself. It is full of metaphoric stories and parables. The Bible is sometimes known as "The Book of Parables". Even a significant one third of The Master Jesus's recorded teachings shows that he often used parables with both believers and non-believers. It was a central and key part of how he would provoke thought and spread Light. For example, in "The Parable of The

Sower", he taught that when a sower sows seeds, some fall on rocky ground – Those that do get lost. And some seeds fall on good earth – where they grow thirty, sixty, and hundredfold" (Mathew 13: 1-23, Mark 4: 1-20, Luke 8: 1-15). Each person will have their own way of interpreting this parable – But, it is very likely that everyone reflecting on its teachings will get some kind of benefit from what he said. All of his parables are like this. They have a double-edged – and often even a triple-edged – aspect to them. The parables of Jesus Christ make us reflect on the highest aspects of Universal Laws. The Master Jesus apparently used them so much that one of his disciples came to him to ask why he often spoke to people in this riddle-like way. His parables demonstrate how high of an exalted spiritual guide he is.

Throughout, The Bible is full of similes, metaphors, allegories, analogies… and also parables. They all are meant to awaken our imagination and teach us about Divine Law. A famous example of a Divine metaphor is "You are the salt of The Earth". A famous example of a Divine parable is when a "Good Samaritan" helps a Jew that has been robbed and beaten. The Samaritan help this man even when a priest would not. The animosity between Samaritans and Jews was a current event in Jesus's lifetime. He shows in this parable that although Samaritans and Jews hated each other, the Samaritan in this story transcends his hate to be a tool of Divine Consciousness for another human being in need.

The word "parable" itself has two definitions; the first definition being "a divine story". The second definition meaning "symbolic". Combing both definitions tells us that a "parable" is "a symbolic divine story". It teaches us, through different forms of symbolism, of some aspect of the Divine Path we are

THE TWO PATHS TO GOD

on to reach our oneness with God. For Christians, parables help quicken their reunion with The Divine Mind. Symbolism gives Christianity its kinetic energy.

Below is a list of the most prominent parables in The Bible and in The Gospels of Matthew, Mark, Luke, and Thomas:

The Growing Seed	The Two Debtors	The Lamp under The Bushel	The Good Samaritan	The Friend at Night	The Rich Fool	The Wise and The Foolish Builders
The Strong Man	The Sower	The Tares	The Barren Fig Tree	The Mustard Seed	The Leaven	The Pearl
The Hidden Treasure	Counting the Cost	The Lost Sheep/ The Good Shepherd	The Unforgiving Servant	The Wedding Feast	The Sheep and The Goats	The Talents / The Minas
The Faithful Servant	The Budding Fig Tree	The Great Banquet	The Lost Coin	The Prodigal Son	The Unjust Steward	The Rich Man and Lazarus
The Unjust Judge	The Pharisees and The Publican	The Workers and The Vineyard	The Two Sons	The Wicked Husbandmen	The Ten Virgins	The Assassin
The Ear of Grain / The Grain of Wheat	The Empty Jar	The Date-Palm Shoot	Drawing in The Net	The Childbearing Woman	The Master and Servant	New Wine into Old Wineskins

Even though parables are commonly found in its teachings, the most prominent and most often used symbol in Christianity is "Amen". Amen not only symbolizes, but it embodies the link between Universal Consciousness and physical matter. Amen symbolizes the cosmic sound within every atom in existence. Amen symbolizes the condensed form of our Universal God into a single word. "Amen" encapsulates

The Five Divine Virtues and The Quintessence of The Akasha. It encompasses also The Five Solar Elements; vitality, warmth, magnetism, Light, and electricity. It is fitting that Amen is the mantra of Christianity, as one of its main transcendent aspects connects us to the symbolic power of The Sun.

In Christianity…
Relics symbolize something.
Icons symbolize something.
Actions symbolize something.
Rituals symbolize something.
Heaven and Hell symbolize something.
Globes, scepters, wheels, white doves, and halos symbolize something.
Hand gestures symbolize something.
Parables symbolize something.
All the different events in The Master Jesus's Life symbolize something.
…And with "Amen", a word also symbolizes something.

    Symbolism is powerful because it is immediate and direct. It activates several regions of the mind all at once. Both the left, analytical brain and the right, intuitive brain are stimulated. The left processes the facts and the logic of the symbol, while the right processes our feelings, our holistic thinking, and awakens our imagination. With symbols, we reflect. We imagine. We compare. We ponder. And, we connect. They awaken both our sensory, abstract thinking (right brain) and our sequential, logical thinking (left brain). Our memory, awareness, and knowledge are heightened when we use symbolism in any form. In today's world, company logos are a reminder of how powerful symbolism is. Even though, 2000 years ago, advertising did not exist – the power of symbolism and the effects of visualization on the human mind were still used in ways to help humanity spiritually evolve. When spirituality and knowledge are the source of the symbolism, we are both grounded and connected to God. The icon, the relic, the religious painting, the ritual, and the symbolic ornament can all trigger memories of a Divine aspect that you have been taught. Within, you cross a bridge from this physical world back into The Divine Consciousness and all of the dynamic parameters that exist within it.

Islam is poetic

It is also possible to see that Islam is a poetic path to God when we observe how Muslims practice their faith and live their lives. Even when we consider The Holy Koran itself, we can see beauty and poetry.

Firstly, when we look at the Koran, it is written entirely in poetic verse. It is written like one long, beautifully, inspired poem. It incorporates many of the same stories found in The Old and New Testament, but in a poetic form. The Koran's most poetic and lyrical text is written in Arabic. Poetry itself has been around for at least 4,000 years - Long before Islam. Ancient poetry is seen all over the world. There are many reasons people choose this unique form of writing, reading, and reciting. Poetry awakens the imagination. Poetry evokes thought. It opens the heart and the intellect. It is a lyrical way of communicating knowledge. So, it must have been for a truly inspired reason that the first Islamic mystics decided to write their sacred book as an extended poem.

However, the poetry found in Islam does not stop there. When Muslims come together in a mosque to pray, they pray in unison. All of the gestures and postures are harmonically done together. Seeing hundreds or thousands of Muslims kneeling on a floor and then bowing in choreographed unison has a spiritual effect on those participating in that prayer and on those observing it. There is a beauty and power that permeate the mosque's atmosphere. Consider for a moment when we watch a ballet; It is seeing its choreography and unison that have a deep effect on us. If we can feel and recognize the poetry in a ballet, then we can feel and recognize the poetry in a mosque.

One form of Turkish ballet is particularly effective, displaying Divine form of dance, originating from Sufiism. "The Whirling Dervishes" are mesmerizing because they epitomize Islamic Poeticism. Through these dancers, ballet and meditation are poetically united.

Poeticism is observed even when a Muslim prays alone. The first thing he or she does is that they use The Sun and The Earth to find the direction facing North, and then, from there, they calculate from where they are in the world to find the direction facing Mecca. In other words, they "choreograph" themselves to The Earth, and then to that Holy City. Five times a day, for each Muslim, there is a transcendent, global, and celestial poetry they are consciously initiating.

When a Muslim moves to a different house or a different country, their inner compass is very active! If they are being shown around a new dwelling, they will first spend some important, unspoken moments finding out where the Sun rises and where it sets. From there they will quickly find the direction north. And then, they will calculate the direction to Mecca. Then, finally, they will imprint in their thoughts what wall, what corner, or what window faces The Holy City of

Mecca in this house and in each of its rooms. It is a disturbing feeling they immediately have when they walk into a new apartment, and they won't feel inner peace until they first find out in which direction they will pray in this new dwelling. Whether or not they pray regularly doesn't make a difference, the "need to know" direction of Mecca is very strong. They may not even mention it or even be aware that they are doing this, but it will be unsettling to them until their inner spiritual compass is satisfied. For most Muslims, it is more urgently important for them to know the direction of Mecca than the number of bedrooms or the price of the rent.

This inner compass is very strong and highly active within those who are practicing Islam. It is poetically choreographed to the rotation of The Earth and its revolution around The Sun.

By knowing, via celestial choreography, which wall or corner points to Mecca, the practice of praying is taken exponentially higher. Prayer is not just haphazardly performed. There are systematic and preparatory steps behind it. This broad type of prayer choreographs the person to The Earth, The Sun, The Moon, their faith, and the dwelling. The Muslim first "aligns" themselves to a spiritually global and interplanetary system. This is poetry on a transcendent and celestial level. Even when a Muslim begins to pray, there are specific steps that they all follow from the laying of prayer rug, to the words they say, and to the way they bow. The fact that they repeat this same choreographed step-by-step prayer five times a day, every day, for the rest of their spiritual life, is poetic in itself.

And yet, the poetry found in Islam does not even stop there! Every Muslim is encouraged to go to The Hajj once in their life. It is their most important pilgrimage. It is meant to cleanse the mind, spirit, and soul. There are 12 steps to The Hajj, including when each person walks counter-clockwise seven times around the Ka'aba. This circular ritual, for one, is poetically choreographed and awakens spiritual unification in those participating in it. Men and women are brought to tears from its poetic power.

The other 11 steps are also choreographed. Muslims feel repeatedly cleansed and reborn, during and after this 5-day pilgrimage. They are filled with Light and joy from this life-changing event. The activated Divinity permeates their soul with spiritual purity. Poetic Grace permeates the soul at many times during The Hajj. They bring this transcendent joy back to their communities throughout the world. From then on, their thoughts, actions, and spirits are forever altered. Like a Christian Baptism or a Hindu's purification rituals in The Ganges, their lives feel more inspired and blessed for having reached the pinnacle pilgrimage of their faith.

The holy month of Ramadan is the ultimate act of poetic choreography and celestial unison. During this intensely self-disciplined time, each Muslim coordinates their actions, appetites, and desires to The Earth, The Sun, The Moon, and God. Through Divine harmony, self-control, and Truth awareness, Ramadan is a yearly event where spiritual purity is highly activated. Even in the weeks and months before and after Ramadan, does a Muslim feel this inner purity reverberating.

They are encouraged to be kind, loving, humble, and giving. Self-control is the motivating factor of the whole Ramadan tradition. Without self-control, the spiritual cleansing would not be as profound. During this Holy Month, Muslims develop the habits of higher contemplation, study, and self-reflection. These feminine aspects of God are re-activated.

It is also good to remember that the word "Islam" is translated to mean "submission to God". In practice, this means "surrender to God". Muslims are taught to surrender to the mystery, or poetic qualities, that God is. A focus Muslims have is to remember that God's actions are enigmatic and His thoughts are unknown. If we were to describe God in one word, for some spiritualists that word would not be "Love" or "Light". That word would probably be "Mysterious". If God is Love, why does he Love? If God is Light, from where does that Light come from? Surrendering to God and the mysterious qualities that every aspect of Him is puts our thoughts in a poetic state.

But, the most significant and poetic aspect of Islam is the palindrome "Allah" itself. Phonetically, Allah is a divine, harmonic mirror. It can resonate in our thoughts both poetically and lyrically – taking them beyond the edges of our galaxies. It harmonizes our thoughts with the mystical flow of The Universe. Allah resonates, through sound and vibration, at a deep level of endless consciousness. "Allah" means "That without beginning… and without end". We can subtly hear its own definition in the word itself. When we consciously repeat it with this in mind, we trigger realms of deep, cyclical resonance within our thoughts. For all life here on Earth, our biggest and most influential symbol of cyclic motion is The Moon – The heavenly symbol that Ramadan is calculated by. It is fitting that Allah is the mantra of Islam, as one of its many capacities is it connects us to The Moon's inner and outer symbolic power.

The word "Poetic" can be defined in many ways. When we say that Islam is a poetic path to God, we define this as meaning a way to harmonize a person's thoughts, feelings, and actions to Universal Consciousness. "Poetic" in the meaning of "harmonic, flowing, mercurial, melodic, and mysterious". And to some extent, "poetic" in the meaning of "beautiful, lyrical, creative, or artistic". As we see the word poetic in many ways, we can see God in many ways.

Again... Ramadan is a month where poetic thoughts and actions are done to awaken spiritual purity. During this time, Muslims are HIGHLY aware of The Sun, The Moon, and The Earth. They coordinate their days and their diets by them. Self-control activates the transformative divinity happening deep within. During Ramadan, Muslims are able to tell you the exact minute the Sun will rise and will set each day. Whether you are Muslim or not, Ramadan aligns the spiritualist with the poetic rhythm of the Moon's cycle. For all of us, each day we see the power of the Moon's poetic rhythm in our night sky and via our ocean tides. Observing them both leads us to think that Divine Poetry is an intricate part of Universal Consciousness. Poetry is powerful because it is flowing - like a river or a wave. It has both the qualities of either going on and on, continuously, like a wave – or rising and receding, as ebb and flow. Both phenomena are described as poetic. At times, we can feel The Divine Energy within and around us flowing like a river or a wave, and at time we can feel it like ebb and flow. We don't necessarily need to be meditating to feel this, as we even feel it during our busy lives. However, for Muslims, through poetically choreographed rituals, like Ramadan, spiritualists are able to synchronize their thoughts and actions with the incessantly poetic realm of The Universal Mind.

Judaism is Mystic

Finally, it is also easy to see that Judaism is a mystical path to God, when we consider its practice of intense self-analysis. Jews look for and are reminded of the mystical meanings behind every ritual, every prayer, every rite, and every word they speak or perform. Every gesture has been divinely analyzed.

Even every letter in the Hebrew alphabet has had the aspects of it spiritually taken apart, individually examined, and then re-assembled. Jews do this not only to increase their mystical knowledge and awareness, but also to get to the heart of the actions they are asked to perform. Actions without much knowledge is rote. Knowledge without much action is pointless. When both come together, there is mysticism.

Mysticism is seen on all levels of Jewish everyday life and in every aspect of Judaism. Rabbis are constantly writing new publications, where they examine and re-examine passages in The Torah and The Talmud and/or elaborate on Jewish customs and celebrations. Once one book is published, there is soon another book that is written with a new idea or a different viewpoint on the same subject. Soon, there are a lot of books by several different Rabbis and Jewish mystics where arguments and ideas are re-explained, supported, or refuted. Once any of these books are written and published, they all get registered in a Hebrew Library. This obsessive examining and re-examining of Judaism is beyond what Priests and Imams do when they give followers an interpretation of The Bible or The Koran, as Rabbis put their arguments and ideas into the written word much more often.

For example, if a Jew is curious about a word, a passage, or Hebrew letter there are several detailed books that have been written interpreting its meaning. A practicing Jew can easily find a lot of written complementary information about anything in The Talmud, The Torah, or The Old Testament. Books are important, because books travel far beyond a small congregation. The shared information in a book travels world-wide. All Jews, especially Hasidic Jews, are encouraged to read as many of these supplementary books as they can. It is to help complete their Jewish education. Today, the enormous number of books available is already *overwhelming*, and each year more and more of these spiritually analytical books get written, dispersed, and archived.

As children and young adults, Jews are encouraged to memorize The Torah and The Talmud by heart – just as other religions require their followers to do. However, if an individual wants to question or explore a written line or word in either of these books more thoroughly, they are not only allowed to do so – but are encouraged to do so – in the form of a book or document. Discussions about their question or idea are set into motion with their Rabbis and Jewish elders. These spiritual debates are highly valued, and are not seen as a means of belittling the questioner's intelligence. If the question is strong and unique enough to pass through the experience of their local Rabbis and Jewish elders, then this student must have been inspired with an idea that is brilliant and useful to many others in the Jewish faith. In Judaism, questions and new ideas are welcomed, as they keep the religion fresh and regenerated. This is high mysticism.

When a situation gets to the point where a question is unanswerable by the local community or an obscure idea is seen to have yet to be explored, what is respected is that to write a book, based on the analysis of a spiritual text, will put several aspects of mysticism in motion – action and knowledge become one. When that book goes on to be shared with others, that is not only high mysticism, but, at times, it can also become Transcendent Alchemy. The writer becomes a channel, and is inspired as they are writing (actually, "grounding") the Divine knowledge and information that is flowing through them. Encouragement and support from the writer's spiritual community helps them to finish the book – which is a HUGE feat in and of itself! Once the book is published, the reader is inspired by the same Light the writer felt as they are informed when reading the words on the page. Both the writer, the reader, – and oftentimes even the listener – are transformed. This happens because Divinity, mysticism, and expanded knowledge come together to activate Transcendent Alchemy. Light is evoked, and the archived book will trigger transcendence for ages. Of course, writing books on spirituality is done in all the other religions, but in Judaism it is especially prominent. Again… the studying and dissecting of different viewpoints within Judaism is a dominant and strongly encouraged part of their practice – in spite of it being done primarily by men.

Writing books that will get archived in a Spiritual Library is actually a deep and collective form of mysticism. By writing, you are forced to put your thoughts down on paper. When something is written, others can examine, question, support, or argue with you about your interpretations. You, yourself, are forced to organize your thoughts and examine your own arguments, regarding the spiritual questions you have burning in your mind. These individual questions are seen as unique to that writer – and, thus, important, as probably others might be curious about the same theme. So, in Judaism, it is good to examine it. It is good to explore it – because it makes the community better, richer, and more enlightened. Ultimately, these mystical books and documents are to help elevate the entire Jewish community. The Hebrew Library awakens not only thought, but also the intellect and will. Intellectual self-examination enriches the Jewish faith. Intellectually divine self-examination is pure spiritual mysticism. The Hanukkah, The Mezuzah, Bar Mitzvahs, and the like are important parts of the Jewish faith… and all of them have been subjects of a mystical Jewish book, article, or essay – as well as a counter-argument mystical Jewish book, article, or essay.

A book stimulates cohesion within a community. In a Christian or Muslim home, there is likely to be one spiritual book. In a Jewish home, there are likely to be several spiritual books. Jews are more prone to research. Added to that, the individual who wrote the book, Rabbi or not, is considered to be highly intelligent for having done so. Their family, friends, synagogue, and Rabbi support them for having taken the time and thought to educate other Jews. It takes a lot of effort to write a book, and that is recognized and celebrated. To be a "good Jew" is to question and to write. A book does both. So, any serious publication on some aspect of Judaism is treated as a jewel.

In his book, "The Mysteries of The Kabbala", The Rabbi Marc-Alain Ouaknin writes (page 383, translated from the French version):

"Contrary to Decartes, The Talmudist and The Kabbalist do not state 'I think, therefore I am', but instead (they say) 'I read, I interpret, I think, I critique, I oppose, I listen, I write, I examine, I respond, I cite, I tell, I name, I discuss, I question, I pray... I learn, I teach, I live, therefore I am' ".

Mysticism is inherent in Judaism. As a metaphor, mysticism is when the engine is taken apart, the pieces are individually examined, and then the pieces are put back together. Each piece of the engine gets dissected and polished. When the driver knows more about the inner-workings of the motor, he then becomes a better driver and can avoid mishaps on the road. Nearly every aspect of Jewish Life involves mysticism. Everything and every action is elevated to something mystical or up to the level of a ritual. To a Jew, there are mystical meanings within things, such as:

- The way they dress (men and women)
- How they dress (men and women)
- Ornaments they have in their homes
- Ornaments they have at the entrance of their home
- Their hair (men and women)
- Their clothes (men and women)
- The rituals around death and mourning
- The rituals when a boy enters puberty
- Every letter of The Hebrew Alphabet
- Numbers
- Gestures
- Phrases
- Stories
- Holidays and celebrations
- Eating and cooking meals (Kosher, Kashrut…)

Mysticism is different than symbolism. In other words, Jewish mysticism is different than Christian symbolism. Of course, there is mysticism found in Christianity and symbolism found in Judaism. But, the strongest tendency in Christianity is symbolism, and the strongest tendency in Judaism is mysticism. Symbolism is triggered through an image – which then inspires thought and imagination. For example, the white dove symbolizes The Holy Spirit or Peace. Mysticism focuses more on acts and the divine interpretation of those acts acquired from religious study. For example, the ritual of kissing the Mezuzah to protect the home. Symbolism is "when I see X… it reminds me of Y… so that I can act out Z…". Mysticism is "when I do A… it means B… and this helps me resonate with God because of C…".

Symbolism is defined as "something representing something else"; For example, fertility, Light, peace, Love, compassion, and The Holy Ghost all have symbolic representations in Christianity. Mysticism is defined as "certain religious, spiritually significant practices and ceremonies". Mystical practices can be "occult, esoteric, ethereal, symbolic, and mysterious". It is when a physical act combines with inspired thought. Mystical practices can also be in the form of art. The more a Jew consciously practices these rites, the higher he rises in the Jewish elite, and the more he feels like an Initiate – That is, like someone who is divinely privileged. An Initiate is someone who has gone beyond basic prayer and meditation techniques. They are people who can use their knowledge and occult tools to manifest their desires and communicate with God. No matter what religion, we all have the possibility to become Initiates.

"AUM" itself is a highly mystical mantra. It is very thought-provoking, as it contains within it both a Trinity and connects us to the cosmic sound. Each letter of "A-U-M" resonates within us in three different ways. It is a powerful tool of Hebrew mysticism and divinity. It can penetrate into our conscious, unconscious, superconscious minds. We can do a lot of self-study into the descriptions of each of its three letters. They have all been profoundly researched in books. In Judaism, "Shin" embodies the "A", "Aleph" embodies the "U", and "Mem" embodies the "M".

The Hebrew alphabet itself is mystical, both in the way the letters are drawn and how they are said. Each letter of this alphabet is impregnated with exalted meanings to help a person evolve. The individual meanings of the letters are kept fresh in the mind of a practicing Jew, via self-study and Rabbinic teachings. Because of the inherent mysticism, every Jew knows that information on any Hebrew letter or word can be easily found. In the West, the meaning of our individual letters has been mostly lost or forgotten. Studying the letters of AUM, and the mantra itself, helps broaden our spiritual knowledge and accelerate our spiritual evolution. In Judaism, the problem is not from a lack of available information, but from an OVERLOAD of available and diverse information. However, mysticism beautifully brings both thought and practice into one to elevate our spiritual knowledge. It is fitting that "AUM" is the mantra of Judaism, as it connects us to the mystical power of The Trinity.

Mysticism is effective because it combines the heart and the intellect through action. It provokes thought – Far-reaching thought to unlock the mysteries of our Universe. The words mystery and mysticism have the same root. Mystery means "secret". Mysticism means "The study of the secrets", or "The unlocking of the secrets". Mysticism combines action (in the form of rites and rituals) and thought (in the form of questions and analysis). If you are not allowed to ask questions, then you are not practicing mysticism. Questions trigger Light – both in the person who is asking and in the person who is being asked. When habitual rites and divine interpretations unite, mysticism is formed. When many daily acts are practiced as a rite or a ritual, then the person can be seen as a mystic apprentice.

What a Marriage helps us to recognize

There is one ritual that transcends all three of these religions, as well as all the other world religions – Marriage. On the surface, it is commonly seen as the union between a physical man and a physical woman. But spiritually, a marriage powerfully symbolizes the loving union between the masculine aspect of God and the feminine aspect of God. These two aspects exist on many levels deep within each and every one of us – within our personalities, characters, talents, thoughts, DNA, and within our True Self. Each person needed a mother and a father to even be born. Each of us is born with both masculine and feminine qualities. If you care about someone, that is a feminine quality. If you've shown assertiveness, that is a masculine quality. Love unifies them both.

Marriage itself has dramatically changed over time. In Europe, the ceremony is unrecognizable today compared to what it was in the Middle Ages, The 1700's, The Renaissance period, etc. Even in other cultures throughout the world, the marriage ceremony has gone through a metamorphosis. And, of course, the fact that women today are better educated and higher-paid than men has created a very new dynamic in regards to marriage. However, what hasn't changed is the central reason two people unite before God in a religious ceremony.

Marriage symbolizes the love and unification we all are building within between our lunar and solar selves. If there is no Love, there is no pathway to God. If there is no God, there is no pathway to a Higher Love – and no matter how symbolic, poetic, or mystic the marriage ritual may be… it is likely doomed to be unhappy and/or unfruitful. When we see a man and a woman marry under the wings of Love and Divinity, it is a physical representation of the highest duality lying deep within our own spiritual realm. It is a unifying ceremony where, in our deepest realm, The King anoints The Queen within, and The Queen anoints The King within. Both sides of ourselves commit to helping the other reach Divine Communion. Both partners commit to helping the other reach Enlightenment, Nirvana, and Paradise. It is a ceremony where we ultimately commit to "Heaven on Earth" in our new and shared chapters of Life.

It wasn't always this way about marriage. The ways and reasons people have married are drastically different now than they were even 50 years ago. Love was often not involved. Women often had no rights. They were given to the husband to do his beck and call. So then, if women and girls had no rights… why did they marry? Why would her family be so adamant in getting her out of the house if they needed her more at home? If people married for power and land, then why did poor people marry? If marriage was for children, inheritance, and to continue the family name… then why marry in a church, mosque, synagogue, or temple?… There is and has always been a deep and spiritually motivating reason to marry. Because of that one reason, this tradition has lasted for ages. The exterior reasons have changed A LOT over time.… But the central, Divine reason has never changed.

When more and more of us are able to see that God is both masculine and feminine… then we will be able to see that the bride is both masculine and feminine… that the groom is both masculine and feminine… and that we ourselves are also both masculine and feminine. When we are able to see marriage this deeply – into the central reason for unifying two souls – then the marriages we attend will not always have to be between a man and a woman. The genders of the two people marrying won't matter. All that we would really need to look for is their Love for each other and their spiritual aspirations to God – Those are the true unifiers.

Three Abrahamic Reactions to tragedy

Examined from the point of view of their strongest traits, we can see that there is a great deal of symbolism in Christianity, poeticism in Islam, and mysticism in Judaism. However, there is a simple way to test whether, in fact, these aspects are truly the central thoughts of the three Abrahamic religions. To clearly see the differences between a Christian, a Muslim, and a Jew, we can examine how each of them responds to tragedy. Tragedies come in different forms and degrees – from a failed college exam, to a bankrupt business, to a car accident, to a fatal disease. But, what is our first conditioned reaction when we are confronted with sudden tragedy? With this question in mind, we can see that The Christian, The Muslim, and The Jew spontaneously react differently to tragedies. These differences are strongly related to symbolism, poeticism, and mysticism.

When tragedy strikes a Christian, he or she is likely to ask themselves "Why is God doing this to me?". In other words, the Christian often looks for the symbolic meaning as to why their flower shop burned down or why they broke a leg on a skiing trip. A Christian looks for the lesson contained in the tragedy. A Christian asks himself "What is God trying to teach me with this tragedy?". When tragedy strikes a Jew, they don't question God's actions. The Jew says, "I have to be a better Jew" – and they are furthermore advised by their family and Rabbi to "be a better Jew". In other words, to keep tragedy at bay and stay in God's favor, they initially feel they have to practice more rituals and mysticism. A Jew uses actions and rituals to transcend their tragedy. By changing their current actions, it is assumed that they will change their future results. When tragedy strikes a Muslim, he neither questions God's actions nor resolves to pray more, instead, he or she is likely to come to the conclusion "It was God's Will". In other words, the Muslim reminds himself of the poetic, flowing, and unpredictable Nature of God. A Muslim accepts God's mystery and tries to align himself to the Will of Divine Consciousness when there is a tragedy. Even though there is much pain from it, saying that "It was God's Will" and thinking in this way helps him or her get back into the Universal and Eternal Flow.

All three of these spontaneous reactions are spiritually helpful. But, there is one thing we can still ask ourselves… "Why can't all three reactions be combined into one?". That is… When a tragic and unfortunate event occurs, we accept God's mysterious flow, while looking for the lesson within our misfortune, as we practice more rituals, prayer, and study. That is an Abrahamic reaction to tragedy.

Again… Christianity is symbolic. Islam is poetic. And Judaism is mystic. They are three pieces of the same heart. In each path, there is more than enough Love to immerse yourself in for the rest of your life. However, by only focusing on our one path and remaining disrespectful and unaware of the beauty in the two other dynamic paths, we miss out on several universal and mind-broadening opportunities. Transcending our ignorance and fear gives impulse to our evolution and sparks our spiritual alchemy. Poeticism, mysticism, and symbolism form a Trinity. Each one is both a tool and a Divine technique. They are three parts of a much larger and all-encompassing Universal Heart. When we are familiar with every nook and cranny of this Universal Heart, transcendent peace and joy will enter our lives to establish their abundance.

Who are The Chosen People?

In Judaism, Islam, and Christianity, there are a vast number of branches, denominations, and trends. In Christianity alone, there are about 40,000 different churches and around 21,000 different denominations. In Islam, there are Sunni and Shiite

Muslims – and a large number of denominations from both. Judaism has The Hasidic, Orthodox, Kabbalist, Talmudist, and a number of other Jewish denominations. Each one of these religious groups sees their path as the right one, and often go on to seeing themselves as "God's Chosen" – a small group of people that will be guaranteed a place in heaven and a seat next to God in The Afterlife. But since there are so many thousands of these groups and so many millions of different members within these groups, for whom are those limited seats next to God reserved? What religion is written on the name tag of those seats next to God?

What we see in all three of The Abrahamic Religions is that, through the passage of Time, they have become splintered. On one hand, this splintering shows the human thirst for Truth and spiritual knowledge… but on the other hand, we must ask ourselves "Did God cause this splintering or did the human mind?".

The overall result of this competitive thinking is that there are three religions simultaneously believing that those tiny number of seats belong to them. Who's right? What's even more confusing is when you factor in the other world religions, where they don't pray to a God who has such a segregated and wrathful way of managing Heaven. Hinduism, Taoism, and Buddhism all also have different denominations, but they focus more on a different aspect of the same faith. They magnify a small aspect of their faith to create a sect. The various yogas in Hinduism and Zen Buddhism are some examples. In Hinduism, the way that yogas "divide" that religion up into "denominations" is by focusing on God's most prominent aspects – Love, Devotion, Work, Thought, and so forth. The idea of "our group is God's chosen and everybody else will burn in Hell" is not a part of their concept. Universal compassion is one of the core beliefs found in all Eastern Religions. In The Abrahamic Religions we say "Unconditional Love", but rarely put that into thought and action. Are we praying to a God of Unconditional Love, or to one that is judgmental, vengeful and is waiting until after we die to tell us we wasted all the joyful and faithful thoughts we had of him to send us straight to Hell?

Chosen people feel that because they have followed their particular path that they will be treated with special favor. That, in some way, God has "favorites" – a favorite child that he loves more than the others. Again… is this a human concept or a Divine concept? Those who feel they are "chosen" feel they will be given heavenly gifts either because of some act they performed here on Earth or by following the doctrines of their one religion. The fact that, after their death, God could say "That was nice… But, try again" rarely crosses their mind.

For many of those fixated on being one of the chosen, even if they did not strictly practice their religious doctrines as they should have, just by saying that they are in a group of The Chosen People (whether Christian, Muslim, or Jew). To many of these believers, they act as if our abundant, limitless, Universal God can only afford a few number of seats – as if God doesn't have enough money to buy extra chairs or room to place a few extra seats for some unexpected guests. We practice faith as if we need to make a reservation for the theater – not as if our daily thoughts and actions matter or are seen.

What gets even crazier is that even the, so-called, Chosen, themselves, cut back on the number of already limited seats and the number of already limited people fighting for these precious few seats. In other words, they start making distinctions within their own group between the "Righteous Chosen People" and "The Unrighteous Chosen People". In their mind, heaven must be the size of a matchbox. Again… is this a Universal and Divine way of thinking – or is it a limited, human, and fearful way of thinking? How disgruntled will these people feel walking around Paradise if God lets in one of the unrighteous chosen or a person from a religion they hated. This isn't the Heaven that they had in mind. Will they feel resentment to God or have to set up a meeting with Heaven's Ombudsman to air their complaints if Christians, Muslims, Buddhists, and Taoists are all walking around in Paradise?

At their earliest beginnings, Jews, Muslims, and Christians were each all persecuted, murdered, banished, imprisoned, crucified, and on the run as refugees. These new faiths were seen to be radically different than to norm or status quo of their day. None of The Abrahamic Religions were immediately met with open arms. They were all considered heretics at first. The societies they lived in despised them, hated them, feared them, and desperately tried to destroy them. In the beginning, those who practiced these new rituals met and performed them in secret. They had to make the choice of either being ostracized from their families and community for this new way they found to love God or to live a lie, constantly denying the joy they truly felt. That joy was felt strongly by all of these original "heretics" – whether they were Jewish, Muslim, or Christian. Each one of them risked imprisonment and death – not for stealing a loaf of bread, but for thought. And prison was no easy place! You would surely be tortured because of this bizarre faith you were following. Fear was a part of it, and no mercy was shown in the prisons of their day, as you were likely to be whipped or beheaded.

Going through all of this hardship must have been extremely trying. They all had to escape armies. Soldiers went from house to house searching for them. They hid out in some sympathetic person's abode, and more than likely practiced in barns by candlelight their first elementary rituals in soft whispers. Constant hunger, thirst, and, at times, near starvation was a part of life. Being despised by people for their faith was the norm. They had no bed to sleep in. No work. No money. Nowhere to turn. And, nowhere to run. All they really had was each other and their common conviction in their prophet and God. What compelled them to keep living under this constant pressure and fear was their common belief that the path they were on was the right one for them.

During these early times of extreme desperation, what probably kept them going through it all was the belief that they were The Chosen People or that God had a place set aside for them in heaven, and for their comrades who had already been caught and crucified. This feeling that they created between themselves was seen as the Divine reward for all of the suffering they were bearing. A feeling that the Ancient Romans might have been able to kill their bodies, but they could not kill their souls and they could not kill their spirits. Telling themselves that "We are The Chosen People", "Our reward is in heaven", or "We are the true believers who are going to heaven to be with God" motivated and unified them during their flee to the next place of safety.

The three Abrahamic religions fight because each one of them thinks that they are "The Chosen People" – The chosen few who, after their death, will easily pass through the Gates of Heaven. They feel blessed to be following such a golden path of Truth as the one they are on. They feel part of a divine and elite group of hand-picked men and women who will live forever in paradise with God. A place filled with angels, virgins, and harps, surrounded by their loved ones and those who followed the same path they did during their lifetimes. Only upon their group does God smile favorably. As for everybody else.... Ha! They will all burn in Hell because they had the chance to come into the Truth, but chose to stay ignorant and blind. God gave them many chances to come onto the right path, but they didn't. When they get to the Gates of Heaven, they will find those doors shut! They will be locked out. They will just have to suffer in the Dungeons of Hell.

Again, this way of thinking can also be applied to each of the denominations within the each of the three Abrahamic religions. Feeling that you are chosen or in an elite group because of your faith, can blind you from truly seeing and accepting the good in others. Someone from another faith might do you a good, honest, and heartfelt deed, but it is never fully accepted, if compared to it coming from someone within your elite chosen group. In these situations, what would God see from his perspective? Who would he say had the most empathy and universal compassion… you or the "heretic" who showed you the heartfelt deed? In whatever way you see this encounter, one thing is true… the "heretic" rose above their hate and fear to show you kindness. Unconditional Love came first. Religion came second. The heretic was the one who went beyond their conditioning and prejudice. They took the first steps towards you with openness and equal vision. It is because of our conditioned mind, that the heretic and their deed are tainted. It is not possible to tap into true universal joy when we see most of the world's humanity as barbarians. How can we see the heavens when we only see the heathens? The Unconditional Love that God IS either shines through you or it does not. The alchemic ability to turn dust into gold is a mental sign of greatness in yourself. Alchemy can turn a heathen into a saint. Prejudice can turn a saint into a heathen. In the alchemic, transcendental state, we can see the same Light in a "heretic" as we do in ourselves.

In times of terror and fear, feeling that we are chosen, selected, or elite can make the members of any group feel protected and self-righteous. But, arguably, for the most part, those times where people are escaping armies and running for their lives because of their faith have drastically changed. Any Ancient Christian, Jew, or Muslim would tell us that what we live now is nothing compared to what they had to go through. Life has greatly improved for all religions. The fact that we have thousands of denominations from a variety of different faiths all over the world testifies to that. Synagogues, churches, mosques, temples, and a wide variety of places of worship are found in both The East and in The West. Yes!... Christians, Muslims, Jews, Buddhists, and Hindus are still persecuted, tortured, and put to death for their religion in some parts of the world... but, globally, we are at the point now in our human evolution to see that this recurring pattern has little to do with religious faith but more to do with human fear. One day we will see that it is enough to just be alive, on Earth, and in human form to feel that we are "chosen". Chosen will mean that you are a Custodian of The Earth, born with the spiritual tools to evolve. Some of God's most prominent aspects are Light, Love, Universal Joy, and Work – by blissfully resonating with any of those, we become like him. And by becoming like him, we all become his "favorites". Using our bliss to resonate with Light, Work, and Universal Joy will replace our need to belong to a specific, organized religious group who feels that it is chosen.

To those who think that they are "God's favorites", what they are really saying is that they don't believe in God at all.

They don't believe that God having given us an able body, a sound mind, and a heart hungry for Truth was enough. For them, Truth is one way – Their way! One narrow path that only they know of. The fact that Truth could be an all-encompassing composite of spirituality and science never crosses their minds. The idea that our various religions create a collage of Knowledge and Wisdom in the map of Universal Truth is foreign to them. We are led to see our religions in a very fragmented way. But, actually, we, as spiritualists, are accumulating Universal Knowledge that can deep into The Cosmic Intelligence. Separately, our religions have failed us... But, together, they can enrich us. This spiritually fragmented-thinking leads us to hate, which has ultimately led to the horrific acts of war and terror in our world. Truth is cumulative. We are all taking part in revealing it. It is not unique to a small group of people who feel that they are chosen. If the Truth they claim to have was really the entire Truth, then it could not be contained. Like Light, Truth spreads and disperses. Truth is like a star. Think of how one star can emit a massive amount of Light throughout an entire galaxy!

The Shield of David is found in all Abrahamic Religions

In Christianity, Judaism, and Islam, there is one symbol that is connected to all three religions – that symbol is The Star of David. It is also known as the Shield of David. It is a hexagon made up of two opposingly directed and intertwined equilateral triangles. One of them is pointing up and the other pointing down. Today we see this symbol and think it has always been Jewish, but, actually, it has not. It was used by both Arabs and Christians before it began to be used by Jews.

In Christianity, it was used in churches as a decorative symbol. Again... symbolism is the hallmark of Christianity.

Christian symbolism teaches us about the many aspects of divinity through depictions and imagery. With this in mind, the priests and cardinals who commissioned the many artisans to depict and carve this emblem into the walls of churches and chapels had to have known of its powerfully symbolic meaning. They wanted it there. Its role in Ancient Christianity was to remind us of something divine. So, the priests, bishops, and popes had to have had a good reason why they wanted their Temple of God to be partly decorated with it.

In Islam, The Star of David was widely used in Arabic literature throughout the middle ages. On the pages of books and poems, readers would come across this symbol. Like priests, in regards to their churches, the early Imams considered the pages of their books to be sacred. A great deal of spiritual thought went into the written work, as well as into the decorative art adorning it. In Arabic writing, the slightest stroke of a brush has a significant meaning. The whole word and its meaning can be completely altered with just one hand movement. Islamic temples, palaces, and mosques are known for their intricate detail. A great deal of thought and sophistication was put into the design and decoration of mosques and Islamic books. Since the first Muslim mystics revered Islamic writing and architecture with such awe and detail, we can assume that the effort that they put into decorating their palaces... they also did in adorning their books. The books were read in the mosques. The book's decorative adornments – that took more time and effort to draw onto the pages than the words themselves – were meant to enhance the words of The Koran as it was being read. The Star of David is one of the depictions that is regularly seen in these ancient books. The many depictions were not illustrations, they were spiritual enhancements. These books could have been written without their many decorative symbols – but, that would have created a totally different experience. To the listeners, the experience would have been the same – But, not to the reader! The reader is always the focal point in the mosque, as they are in the church, synagogue, or any other temple. When a person is reading from an adorned Koran, he is inspired by both its words and by the depictions. The Shield of David is one of the depictions he sees on the page. In Ancient Islam, The Star of David helped to spread Light to many others through the one person reading from The Koran.

The Star of David has not only an ancient history, but can be found in our recent history, as well. It has been used on both the flag of Morocco and the flag of Israel. It has been used during the Holocaust to identify Jews, as well as on emblems and tombstones. It has been carved into the stone of synagogues and the hard cover of books. There is no simple way of writing it without lifting your pen. You need two strokes to draw it correctly, causing the mind to consider both the involution and evolution of its global meaning.

David was the young boy who defeated Goliath with his sling and then went on to become one of the most important Kings of Israel. Goliath was a strong, powerful, and sinister giant. David was known for his strength, intelligence, and his faith in God. The story of their battle is one of the most well-known in spirituality – even beyond The Abrahamic religions. David went on to write some of the Psalms of The Bible, and is highly revered in the spiritual books of Judaism, Christianity, and Islam.

With nothing but his sling, a rock, and precise intention, David killed Goliath. Today, to defeat Goliath can also mean that an underdog has defeated a powerful adversary. Yet, in the spiritual realm, it can symbolize how, through focused effort, faith, and intelligence, we can defeat our darker forces, traits, and entities. Through Light, we can reach our birthright as spiritual Kings and Queens.

To call this symbol "The Star of David" or "The Shield of David" is highly significant. A star gives Light and a shield gives protection. But the truest and deepest aspects of this simply drawn symbol lies in the directions of its two equilateral triangles. One points upwards, signifying our "Evolution". These are our actions towards oneness with God. Things like prayer, meditation, and all of the spiritual techniques, rituals, and thought we put into ascending from man to God describe the steps we take in our evolution. The other triangle points downwards, signifying "Involution". These are God's actions towards us; grace, blessings, inspiration, serendipity, and answered prayers show us how God is descending into our lives. But also rainbows, The Sun, The Earth, "un-requested answered prayers", and how God supports and maintains all Life in The Universe are some other signs of involution at work.

The Star of David shows us that when evolution ("I am God") and involution ("God am I") meet, there is Light and protection. Finding signs of both evolution and involution within and around us elevates our thoughts. For example, praying while simultaneously realizing that your heart, breath, and all your bodily functions are operating beyond your conscious participation. In other words, the realization that you are sending a message to the same God who is supporting your heartbeat. When we connect with something greater than ourselves, both triangles in our inner Star of David combine to evoke Light.

The Two Universal Constants

The Two Paths to God

The two complementary paths can be combined into a "Paired Mantra". There are 12 paired-mantras. Each one is unique. All elevate our thoughts and evoke the same Light within us, but each does so in a very different way. Pairing a Cosmic Sound-mantra with an Eternal Field-mantra generates a multitude of beneficial effects on every aspect of our being. The Trinity and The Paired mantra both use synergy to empower thought. In other words, when different elements are brought together, they are more powerful than they are individually. When both mantras are used as one, our thoughts consciously dance on the edge between the manifested and un-manifested realms. Both aspects exist within and around us. They evoke Light, peace, and understanding. Practicing with them, helps us exude these qualities. With a paired-mantra, we emit Light from our body, mind, and spirit – and our thoughts are extended to the outer limits of our galaxies.

Our ultimate goal is to re-examine the mantras we've developed and enriched in this Age of Religion. Why? It is because we are beginning a new age… An age we can describe as "The Age of Light".

The Two Universal Constants are the manifested and the un-manifested realms

Science and religion have developed techniques that work with the same one reality. Both the scientist and the spiritualist attempt to activate an action-reaction-response with our Universal Consciousness. With science, it is easier to see the results of our efforts. Our desires from science are often very small, or will often involve the natural laws of Nature. Take for example, the light bulb. Today, we flip on a switch without even thinking about it. Yet, Thomas Edison spent years sweating over this invention he wanted to bring into the world. Edison worked with waves and particles to bring his idea to fruition. J. Robert Oppenheimer's atomic bomb invention is also small, as he focused on atoms, nuclei, and molecules. But the results of his work have had catastrophic consequences in the world; Destruction, fear, and death are some of the results of his work.

With religion, however, our desires are often very BIG. We connect to Divine Consciousness to pray for healing, wealth, and to save our own or someone else's life. But, the difference between us and Oppenheimer, we quickly lose patience. Research scientists are trained to have tons of patience. It is an essential requirement needed to unearth the manifested from the un-manifest. Like when Thomas Edison tried hundreds of experiments before finally finding that one combination that would develop the light bulb, we also need faith, persistence, and patience when praying.

In general terms, science and religion lead us to two different realities - one that we see and one that we sense. Science leads us to interactions with the manifested reality. Religion leads us to interactions with the un-manifested reality. Both overlap and interact with each other. Both are complex, unlimited, and constant. One side is eternal, from whence Life is born and returns. The other side is transient, in where Life exists and is conducted. One side is abundant with Universal intelligence and Divine potential. The other side is abundant with free will and is teeming with innumerous forms of Life. Both Universal intelligence and free will come from Thought.

In the first sections of this book, we have seen how "Tao" and "Allah" take our thoughts to a constant and eternal realm of thought – and how "Amen", "AUM", and "Om" take our thoughts to a dynamic vibrational realm of thought. With "Amen"/ "AUM" / "Om", we see that this dynamic and vibrational realm is constantly emerging, merging, and re-emerging from the constant and eternal realm of "Allah" / "Tao". This flux is going on at this very second throughout the entire universe. Astronomers can see stars being born and dying – and hundreds of women throughout the world have just discovered that they are pregnant. In other words, Universal Consciousness is not only doing this an INFINITE amount of times throughout the Universe… but also an infinite amount of times within our own body. In each of our bodies, we have an innumerable amount of cells and atoms in this flux of birth and decay. Imagine for a moment the VAST number of atoms being born in the Universe at this very second… and the VAST number of atoms that are dying in the Universe at this very second. Even though it is unthinkably HUGE, there must be a number. That number is so infinitesimally BIG and fleetingly mercurial that only Eternal Consciousness knows what it is at this very second. As for us, it is immeasurable. We can only think about it in hypothetical terms. To our scientists, it is incalculable. We have no way – and will have no way – of calculating, second by second, every atom on all of the multi-trillions of planets, stars, moons, and asteroids throughout our entire Universe; Nor of their inhabitants, environment, and food sources. We don't even have the capacities to calculate that here on Earth, or even within one human body. Besides that, it is a number we do not need to know. Only knowing that at every second a dynamic and Universal number exists is enough.

Awareness of this phenomenon, and its scientific and mathematical truth, opens our thoughts to a dynamic realm within and around us. The fact that we can imagine this number being SO ASTRONOMICALLY HUGE, UNIVERSAL, FLUCTUATING, and INCESSANT… gives rise to its momentary existence. Because of that, we can call it a Universal Constant. It is our "Variable Universal Constant". It is our manifested reality. Our "Invariable Universal Constant" is Divine Consciousness itself. It is our un-manifested reality. As long as we have a Universe that we can see, feel, taste, smell, and hear we will have two constants – one that is eternal and one that is dynamic.

Our mystics tell us that before the creation of this manifested reality, there was only one constant – The One Eternal, Pure Consciousness. For reasons unknown, The Eternal Field gave birth to The Cosmic Sound. When that happened, this second constant came into being – because The Circle of Life came into being. Cosmic Sound and Universal Intelligence are the more likely components that developed life in the universe. It is hard to imagine, as many Big Bang Theorists do, that planets, galaxies, and star constellations were violently spewed out whole from The Eternal Void. God shows himself to be calmer than that – especially when He's creating. If whole galaxies and planets did, in fact, suddenly explode out of The Cosmic Void all over our entire Universe, then how does that explain the circular motion we see everywhere? Our Earth circularly rotates on its own axis. All the planets in our Solar System circularly revolve around the Sun. And images of our Milky Way Galaxy show that the trillions of its stars, planets, and moons are moving in a circular motion. If whole planets and galaxies haphazardly exploded out all over the Universe, there would not be this circular motion inherent in every celestial body and star configuration. But, the fact that there IS ALWAYS clockwise or counterclockwise movement found on some, or all, levels of a celestial body show that there is Cosmic Intelligence at work. On the level of circular celestial movement, our Universe operates like the innerworkings of a pocket watch; some wheels turn clock-wise and other wheels are turning counterclockwise. But, together they operate as one. All of the little individual wheels effect the others – no matter how big or small. Each wheel's individual manoeuvre has a purpose, a function, and a significant meaning… otherwise "The Watchmaker" would never have put it there.

Paired Mantras combine Cosmic and Universal Vibration with Divine and Eternal Intelligence. When we consciously repeat "AUM-Tao", "Allah-Amen", or any of the 12 mantras, our thoughts dance between two constant realms – The manifested realm and the un-manifested realm. There is only one absolute God, however when something is born, the state of existence changes as it has passed through the various stages in the cycle of life and death. It is no longer in its absolute state. It has taken a body – a temporary form. Reincarnation recognizes how our souls repeatedly pass from the un-manifested realm, into the manifested realm, and then back into the un-manifested realm – taking information and experiences along with it to evolve. By combining both the Eternal Field and The Cosmic Vibration, we combine both the constant and the dynamic realms within us. We align our Lunar and Solar selves. We create an Inner Eclipse that can evoke tremendous Light.

When we align our Inner Sun with our Inner Moon to form an Inner Eclipse, we focus our thoughts between the realm of constancy and the realm of fluctuation. Our Inner

Sun is active and dynamic, while our Inner Moon is silent and passes through various phases. Paired Mantras create an Inner Eclipse – aligning within us a realm that is variable and one that is invariable. A realm that is incarnate and one that is immortal. With a paired mantra, we become Spiritual Kings and Queens, with a reign over our Inner Universe. Furthermore, the more we practice expanding our thoughts and focusing on these two ever-present realms, the more we begin to see that the constant is dynamic, and the dynamic is constant. Our thoughts and inner-vision can connect to either of these aspects of God or merge them into one at will. Working with the two Universal Constants accelerates our vibration to a high level. Once our thoughts and practices get to this point, we can be sure that the Light we evoke within and around ourselves is extremely bright... and itself becomes a constant!

Again, with any of the twelve paired mantras, such as "Om-Tao", our thoughts dance between the manifested and un-manifested parallels. When we use techniques to consciously unite these two realms within, our mind merges with The Absolute, our body merges with The Absolute, and then our actions and whole Life merge with The Absolute.

Light is a particle and a wave... and The Universe is a particle and a wave

God is often described as Love... But, He is also often described as Light. So, if God is Light – What is Light? Scientists who study it have difficulty describing what Light is when conducting their experiments and research. Some describe it as a wave. While others describe it as a particle. It acts differently, depending on the experiment. But, what seems to be the current theory is that it is the scientist's own thoughts and expectations which will influence whether light will act like a wave or like a particle. Light itself is both.

The light we see is a small part of the entire Light spectrum. Invisible light encompasses several times more space. Most Invisible light is un-manifested, not counting the Ultra-Violet and Infra-Red. The Visible Light we see every day is manifested. Visible light can be experimented with. What is prayer other than experimenting with thought to trigger a result? However, when we use paired mantras, we resonate at a higher frequency that evokes Light from the invisible light spectrum. In this state, our prayers become more powerful.

As for God being described as Light, this is probably a good metaphor. It is our thoughts and expectations that influence what God for us is. If we see him as wrathful and judgmental, we see him as conditional. He selects. He condemns. He has "good ones" and "bad ones". But, who is selecting and who is condemning – God or our own thoughts? It is our own thoughts, teaching, and free will that have created him this way for us. No wonder we think he rarely answers our prayers, He is too busy sending the sinners he hates to Hell!

A different way to focus on God is to base our thoughts on the Universal Abundance and Cosmic Intelligence we see within and all around us. God is The Eternal Field and The Cosmic Vibration. The Eternal Field is like a "wave" of Light. The Cosmic Sound, like a "particle" of Light. God is both. It is our own thoughts that can determine into which realm we can come into oneness with his Divinity. Light would not be Light if it were only a particle. Light would not be Light if it were only a wave. Light is both. And, using Light itself as an example, we can consciously combine two aspects of God into one by use of the paired mantras.

A More Scientific View Of God

A lot can be said for simplifying our connection to God to five words. When we do, much of the folklore, stories, parables, and rituals that our religions use in their practices are removed. The Five World Mantras keep our thoughts focused on the here and now. By awakening the solar and lunar aspects of ourselves, we connect to Divine Intelligence in two unique, and interconnected, ways. These words we have empowered with our highest thoughts and aspirations for several millennia. Our religious festivals evoke collective joy to help empower them even more.

The Sun, giving the world vitality and electromagnetic energy, reminds us of God as "The Cosmic Vibration". The Moon, influencing the world's tides and gravity, reminds us of God as "The Eternal Field". Remembering God in these ways removes our sentiment about God and helps connect us to the deeper aspects of who we are. We don't see him as a judge, punisher, or condemner. We don't fear Him. We don't hate Him. Rather, our thoughts are united with Him here, now, in this present moment. At any time, we can stop for moment to see God that is beyond what is visible to the eye and where He exists in The Eternal Field – here and now. And then, simultaneously, we can look at the part of Him that lies within the deepest Cosmic Vibration of our own body cells and within every manifested thing we see around us – here and now. The present moment is the most productive time to use for transcendence and transformation. Our thoughts in neither the past nor the future can do what the present moment can. It is a time we can use to spiritually evolve because it can take us directly into Eternity. It is when our thoughts are in the present moment that Time itself seems to stop for a split second.

When we begin to experience Divine Consciousness in this way, we use our capacity for scientific thought. We don't have the university credentials of a PhD scientist, but on our spiritual realm we are applying many aspects in their way of thinking to analyze Divinity. In this way, we open our thoughts to the four major areas of Science; The Natural Sciences, The Social Sciences, The Formal Sciences, and The Applied Sciences:

We not only become like Social Scientists who study theology, law, and health, but we also become like Natural Scientists, who apply a scientific method in order to study the Universe. These are scientists who try to clarify the rules that govern The Natural World. Physical scientists study molecules, atoms, and their behavior. Physicists study the behavior and the phenomena of The Universe. Ecologists study living organisms and their relationships with each other. Earth scientists study physics and The Natural Laws. Astronomers study the stars, moons, and planets. We trigger the aspects of these scientific disciplines when we incorporate what The Moon and The Sun can spiritually represent to us in our prayers and rituals.

In the next chapter, we will learn about "The Clock of The Twelve Paired Mantras". Like how the elements of an analog clock work together, the elements of The Five World Mantras work together. With this Clock, we become like Formal Scientists who study mathematics, logic, information, and theory. The Clock also helps us become like Applied Scientists who use theories and systems in their practices. Using this Clock in our prayers and meditations, is like how an applied scientist actively tests out his or her theories on or in a system. It is the use of scientific knowledge in a physical environment.

Recognizing that there are two Universal Constants and applying this knowledge in accordance to our Sun and our

Moon can trigger many aspects of scientific thought. Some scientists are already experimenting with this. Namely, Quantum Scientists observe how the smallest independent units in our Universe – such as thoughts, energy, ideas, intentions, and electromagnetic radiation – can generate phenomena that will influence the physics in our world.

But, the science that triggers the most direct lunar and solar benefits to the analyst is Alchemic Science. The science of transforming one's own spirit. Since we are working with celestial bodies and subtle thought, prayers, meditation, and affirmations perfectly correspond to this realm of activity. The Sun and The Moon are gifts from God to us all here on Earth. Life as we know it would not exist without them. We need them both, as they are both part of us. Before the existence of The Abrahamic religions there were civilizations that worshipped The Sun or The Moon. Ancient Egyptians, for example, were Sun worshippers. They even had a name for The Sun God – "Ra".

Today, it is easy to take for granted the importance of The Sun and The Moon in our busy lives. But, we can also stop for a moment and try to look closer at these celestial gifts. As with almost anything, using a more scientific and analytical approach can help us better understand and improve our experience and knowledge of it.

Lunar And Solar Medicinal Healing

As we enter into "The Age of Light", it can be argued that in The Age of Religion some of our most prominent problems were racism, sexism, homophobia, Islamophobia, Anti-Semitism, etc. All of these were based in fears and biases that originated from how people were taught to think of God and follow the world's religions. Many people were led to think of them selves as sinners. This led to fears, hate, and a lot of destruction. Phobias came from fears. Fears closed down our vision and our minds. A closed mind created pre-judgements and hate. Hate prevented many people from seeing the diversity that is God and his creation of Life. And often, much of this originated in the teachings in our spiritual institutions. Focusing on The Five World Mantras and the Two Universal Constants changed that. The Sun and The Moon became the catalysts for this.

Incorporating The Sun and The Moon into our spiritual practice does one major thing – It expands our thoughts. By thinking in an "expanded environment", we begin living in an "expanded environment". We multiply the opportunities we can potentially attract to ourselves. By using them, no longer do we live our lives unaware of their spiritual importance, but we also awaken The Two Universal Constants within and around us. To bring balance into ourselves and into our thoughts, we are compelled to remember both the lunar power and the solar power we were born with.

In fact, there are neither open minds nor closed minds – rather there is a DEPTH of mind and vision. Depth of mind also puts us into the present moment. Depth of mind and vision gives us more self-confidence. Confidence in The Self – In other words… Trust in God.

When God fills our thoughts as being "The Cosmic Sound" and "The Eternal Field", there is no room for sin. Life just is. Everything and everyone can remind us of our own eternal connection to Divine Consciousness. As our thoughts begin to frequently dip into the eternal, dynamic abyss, we come out of it rejuvenated. There is no room for "God hates me" or "I hate God". Even the thought "God hates me because I am a sinner" doesn't even come to mind. If God hated people who think they are sinners, billions of us would be outcast. Do loving parents conceive a child to hate it?

The Moon and The Sun taught us to free ourselves from judgements. They showed us how to awaken harmony and Transcendence – and the world became a more peaceful place.

The Clock Of The Twelve Paired Mantras In The Age Of Light

As Luni-Solar beings, we can explore the spiritual and synergistic value of the Two complementary Constants existing in The Universe. Our Five Individual World Mantras are the keys that can be combined into "Twelve Universal Paired Mantras". Any of the Paired Mantras create a powerful and multi-dimensional synergy within our hearts, thoughts, and prayers. One mantra takes our thoughts into Eternal and Divine Potentiality and the other mantra takes our thoughts into Dynamic and Incessant Activity. Both are complementary because, when used as one, our thoughts consciously dance on the edge between the manifested and un-manifested realms. Our thoughts go beyond the limits of our galaxies and into the depths of our own spirit.

Our world is now entering a new age – "The Age of Light". An Age where abundance, transcendence, Pure Joy, and knowledge are experienced exponentially. A new era where scientific and spiritual knowledge combine for the common good. In this Age, every conscious and spiritual individual can evoke a powerful tool to accelerate their spiritual evolution. This tool is known as "The Clock of The Twelve Paired Mantras". It is the map that humanity has invested its spiritual resources into creating for more than four millennia.

The Inner Eclipse – When Our Moon And Our Sun Align

Allah and Tao complement Amen, Om, and AUM

The most dynamic words we can use with "Allah" or "Tao" is either "Om", "AUM", or "Amen". As we will see in the next section, "Allah" and "Tao" are more "Lunar". "Om", "AUM", and "Amen" are more "Solar". Aligning them together creates an "Inner Eclipse". Allah and Tao bring our thoughts to God's dynamic immortality – while Om, AUM, and Amen help us to remember how God created this incarnate Universe we live in. When aligned, using two of these mantras bring us into the present moment – The NOW. The "present moment" is a gift, when we remember both the contents and the gift wrap.

    These five mantras bring our thoughts - and, by extension, our prayers - to the same Divine Source in uniquely different ways. With Allah, our inner vision looks into and beyond the beginning of creation and then into and beyond the end of creation. We fall into an eternal realm where we become a *conscious* part of The Cosmos. The space between "Aaah" and "Laah" is VERY important. So, it is often not good to say "Allah" too quickly. It is INFINITELY BETTER to repeat it <u>*very slowly*</u> – with both of its root meanings in your thoughts. "Aaaaahh…"/ ("That without beginning…")…. "Laaaaaah…"/ ("…and without end…."). We can also use "Allah" in conjunction with "The Un-born" and "The Un-dying" to reach the same realm of Endless Eternity.

All five mantras fill us with Light. We evoke this Light by remembering that they lead us to the Eternal Field behind the façade of material manifestations and The Cosmic Sound vibrating within every molecule. With both, we remember the One, eternal and limitless realm that permeates all existence. The realm of Life that we can truly call "alive". The realm that is creative and dynamic. Intelligent and mysterious. Where The Eternal Field and The Cosmic Sound become the two definitions that come as close as we can think of to describing our indescribable God.

We evoke Light even more when we remember that Mosques and Taoist Shrines are Temples of The Moon. Temples where knowledge, poeticism, and The Five Virtues thrive. We evoke Transcendence when we remember that Churches, Synagogues, Buddhist Temples, and Hindu Shrines are Temples of The Sun. Temples containing a concentrated amount of Cosmic and Universal Vibration because of the intense Faith and Love practiced within them. What more power can you get from two eternal mantras that help us feel the alchemic and omnipresent realm within and around us?

With "Allah" and "Tao", we come to the field BEHIND everything. With "Om", "AUM", and "Amen", we resonate with the cosmic vibration WITHIN everything. When used together, they awaken immense TRANSCENDENT power!

The Inner Eclipse that Allah/Tao and Om/AUM/Amen create together can also be found in certain profound sayings. For example, "You are the sky... Everything else is the weather". In this metaphor, Allah or Tao is the sky and Om, AUM, or Amen is the weather. Both the sky and the weather are intertwined. Clouds emerge from the sky, exist in the sky, and merge back into the sky. If only the sky or the weather existed, we would not be able to appreciate Nature as we do. Imagine if all we had was rain. Imagine if all we had were cloudless days. If that was the case, then why would we ever need to look up?

Repeating both Tao or Allah with Amen, Om, or AUM in the same breath with our renewed understanding, ignites cosmic synergy. Together they amplify our thoughts, our intentions, and - most importantly - our prayers. The rest of this book is dedicated to a technique that does just that.

The Twelve Paired Mantras

Synergy, The Paired Mantra, and The Trinity

Trinities are found throughout our world religions. Later in this section, we will explore the many trinities that are found throughout the Eastern Religions in Asia. The phrase "As above, so below" can readily be applied to any discussion on Trinities, as they are not only found in the basic practices of our rituals, but also in the higher planes of our Collective Consciousness.

Synergy is the hidden power in both The Trinity and The Paired Mantra. Synergy is the mystical phenomenon occurring when two or more "Divine Elements" are brought together, and how they then become greater than what they were individually. A Divine Element can be an idea, a rite, a word, or a mantra. It is our thought and understanding that triggers this phenomenon and the Transcendence we feel. Again, every human being is both Lunar and Solar. He or she can consciously combine both aspects of themselves to trigger an exalted, abundant, and synergistic level of consciousness. The conscious and spiritual man can create an "Inner Eclipse".

As for the Trinity in man, what occurs in the third, empty space between a lunar and solar mantra of a paired mantra, is like the force that occurs between a magnet and steel. The magnet is the Eternal Field, steel in the Cosmic Vibration, and the force created between them is the synergy and transcendence of any of the paired mantras. Take a refrigerator magnet and place it a half of a centimeter in front of a refrigerator door. You can feel the power between them. With a paired mantra, we also create a powerful force. We take our thoughts to a realm to where we are able to manifest joy, abundance, and Light. Incorporating this realm into our prayers, affirmations, and actions enhances everything we do and want to achieve. A few daily, habitual, transcendent thoughts from this spiritual realm are worth hundreds of actions on our material realm.

The two Universal Constants and the five world mantras are all interconnected. Mankind has empowered these mantras with Cosmic thoughts and Divine aspirations. When we pray, we use one of the mantras to resonate higher. Even the knowledge and awareness of their ability to change our spiritual vibration can already amplify our prayers. Each mantra empowers our communication with Divine Intelligence. Through thought, we can connect to The Incarnate resonance of God with "Om", "Amen", and "AUM" – So too, can we also connect to The Immortal resonance of God with "Tao" and "Allah". However, by combining both aspects of God into one mantra, we create a spiritual elixir within. A cosmic cocktail formed from synergy. When we activate this, we become a fountain of Transcendence and Light.

All Faiths tell us that practice and study is its own reward. The Talmud, for example, makes the study of Torah a cardinal virtue in Judaism and summons all men to engage in it. "Whoever labors in the Torah for its own sake," declares the Mishnah "merits many things; and not only so, but all creation is vindicated through him. He may be acclaimed as friend, beloved, a lover of the All-Present, a lover of mankind. It clothes him in meekness and reverence; it enables him to become just, pious, upright, and faithful; it keeps him far from sin, and brings him near to virtue. Through him the world enjoys counsel and sound knowledge, understanding and strength. ... It also gives him sovereignty and dominion and discerning judgment. The secrets of the Torah are revealed to him. He is made like a never-failing fountain, and like a river that flows on with ever sustained vigor. He becomes modest, long-suffering, and forgiving of insults; and it magnifies and exalts him above all things".

Taoism, Confucianism, Buddhism, Hinduism, and more also encourage both the practical and the abstract study of Divinity. This method evokes the most Light within us. The twelve paired mantras do the same by combining two paths to God into one. The second thoughts we have from our new understanding of each word's root meaning awakens everything written in the Mishnah above.

The Five World Mantras and their Geographical Ties

What is interesting is when we look at the linked history of a few of these coupled mantras and where they resonate most today. For instance, "Om" and "Tao" resonate a great deal in Asia. "Amen", "AUM", and "Allah" resonate a great deal in the Middle East. When we look deeper, we see the two different approaches to Divinity originating in the same area of the world. And still today, the same two different approaches to God exist in the same region. Om and Tao are concentrated in China and Japan. AUM, Amen, and Allah are concentrated in Israel, Palestine, Egypt, and throughout the Middle East. This can be no coincidence, as God is the source of all inspiration and so must have intentionally inspired people, or the migration of people, in the same region to unite with him in these two different ways. Of course, today Hindus, Muslims, Jews, Christians, Buddhists, and Taoists exist throughout the world. But, looking at their religious beginnings helps us to see how two complementary views of Universal Consciousness came to "coincidentally" establish in the same area of the world.

The beauty of having these two complementary aspects of Divinity in one area is that people living in this region are exposed to both practices. Both religions have likely heard the complementary side's mantra being repeated with Love. They have been exposed to both the devoted thoughts of their own mantra and the devoted thoughts of a complementary mantra. When we look past our ego and fear, we can see how enriching this is for all involved. Because these religions may have been enemies, does not mean that they have to stay enemies. Even though many consciously try to block out a different mantra, empowered mantras are strong enough to penetrate rock, steel and human flesh. To someone living in these regions, the other mantra is already within their hearts – but, dormant. Its unique and universal sound vibrations are just waiting to be activated.

Finding Your Paired Mantra

An Introduction

As has been mentioned before, "Amen", "AUM", and "Om" lead our thoughts to the Solar aspects of ourselves, while "Allah" and "Tao" lead our thoughts to the Lunar aspects of ourselves. When we combine one of the 3 Solar mantras with one of the 2 Lunar mantras, we create 12 different combinations of a paired mantra.

The 12 paired mantras are as follows:

1. Om-Allah	7. Allah-Amen
2. Om-Tao	8. Tao-Amen
3. Allah-Om	9. AUM-Allah
4. Tao-Om	10. AUM-Tao
5. Amen-Allah	11. Allah-AUM
6. Amen-Tao	12. Tao-AUM

Slowly read all twelve paired mantras with the root meaning of each word in your mind. Read the first word out loud and then contemplate its meaning for a moment. Then read the second word out loud and contemplate its meaning. "AUM" could trigger three thoughts in that one word (conscious, unconscious, and superconscious states). "Allah" could trigger two thoughts in that one word (That that is without beginning... and without end). "Tao" could trigger three thoughts (The Eternal Field, The Universal Mother, The Divine Virtues). And "Amen" and "Om" may lead our thoughts to the Vibrational Field permeating every atom in The Universe. Whatever thoughts this exercise triggers in your imagination, you will be consciously awakening a tremendous amount of Inner Light. The more you practice it, the more intense the light becomes.

Another thing we can do is to go through the list again and focus on the empty spaces within the mantras and between the mantras. There is power in The Emptiness. Just as with Light the two components of a wave and a particle synergize, emptiness and the paired mantras synergize. In these little spaces, there are many various and subtle signs we can notice happening within our body as we slowly and consciously reread the list. For instance, notice if your lungs spontaneously inhale... Notice if your spine suddenly stretches and your head is held high... Notice if there is a "popping" sound in your ear... Notice if you feel energy and light entering your head or body... Notice if you see sparks of light (white, black, or blue) coming in and out of your vision... etc. These spontaneous, subtle changes in our body and vision come to us from beyond thought and reason. They are blessings. They are Grace, and they only thing we can do with them is to feel eternal gratitude. A selfish rich man can live his whole life without ever feeling the entranced wonder of one Blue Pearl. A pious poor man can be blessed with regular visits of The Blue Pearl in his daily meditations, and would not change that experience in his life for any amount of money offered him. In Hinduism, all of these little signs are called "Kriyas". They happen to us when our entire being resonates at a very high spiritual frequency. People of all faiths experience kriyas. Some Christians call it "Being filled with The Holy Ghost". Some yogis see it as "Expressions of The Shaktipat". What they ultimately are are a confirmation that we have done a lot of spiritual work in our current and past lives. They are some of the rewards from our efforts, and signs that we are on the right track.

Kriyas are the phenomena of little divine "explosions" throughout our physical and sensory world. They come in all types and degrees of intensity. They cannot be forced or manipulated, but are more prone to appear when we've created a conducive inner environment for them. You'll know when you get one. They percolate to the surface on their own and in their own time. They happen involuntarily and unprompted. They have a mind of their own, as they come from a realm beyond our own thoughts.

After doing the first two readings above, slowly read the paired mantra list out loud for a third time. By now, one of the pairs should "attract" you more than the other eleven. To find it, listen to your body. Which one resonates strongest with you? You may end up finding that the one that resonates most may not even contain a mantra from the religion you've practiced thus far in Life. That, in and of itself, is a sign of how far your heart and mind are already opened. The spiritual definition and the root meaning each of the two mantras symbolize for you are what's most important. The power that they ignite together in your heart comes from beyond your own thinking. Trust your inner voice. It will help you choose the one you will be working with most.

Finding your paired mantra is the first step of The Six Steps of Scientific Prayer. This Scientific Method of Praying takes us through a deeper process than spontaneous, un-prepared prayer. This process can be described as "Spiritual Transcendence" (step one)… "Inner Activation" (step two, three, and four)… and "Conscious Prayer" (steps five and six). These Six Steps take us through three phases of preparing our thoughts for prayer, activating our inner resources, and then sending our thoughts and desires into The Cosmic Mind.

The paired mantra is first in The Six Steps of Scientific Prayer, as it channels a large amount of Light into our world. It not only changes our thoughts, but also the atmosphere around us. As we are all transmitters and receivers, people feel the cosmic energy we emit. Some of the inner antennae that we all have can sense when someone is either filled with Love, Hate, or Fear. They often don't even have to say a word for us to see it. Their thoughts are habitually consumed by something they love… or something they fear… or something they hate. However, all three of these feelings are triggered by an "object" (meaning a person, thing, idea, etc.). Love, Hate, and Fear occupy a lot of our time. But, a paired mantra is transcendent because it takes our thoughts beyond all three.

Discovering your paired mantra is the initial step towards sending much more precise and powerful prayers into The Universal Mind. You use two empowered mantras – one solar and one lunar – to complete each other and evoke spiritual wholeness. This focus of thought you develop helps activate the Universal Law of action-reaction-response. With practice, we eventually come to a new life situation where we start seeing around us "Un-Requested Answered Prayers". In other words, by habitually uniting our Lunar and Solar selves during the day and as we pray, we send Light into The Cosmic Intelligence. That Light will eventually come back to us in abundant ways we did not specifically pray for – i.e., The Un-Requested Answered Prayer. This is a life where we have sought first The Kingdom of Heaven… and how the rest gets added onto us.

The Difference between Involution and Evolution

After finding your paired mantra, examine what type of mantra it is. There are six Evolutionary Mantras and six Involutionary mantras.

Evolutionary is from Man to God (i.e., going from the vibratory state to the eternal state). Involutionary is from God to Man (i.e., going from the eternal state to the vibratory state).

As was said before, consciously repeating AUM, Om, or Amen gets us to resonate with The Cosmic Sound, with which everything vibrates. Consciously repeating Tao or Allah connects us to the Eternal Field within us, and from whence everything in The Universe manifests. The Cosmic Sound is incarnate. The Eternal Field is immortal. Depending on if your chosen paired mantra starts with "The Cosmic Sound" or with "The Eternal Field" will tell you if it is evolutionary or involutionary.

When something is "born", the first step out of The Eternal Field and into existence is the creation of vibration. Some mystics claim that in the split second a baby is conceived there is vibration and a spark of Light. Cosmic vibration is the beginning of its development into physical matter. When something "dies", the last thing to be lost is this same Cosmic Sound. Before a person finally merges back into The Eternal Field, the vibration in their atoms is slowly subsiding. Their heart may have stopped and their lungs may not be breathing, but their cells are still full of Cosmic Vibration. This is exhibited by a lot of saints and spiritual masters who've "died" (or "left their bodies") after spending their lives in love, service, and study of Divinity. Cosmic Vibration came with their constant, decades-long communion with The Universal Mind. Because of that, their bodies stay longer intact after death – sometimes for years. Saint Basil of Ostrog in Montenegro and Sri Paramahansa Yogananda are two examples.

As was said in the second section of this book, The Star of David (or The Shield of David) is a symbol depicting both the evolutionary and involutionary directions man is a part of. One triangle is pointing up, signifying evolution – and one triangle is pointing down, signifying involution. The two equilateral triangles shown in The Star of David symbolize a unification of both paths. Each triangle in The Star of David corresponds to six of the twelve paired mantras.

Six of the twelve paired mantras have an emerging (God to Man) tendency. And, six of them have a merging (Man to God) tendency. For example, if your paired mantra is "AUM-Tao", it starts from The Cosmic Vibration and flows towards The Eternal Field. This is an Evolutionary paired mantra. It means that AUM is the last vibration that subsides before we merge back into the Eternal Tao.

Again, Involution is the first step when Universal Sound emerges out of the Eternal Field. Evolution is the final step before Universal Sound merges back into the Eternal Field:

**The Six Paired Involutionary Mantras
(Those that emerge from Source):**
"Allah-Om", "Tao-AUM", "Allah-Amen", "Tao-Om", "Allah-AUM", "Tao-Amen"

**The Six Paired Evolutionary Mantras
(Those that merge into Source):**
"Om-Allah", "AUM-Tao", "Amen-Allah", "Om-Tao", "AUM-Allah", "Amen-Tao"

The Cyclic and Transitional Phases of Emerging, Merging, and Re-Emerging

The transitional steps of both involution and evolution are very mysterious and complex. But, as they do, there are definite phases they will go through. If we consider bodies, cells, molecules, and atoms as being "transitional phases", we can see how Divine Thought is able to construct, deconstruct, and reconstruct physical matter.

Involution is when the end result is matter – i.e.; starting from Universal Consciousness… then its forming of cosmic vibration… then the forming of atoms and molecules… then cells… then physical matter. Evolution is when the end result is Universal Consciousness – i.e.; first with the cellular break down (or deconstruction) of physical matter... the decay of molecules and atoms... then the liberation of The Cosmic Vibration contained within the atoms... and finally, the merging with Universal Consciousness. With either direction, Divine Thought is the driving force. It is Divine Thought that keeps "The Wheels of Involution and Evolution" turning, as we pass through the different stages Life takes us.

In Hinduism, the three major Gods describe the three universal states on this Wheel of Involution and Evolution – They are Brahma (Creation), Vishnu (Preservation), and Shiva (Destruction). These three are together known as "The Trimurti". However, these Gods only come into being when they are separate from The Trimurti. In other words, they are activated when something has come into existence. The cycle of birth and death only commences when Life is created. If there were no objects, people, or beings that came into existence, then Brahma, Vishnu, and Shiva would not be activated. Only by coming OUT of The Trimurti, or Universal Consciousness, do the powers of creation, preservation, and destruction begin to operate. It is physical matter that triggers these three Gods. Physical matter kickstarts the cycle of creation-preservation-destruction out from and back into Universal Consciousness – The cycle of emerging from and merging back with The Divine Mind. Physical matter is the catalyst that turns the wheels of the universe within and all around us. But, unlike a catalyst, the physical matter we are is also affected.

Combining both "The Wheel of Involution and Evolution" with "The Trimurti" opens our thoughts to two powerful processes that are in incessant motion in our Universe:

THE TWO PATHS TO GOD

VISHNU
Preservation
Physical Matter

BRAHMA   **INVOLUTION**      **EVOLUTION**   **SHIVA**
Creation   Destruction

TRIMURTI
The Eternal Field
Universal Consciousness

Each of the twelve paired mantras has a mirror, or complementary mantra. For example, "AUM-Tao" is evolutionary and "Tao-AUM" is involutionary. Again, we should remember the empty space within and between the individual mantras. These empty spaces add immense power to our thoughts and prayers. When we remember the emptiness contained within the evolutionary or involutionary mantras, our imagination dances between three realms – The Cosmic Sound, The Eternal Field, and Transcendent Emptiness. The transcendence we feel in the Eternal Emptiness ties both mantras together.

Working with the root meanings of our chosen paired mantra and its involutionary or evolutionary complement taps into many of our spiritual reserves. We come to see that our mantras do not oppose each other, rather they support each other. They are not competitive, they are cooperative. When you activate The Trimurti within you, your spiritual garden starts to grow. Om, AUM, or Amen are the seeds. Tao or Allah is the soil. Their root meaning is the water. The empty space between the mantras is the Sunlight. And your thoughts and actions through daily practice are the fertilizers.

Xavier Clayton

The Number Twelve Is A Path Into The Divine Mind

Here on Earth, The Sun is our Father and Twelve is our Mother

Since the birth of our planet, The Number 12 has been giving its influence on everything here on Earth. When man developed a numerical system, it helped identify the power that it was having on the Earth's rotation, Four Seasons and revolution around the Sun. From the Earth's position in our Solar System, twelve is the number that easily calculates our days, our nights, and our years. The 12-cycles of The Moon were also at our planet's conception, giving its influence on our world. The Earth's revolution and rotation were and still are calculated by 12. The three months of each of the four seasons also generated a cycle of twelve. Christian, Muslim, Hindu, and Jewish Mystics all seem to have recognized this number. Ancient Chinese and Greek sages and philosophers used twelve in astrology and their representation of The Gods. Twelve is a tool. It is a spiritually powerful and deeply alchemic tool with the ability to connect us to The Earth and, thusly, to The Universe. Even if our planet was still molten lava, this mystic number, that can help lead us to our Perfect Good, would still be inseparable from it.

The Number 12 is all around us

Numbers serve several functions. They are not only just used for counting. Ancient mystics have used them to awaken Divine Thought and to help us spiritually evolve. Numerology is a metaphysical science that is used within and in conjunction with Astrology. Numbers are mystical and symbolic. They can be teachers, as well as reminders, of the spiritual beings we truly are. When a number, like The Number 12, is repeatedly seen at the highest echelons of our spiritual life, we can say that this number is a portal into The Divine Mind.

Twelve is the number of spiritual perfection here on Earth. Being born on this planet activates a cascade of twelves within and around us. Below is a list of some of the many places it is seen in our spiritual lives, and throughout our daily lives. Each item on the list has a far-reaching and life-long impact. The 12 months of the year, for example, affects everything we do. We would not be alive were it not for our 12 major organs. And depending on our faith, our prayers and communication.

Earth has a connection to The Number 12 through Time even before we are born...

There are 12 months in an Earth year.
It takes twelve months for the Earth to travel around the focal point of our Solar System.
There are 12 hours in a day.
There are 12 hours in a night.
A year is best calculated by the number twelve.
An hour can be divided by twelve.
A minute can be divided by twelve.
The Earth has four seasons with 3 months each.
Our moon passes through twelve cycles each 12 months
(12 full moons, 12 new moons).

At birth...

We are born under one of the twelves signs of the Zodiac.
We also have a connection to the twelve Chinese astrological signs.
And a connection to the 12 Native American Astrological signs.
We are born with 12 major organs (stomach, heart, liver, kidneys, etc...)

Throughout life...
Time is based on calculations of twelve (minutes, hours, days, seasons, and years).
The music we listen to throughout our lives has 12 notes (Do, Re, Mi... + the five black notes).
We ponder the moon and the sun throughout our lives.
The number 13 is considered "unlucky" because it comes after The Number 12.

Beginning our spiritual quest, there are many 12's incorporated into many religions...

Twelve Laws of Karma (Buddhism)
The Twelve Apostle's Creed (Catholicism)
The Twelve Disciples of Christ (Christianity)
The Twelve Tribes of Israel (Judaism)
The Twelve steps of The Hajj (Islam)
The Twelve Vows of Taoism (Taoism)
The Twelve Laws of The Universe (New Age)
The Kumbh Mela Pilgrimage (Hinduism)

Even in science we encounter twelves...

The String Theory's twelve-dimensions of The Universe

These are just a few examples – But, even in this short list, we can see how twelve is operating in many parts of our lives. For us, it must have a great important meaning for The Earth, The Sun, our bodies, our Zodiac, and our Religions to be using it so liberally.

Numerology is a very powerful practice. Like astrologists, numerologists can tell you many things about your Life based on the numbers around your birth and the letters of your name. Letters and numbers are connected to The Cosmic Sound. Both are attached to a form and a thought. They awaken an idea. And, thusly, both letters and numbers contain a vibration.

Certain numbers are unique, as there is a word that symbolizes the number itself. Twelve is one of those numbers. Take, for example, the word "dozen". How did it come into being? It is a word and a number that has no correlation to the fingers we use to count with. So, why was it important enough to have a word describing it? The word "dozen" not only exists in English, but also in French, Dutch, Roman, and Greek. One reason for this could be that this number is very mystical. It is symbolic and auspicious. We are all familiar with "duos", "trios", and "quatros". But, between "octo" and "dozen" there are not so many word-numbers we regularly use. And after the twelve of a "dozen", there seem to be no word-numbers until we get to 1000 - a "grand".

Numbers like 3, 5, 22, 23, 26, 32, and 108 are revered in many spiritual practices. In yogas and in the highest echelons of some religions, certain numbers help us to connect to The Divine Mind. The importance of many of these numbers are taught to spiritualists in subtle ways; For example, the Trinity and The 5-pointed Star. When we examine the numbers 23, 26, and 32, Jewish and Hindu Mystics will tell us that they all relate to the pathway to God between the second dimensional world and the third dimensional world. Mathematics are also related to these three numbers in square^2 and cubic^3 symbolism. The Hebrew "Tetragram", symbolized by the number 26, is seen as a pathway to God because it is the only number in existence that comes between a squared number ($5^2 = 25$) and a cubed number ($3^3 = 27$). In Siddha Yoga, the 2's and the 3's in the numbers 23 and 32 represent outright this squared and cubic symbolism; in other words, the pathway to God between the second and third dimensions. The second dimension is a flat plane (X by Y) or (length by width). The third dimension is cubic (X by Y by Z) or (length by width by height). The fourth dimension incorporates thought and action. Consider the following statement from the writer Neal Cassady:

> "We are actually fourth dimensional beings in a third dimensional body inhabiting a second dimensional world!".

Mr. Cassady is saying that we are all spiritual beings in a physical body, who all have the ability to manifest our desires in this world we live in.

Numbers contain power – sometimes even Universal Energy. Albert Einstein's $E=mc^2$ is a number that contains Universal Power. His famous equation says that Universal Power is created when physical matter is multiplied by an extremely high amount of Universal Light. Numbers play an important role in our Universe, and therefore in our lives. Like a mantra or a word, it is the meaning behind the number that gives it its power. With the number 108, it represents the 108 names of God that mankind has called Universal Consciousness; Jehovah, Yod, Krishna, etc. 108 is also the number of prayer beads on many rosaries and mala necklaces. These aesthetic numbers are enigmatic. When spiritual guides speak of the meanings they encompass, it is to help our evolution.

Some of Life's Twelves we overlook

The number 12 is not only one of the highest auspicious numbers, but also one that we all can relate to, resonate with, and use to empower ourselves. Whoever you are, whatever religion you are, and wherever you live, you are working with the number 12. It is operating in Time, our music, bodies, and seasons. It is found in unexpected places – and is there to help us grow in understanding, wisdom, and Universal Light. The Number 12 is a pathway into The Divine Mind. Using mathematics combined with Spiritual Thought, opens these regions of our hearts and thoughts. For instance, the two central and interconnected dogmas found in Buddhism (The four noble truths and the eight-fold path) add up to the number 12. As another example, The Koran mentions Jesus Christ 12 times. Awareness of this connects the Lunar aspect of Islam and the Solar aspect of Christianity through the power of the number 12. Lastly, the number twelve is deeply hidden in The Old Testament, where is says that "God made the Universe in six days and on the seventh day he rested". When we think about this sentence, it doesn't really make sense. Why would God need to rest? God never rests. It is man that needs rest. Divine Consciousness is continuously active. If God took a break, then the Universe would die. And furthermore, if God rested for a day, then who was operating The Universe and all of its innumerable and multitudinous activities on his day off? There is a possibly different reason for that seventh day. At first, the importance of it is to help us calculate the cycles of The Moon and The Earth's rotation around The Sun. We need that seventh day in the week to help us calculate a year. So, even if that passage says that God rested for a weekend, or God worked for all seven days, we would still be able to calculate a calendar year. But, the passage says that God "made The Universe in six days". Why six? Why six days? They could have written six minutes or six hours... or, even six years. But, The Bible says six "days". The mystics that wrote this surely knew of the 12 Tribes of Israel, The 12 Apostle's Creed, The 12 hours in the day, The 12 hours in the night, The four seasons, and they possibly even knew of The Kumbh Mela Pilgrimage in India. So, there could definitely be a mystical reason for saying that God made the Universe in six days – a reason we could correlate to the number twelve. When we do this and examine this passage in a spiritually numerical way, we see that it reveals TWO twelves to us. It just so happens that six days contain 144 hours – and 12 x 12 = 144. This is a "12 x 12 number" also found in the Kumbh Mela Pilgrimage. A very powerful number, where spiritual cleansing is done on The Holy Ganges river. Divine Baptism is done every twelve years for this pilgrimage. However, the 12th time it is done (meaning every 144 years), it is the most auspicious Kumbh Mela Pilgrimage of them all. We don't know, in fact, if it was the hidden intention of our Christian Mystics to imply that the 144 hours in six days is meant to correlate with all the 12's we have within and around us... But, what we can say is that it is a mathematical fact that would not be there if they had written that God created the Universe using any other combination of numbers, days, or hours that make up a 7-day week.

If two twelves appeared in these higher metaphysical realms just once, we could call it a coincidence. If it happened twice, we could call it fluke. But, that the number 12 is routinely seen throughout our world religions, as well as in the cycles of our Earth, Moon, and Sun, means that the symbolism of it is beyond faith, dogma, time, and chance.

The Number 12 is inextricable from Life on Earth

There are many other twelves within and around us:

1) 12 months
2) 12 astrological signs (zodiac)
3) 12 Chinese astrological signs
4) 12 Native American Astrological signs
5) There are 12 hours in a day
6) There are 12 hours in a night
7) An hour is divided into 12
8) A minute is divided into 12
9) A year that is calculated by 12 better than by 7, 8, 16, or any other number
10) Earth's yearly orbit around The Sun is best calculated by the number 12
11) The Moon passes each of its cycles 12 times (12 full moons, 12 new moons, etc...)
12) Four seasons with three months each
13) Twelve notes of the musical scale (Do, Re, Mi, Fa, etc. Plus the black notes)
14) 12 laws of Karma (Buddhism and Hinduism)
15) The 12 Apostles Creed, The 12 Apostles of Christ – "Apostle" means "I send out a message"
16) The 12 Tribes of Israel (Judaism)
17) The 12 Steps of The Hajj (Islam)
18) The 12 laws of The Universe
19) The number 13 is considered unlucky because it comes after the number 12
20) The 12 Vows of Taoism
21) The 12 main organs of the body (kidneys, pancreas, lungs, heart, spleen, etc.)

Twelve is an extremely high, mystical, and spiritual number. It is inextricable from Life here on Earth. It is also very accessible and has been used in numerous ways. Compare the Western Zodiac with The Chinese Zodiac. Because there are 12 months in a year, it is easy to deduce that we would logically have 12 signs in The Western Zodiac; Aries, Scorpio, Capricorn, etc... However, when we look at The Chinese Zodiac, they also have 12 signs; The Dragon, The Rabbit, The Monkey, etc. Yet, the cycle of The Chinese Zodiac is every 12 years. There is no other parameter, like the 12 months of the year, that would confine the 12 Chinese Astrological signs to the number twelve. Why would ancient Chinese mystics not have 9, 15, or 37 signs in their Zodiac? Again, we see the number twelve. Awareness of the mysticism of 12 transcends cultures, countries, and religions. Twelve is an open window into The Divine Mind. All we need to do is to climb through it.

The Clock Of The Twelve Paired Mantras

The Clock of The Twelve Paired Mantras is The Heart of this book

The number twelve is not only related to various religions and aspects of Time here on Earth, but it also reveals itself when an Eternal Field mantra and a Cosmic Sound mantra are combined. The five world mantras create twelve paired combinations. There are 6 involutionary mantra combinations and 6 evolutionary mantra combinations. Seen in another way, there are 6 "Sun to Moon" mantra pairings and 6 "Moon to Sun" mantra pairings. These twelve mantra combinations, or "Paired Mantras", can be arranged in the form a clock. This arrangement is a clear and easy way to not only see all twelve pairings, but to also feel their overall, transcendent power when they are aligned in an ordered and mystical way. Arranged in this way, we can see their relations to each other both individually, in pairs, and in groups. We can bring Astrological aspects into this clock. We can bring numerical aspects into this clock. Once our individual mantras are placed in an ordered and metaphysical diagram, we've taken our thoughts and aspirations higher. We've exponentially added Universal Power to our prayers and our ability to manifest our desires. Order and the understanding of each mantra's root meaning are the Divine Parameters that get this clock to work. The six involutionary and the six evolutionary mantras contained in the clock trigger Light and Universal Abundance within us. When these twelve Solar/Lunar combinations are organized in this simple and effective way, it is called "The Clock of The Paired Mantras".

Again, "AUM", "Om", and "Amen" direct our thoughts to our Inner Sun. The Solar aspect of ourselves. The Cosmic Vibration within and around us. "Allah" and "Tao" direct our thoughts to our Inner Moon. The Lunar aspect of ourselves. The Eternal Field within and around us. Whether your paired mantra is "Sun to Moon" or "Moon to Sun", each pairing can activate an Inner Eclipse. When the twelve paired mantras are seen together on the face of a clock, their relation to each other, and as a whole, becomes very pronounced. By using a familiar and well-known diagram, we are transported to a higher realm than we are by just the telling of Time. The twelve equal segments of a clock are very familiar to us all. Just as all twelve numbers on a clock are different, all twelve paired mantras on The Clock of The Paired Mantras are different. Each pairing brings our thoughts to the same field of Universal Consciousness, but in its own unique way. The five individual world mantra keys have become 12 unique paired mantra key combinations. The clock "works" when we add the meanings behind each of the individual mantras we see in each pairing.

"The Clock of The Twelve Paired Mantras" is the heart of this book

To draw this Clock is very simple. Learning to do this, in and of itself, is both mind-expanding and eye-opening. The process of drawing it can take us deep into our own consciousness, where we are systematically examining ourselves as both incarnate and immortal beings. A visual and organized drawing of our five world mantras teleports our thoughts to the pinnacle of our spiritual self.

How to draw The Clock

First start with three circles – To do this, start with a small circle, then draw a larger circle around the first circle, then draw a third circle around the second circle. The three circles should look like two wheels – with an outer wheel and an inner wheel.

Once you've done this, divide the two wheels into four equal segments. To do this, connect the first circle to the third circle by using four lines – one north, one south, one east, and one west. It is as if you are tying the outer wheel and the inner wheel together and leaving the space in the middle empty.

Once that is done, divide each of the four segments into three smaller segments to create 12 segments in total. Always leave the space in the middle of the two wheels empty.

When you finish, you will see an "outer wheel" of 12 parts and an "inner wheel" of 12 parts.

How to add The Solar elements

Check to see if your clock has 12 segments and is divided into 2 sides – a right side and a left side. Again, it should also have an "inner wheel" and an "outer wheel". The twelve segments are exactly like those on the face of a clock. It should have a segment for 12 o'clock…one for 1 o'clock, 2 o'clock, 3 o'clock, etc.

The Solar elements are on the outer wheel on the right side of the Clock, and on the inner wheel on the left side of The Clock.

Starting on the "right side" of the clock, in the "outer wheel", there are three different segments. These three segments go from 12 o'clock to 3 o'clock. Write "Amen" in the first outer segment, "Om" the second outer segment, and "AUM" in the third outer segment. Then from 3 o'clock to 6 o'clock write the same "Amen", "Om", "AUM" sequence in the outer wheel. Again… for the Solar elements, use the outer circle on the right side of the clock.

Then, in the "inner wheel" on the left side of the clock, continue in this "Amen", "Om", "AUM" from 6 o'clock to 9 o'clock… and then finish the same sequence from 9 o'clock to 12 o'clock all on the inner wheel. Only use the inner circle on the left side of the clock.

How to add The Lunar elements

The Lunar elements are on the inner wheel segments on the right side of The Clock and the outer wheel segments on the left side of The Clock. However, instead of using three mantras to fill these clock segments, we will only use two – "Tao" and "Allah".

In the "inner circle" on the right side of the clock, from 12 o'clock to 2 o'clock, write "Tao" in the first inner segment and then "Allah" in the second inner segment. Then from 2 o'clock to 4 o'clock write the same "Tao" then "Allah" sequence. Then from 4 o'clock to 6 o'clock repeat this same "Tao" and "Allah" sequence. Again… for the Lunar elements, use the inner wheel on the right side of the clock.

Then, in the "outer circle" on the left side of the clock, continue in this "Tao" then "Allah" sequence from 6 o'clock to 8 o'clock… then from 8 o'clock to 10 o'clock and then finish the same "Tao" then "Allah" sequence from 10 o'clock to 12 o'clock. For the Lunar elements, use the outer wheel on the left side of the clock.

As we all had to learn how to read a clock in order to tell Time, reading The Clock of The Paired Mantras is also easy to learn. All you do is read the outer segment first and the inner segment second. No matter where you are on The Clock, by always reading it in this systematic way, it will lead you to the six involutionary/evolutionary pairings, your complementary paired mantra, your paired mantra's Trinity and Lunar counterparts, and your paired mantra's two Solar paralleled combinations. Many exercises in Divine Science will help us get proficient at finding all of these combinations and more.

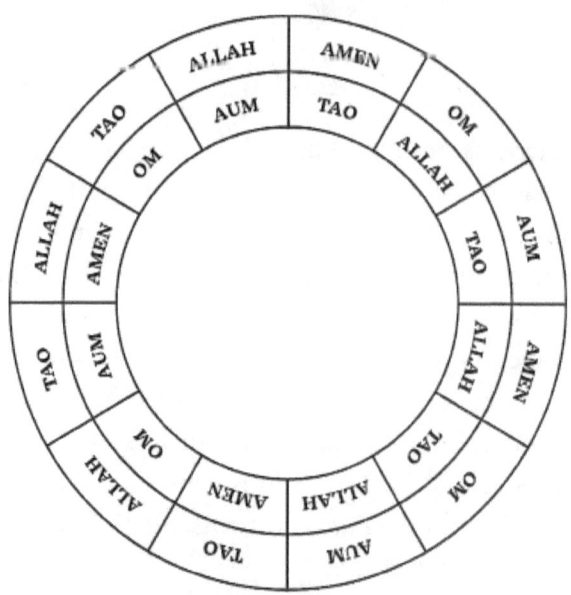

THE TWO PATHS TO GOD

Spend some time with this Clock.

Note the time and day you first drew it to put into your Equinox Journal.

One thing you can notice about this Clock already is that the involution and evolution pairings are polar opposite to each other. For example, "Om-Tao" (evolutionary) is directly opposite to "Tao-Om" (involutionary).

Sketch this Clock a few more times.

Try drawing it without the directions.

Contemplate it for some quiet moments. Think of the meanings you have given to each of the five mantras and to the pairings.

What you have done, and what you do each time you consciously sketch out The Clock of The Twelve Paired Mantras, is something quite remarkable and rare. This Clock is a Clock that goes beyond Time. One side of the clock leads our thoughts to the incarnate, while the other side of the clock leads our thoughts to the immortal. One side of the clock lets us touch the power of evolution, while the other side lets us touch the power of involution. It has a Solar-Sun side and a Lunar-Moon side. Each of the twelve pairing has both an Eternal Field aspect and a Cosmic Vibrational aspect.

A Clock that does more than tell Time

To draw it, we use the familiar reference of a normal clock telling us the Time here on Earth, but actually, it takes us on a trip throughout The Entire Universe. The Clock of The Twelve Paired Mantras is, in fact, …

A map of our inner cosmos.
The wheel of universal abundance.
The fountain of youth.
The power source of our collective consciousness.
A prayer amplifier.
A mind and heart expander.
A spiritual purifier.
A Light trigger.
A transcendent "Synergizer".
Pure energy.
Qualities of The Holy Grail.
A destroyer of fear, hate, and judgement.
A harmonizer of spirits and a unifier of men.
A lighthouse, guiding us through the second and third dimensions.
Six man-made solar eclipses and six phonetic lunar eclipses.
Mathematical and astrological.
Spiritual and practical.
Divine and man-made.
Involutionary and Evolutionary.
A powerful force for Good.
Universally symbolic with its circle with a dot in the middle – a nucleus, cell wall, and cytoplasm.

At first, the Clock may seem like a simple drawing that unifies the world religions through their mantras. However, as we study and work with it more and more, we come to see and feel its immense power. What we search for in The Holy Grail – Wonder, Grace, Power, Infinite Abundance, Light, and Eternal

Youth – we find in The Clock of The Twelve Paired Mantras. Drawing it for the first time opens many new areas within each of us. It opens a gate into our Collective Consciousness and a door into the Wonders of our Universe.

How The Clock of The Paired Mantras can help our Collective Spiritual Future

Look at our world today and decide for yourself if this is the most harmonious point that human history has brought us to. Throughout our human history, we have all said we want Peace. Some of us want peace through construction and others want peace through destruction. Both the atheist and the spiritualist want peace. Peace is part of our True Nature. Peace and harmony are part of who we are and what we see. The most calculable and prominent aspects of Divine Intelligence are harmony and balance. From our four seasons to our star constellations, we can see the immense tendency towards divine equilibrium at work. Peace is an aspect of God that we all religions encourage their members to practice through greetings, words, mantras, gestures, thoughts, and even handshakes. In everything – even out of the reach of man – we see that God strives and supports harmony and balance. And as we are living in the Universal Consciousness he created, we cannot avoid needing balance and harmony, as well. Again... harmony, peace, and balance are a part of what we see, what we experience, and who we are.

Outwardly, it seems that we can make steps towards this universal harmony through our political organizations, marches, and voting. We want to restore equilibrium when we feel something is "out of balance". The real balance that we want to achieve collectively starts individually. Any conscious steps we take in our individual lives towards balance and harmony will collectively affect those around us. Balance and harmony start from inside ourselves.

Aligning our spiritual evolution with Universal Harmony is what will bring balance into our world. Our future is dependent on bringing peace to our planet. It is up to us to decide how we are going to achieve it. In regards to our collective spiritual evolution, it seems that we have one of four ways that our world could consciously evolve into a more peaceful future for us all…

The first way is that we could keep going in the pattern we are living now. Fighting each other and living side-by-side with borders, walls, mistrust, and fear. We know our neighbors. We don't wish them any harm. But, we don't agree with many aspects to how they live. The resulting "Peace" we head towards in this way is no more than tolerance. Tolerance through familiarity is what we are encouraged to incorporate into our daily lives. But, then the question is… Does tolerance or hiding something you begrudge lead to True Peace?

The second way is that one religion will dominate all the others by annihilation or conversion. We all know that this has been tried by the greatest of Kings, with the greatest of armies, throughout our human history. Ethnic cleansing has never worked. It always leaves destruction, pain, and animosity. This leads us to a second question… Is peace through war and destruction True Peace?

The third way is that we give up religion completely and all become atheists, iconoclasts or soul-less half-man/half-computer androids. However, the divinity that we are and see around us will ALWAYS be evident to most of us. Because of our own Divinity do we enjoy a sunset. When the spiritualist talks to the atheist, it feels to him like they are two fish at the bottom of the ocean – with the atheist fish asserting to the spiritualist fish "I don't believe in this water you are talking about! I have never seen water. I have never tasted water nor have never touched it. So, stop talking about this water, because to me it's just silly!". This result leads us to the third question…. Does ignorance and blindness lead us to True Peace? Or… Is Peace only found when the spirit and soul are removed?

These are the three options most commonly discussed when we talk about obtaining peace in this world we share. However, there is a future fourth option! An option not so commonly discussed…

The fourth option is a future where we can unbiasedly look back at all the knowledge we have gained from our various faiths and scientific fields. In that way, everyone's thoughts and efforts have contributed to one goal – A better understanding of The Divine Mind. Scientists and spiritualist both can agree that there is SO MUCH to learn from The Divine Intelligence. So, if we are ever going to really live as active and abundant components of The Divine Mind we are all operating in, the best way is to compile all of the spiritual and scientific knowledge we have gained. That idea in and of itself will create Peace, because from that realm of thought there are no enemies.

Through both Faith and Science, we have developed various techniques to communicate and understand The Divine Consciousness we live in. It is we who keep them separated, when, in fact, they are complementary. More than that, when science and spirituality come together, they are synergistic.

This fourth way is about merging our spiritual knowledge with our scientific knowledge, non-judgmentally. Peace, then, does not become a goal – It becomes a by-product. Peace becomes one of the many beneficial results from a vast spiritual knowledge and a wide scientific experience. In the future, if humanity is spiritually evolved enough to unbiasedly look back on its past, then we can make real steps towards World Peace and True Abundance for each of us.

In the past, we can point to countless examples of how fear and hate between religions have led to destruction. Some examples are The Spanish Inquisition, World War Two, The 100-years war, Northern Ireland, The creation of Protestantism, Conflicts between Hindus and Muslims, "Defensive war" conflicts between Buddhists and Taoists, Wars against the Ottomans, The Unia in The Balkans, Wars between Israel and Palestine/Iran/Egypt/Syria, etc. Looking back on our past as a whole, we can see that these religious conflicts have been part of The Age of Religion we have lived in for the last 2000+ years.

In our world today, there are many new wars, brewing wars, on-going wars, and lingering begrudgements. Wars do not only exist between nations, they exist between people as well. Overwhelmingly, many of these wars are based on the differences between religious faiths. In many countries, there are several wars existing between just two people. Neighborhoods, families, and work environments become toxic because of this animosity.

The Divine Intelligence we all live in has often been described as an "Ocean of Consciousness". Each of us is likened to a "fish" swimming in these waters of Divinity. Conflicts occur when we forget we are all supported by this same ocean of consciousness. We create wars between fish that have been living in salt water and fish that have been living in fresh water. But, water is water. All water comes from God – and the ocean of consciousness we are all swimming in is the same.

Using "The Clock of The Twelve Paired Mantras" is like putting out thoughts directly into this Ocean of Consciousness. Why? Because we are triggering our highest and most Divine thoughts and afterthoughts. We are consciously uniting the two Universal Constants within. We are using empowered words to evoke joy, Light, and Cosmic Abundance. Our thoughts and hearts are expanded. The clock takes our mind to both a deeper and higher realm of existence where there is no fear or hate. We consciously put our thoughts on abundance and unity. Any two things that have become united was done with effort and intention. Using one or more of the twelve paired mantras creates an inner eclipse that triggers unasked for answered prayers. If we are habitually using a paired mantra in our daily prayers and affirmations and are also seeing unasked for answered prayers happening in our lives… then we have sure signs that we are on an exalted Lifepath.

Religious conflicts and war lead to chaos, suffering, and unimaginable pain. What would cause one spiritually-aspiring human being to kill another spiritually-aspiring human being? The answer is fear. Fear has two sides – it comes from the unknown and leads to hate. It is an effective tool that is used by both Church and State. Millions of people from various backgrounds and walks of life can all be manipulated by one common fear. Religious wars have their roots based in fear. Like a plant getting its nutrients from soil and sunlight, religious wars get their nutrients from hate and fear. Or, if compared to walking on a long road, when the first steps of a religious war are started with hate and fear… the last steps will likely end in destruction and pain. In religious wars, all sides are affected. All sides suffer. No one is unscathed.

The Clock of The Twelve Paired Mantras breaks through our fear. By looking at The Five World Mantras as Lunar and

Solar, we look higher than our religions. We awaken the two most prominent celestial aspects of who we are as human beings here on God's Earth. The twelve inner eclipses are ways we can consciously evoke Light and transcendence. At this exalted level of consciousness, there is no room for fear and hate – only understanding, expansion and awareness.

Although much suffering has been the result of religious war, there is one, small, positive element to the destruction we have experienced – it has brought with it integration and exposure to other cultures. For some of us, it has brought knowledge and compassion. Yes, there is fighting and violence – but, because of that, there is also unavoidable integration and exposure. A war without intermingling is not even an argument. Many of us have come to put down our arms to instead raise our hearts and open our minds. With that, we have inspired our souls. Those that have done this get beyond the preferences of their own religion, and their pre-judgments over another religion, to see the beauty in both. This book was written to help more people experience this realm of non judgement and peace.

One day in the future – 20 years, 50 years… or 100 years from now – we will abandon this dark, destructive Age of Religion and live in a new, constructive Age of Light. In The Age of Light, we will look back on this time we have spent fighting as also a time we have spent developing. We've learned and created much in regards to our faith and concepts of God. Time we've spent using our prayers and aspirations to enrich ourselves and bring Light into our collective consciousness. Through our combined prayers and aspirations, we have been filling the coffers of our collective spiritual bank. Our various prayers and religious techniques are all ultimately filled with love and light. This pure joy has been filling our collective reserves with divine treasure.

Many of the religious techniques we've developed in the world are to learn how to contact and evoke a response from a Universal God we sense is Pure Thought. Even the spiritually intimate techniques, where it is to come into a more closeness or oneness with Divinity, we still hope to trigger a response of abundance and joy. We have put a lot of work and lifetimes into developing a multitude of ways to trigger a response from Divine Consciousness. Not only the spiritualist has worked hard on this, but the scientist as well. With a paired mantra, we dig deep into the work we have done in our current lifetime and in our past lifetimes. The complementary book of Divine exercises and experiments will awaken our spiritual reserves even further.

The handful of things religions have discovered through thought and prayer, and science has used in experiments and applications, will be compiled in The Age of Light. The pieces of the puzzle will be collected and put into their right places. Once this knowledge is collected, from both the fields of science and the fields of spirituality, humankind will benefit from this more collectively enlightened state. A bigger picture for all of us emerges.

Not everyone will have, need, or want an encyclopedic knowledge of science and spirituality. But, the world will have new, simple, and synergistic techniques to trigger transcendent joy and universal abundance. We urgently need to compile this knowledge for our own well-being. The Universal Intelligence that is operating our inner and outer worlds is both invisible and incessantly active. Both the scientist and the spiritualist tap into it. Both have documented the knowledge they have learned. As divine human beings, we are both scientists and spiritualists when we pray. And... we are both scientists and spiritualists when we analyze the responses we get from God. Scientific knowledge helps us become better spiritualists in our communications with Divine Intelligence. Spiritual knowledge helps us become better scientists in the laboratories we call "Life". Scientific thought helps everything.

But, what's preventing us from living in The Age of Light now? Transcendent abundance is right here now... It has always been here. We have always had the ability to tap into it in various scientific as well as various spiritual ways. The fact that it reveals itself to us in science, spirituality, and Nature in a multitude of ways demonstrates its limitlessness. But, what's blocking it from its full radiance in our lives are our fears, ignorance, pride, ego, and prejudice. When focused on one path, the most fervently pious of us can spark some Light from our merciful God. To produce Light, that kind of tunnel vision focus can reliably work, but it takes a lot of effort. To get there, you have to block out a lot of knowledge and experiences that could have also benefitted your specific personal growth if you had a more open heart. It takes a lot of digging to see the same aspects that a simpler and wider view of the world offer. Our spiritual world is like a field of wild flowers. We can pick one type of flower and then look deep into its stem to see its various colors. However, the most colorful of us have picked a bouquet with flowers that are red, blue, yellow, white, and lavender. It puts a more fragrant collection into our hands.

Another factor blocking us, are our thoughts of God as a condemner, a punisher, and/or judge. These thoughts help trigger the fear that prevent us from fully experiencing all that we truly are. How can you be all that you truly are when there is a Divine Punisher, a Cosmic Judge, and a Vengeful God? Where could we turn to to find Divine Love, Cosmic Joy, or Universal Abundance? The Clock of The Paired Mantras are twelve different paired-concepts of God that are a more true and fear-less way of looking at him/her. With many of our biggest fears out of the way, we open our thoughts and hearts to what Life can teach us in the short time we are here.

God as a condemner, punisher, or judge triggers friction, hate, and fear between men. Fear is what we see when we look beyond humanity's hate. The antidote to fear is experience. Using The Clock of The Paired Mantras gives us exalted experiences. It gives us twelve ways to consciously connect us to the harmony and balance we see throughout The Universe. The concepts of a vengeful God go against the equilibrium we so clearly see in his creations. These thoughts block The Light we were born with and born from. Universal Light can be awakened in our lives as easy as letting a feather drift down into our hand. These habitual and perpetuated thoughts of God as a condemner/punisher/judge have all our fears attached to them. Our spiritual texts – Like The Bible, The Koran, The Tao Te Ching, The Vedas, The Bhagavad Gita, and The Talmud – are Eternal because they have shown us to see God as "The Eternal Field" and God as "The Cosmic Sound". Our fears are what turned Him/Her into the punisher.

The Clock of The Twelve Paired Mantras and this book are to help us examine the source definitions of the five world mantras. When we see God as "The Eternal Field" or God as "The Cosmic Vibration", we align our thoughts to his true Nature of Eternal Equilibrium. We cannot attach the labels of fear, sin, or judgement to these definitions. Punishment is erased. These two concepts of Universal Consciousness are "The Two

Paths to God". These two paths are inspiring, mind-expanding, and bring with them an epiphany of Light, transcendent joy, and abundance – not our fears, guilt, hate, and prejudice.

In The Age of Light, we will start compiling and practicing with the new knowledge we have gained and continue to gain. Living in The Age of Light, we will see further and deeper than we did in The Age of Religion. The Clock works like a flywheel. It takes some effort to get it started. But, once it starts spinning, it goes faster and faster with very little effort. Spiritual and scientific knowledge evoke Light within each of us. Together, we will naturally grow into more loving, abundant, and well-rounded individuals. Individuals form a society. Societies form a country, and countries form our world.

This fourth option leads us to the last question... "Does a new, limitless, non-judgmental concept of God combined with scientific knowledge and active spiritual practice lead us to True World Peace?".

We can go back and re-examine all four questions to decide what would be the best option for ourselves, our neighbors, and our world. It has always been up to us – consciously or unconsciously. In the supplementary edition of this book, "Exercises in Divine Science and Experiments in Multiplicative Joy", we will discuss how each of these four options are linked to an area of Mathematics.

Using The Clock Of The Paired Mantras To Amplify Your Prayers

The Theme of this book can be said in three words "Awakening Divine Synergy". We can do this in our thoughts, in our actions, in our world, and in our prayers and affirmations. Mantra repetition, or Japa, is seen in how great saints lived and taught. The Master Jesus and The Master Gandhi are two of the many who are known to have practiced it. Japa is a direct connection and remembrance to an aspect of Divinity. It awakens pure and instant Joy. With our new knowledge of the five world mantras, practicing Japa with a paired mantra exalts our thoughts and actions even more profoundly.

One way we can look at The Clock of The Twelve Paired Mantras is as we do the components of a car engine. There are many components to a car's engine; the piston, the cylinder, the rotor fan, the carburator, valves, spark plugs, and pumps. But only when we know how to put them together, do these auto parts make sense and fulfill their intended use. Mechanics are taught how these components fit together. Like a mechanic, when we see how the five world mantras are interconnected, then our engine starts to run!

The most often asked question about "The Two Paths to God" is "What is this book supposed to help the reader to do?". From the writer's perspective, there are many answers to this question...

One of the first and foremost answers to this question is to realize that we are blessed to be alive, on Earth, and in human form. If we also possess a sound mind, an open heart, and a determined will, then we are in the best position to capitalize on these three blessings even more. This book shows us that the Five World Mantras we use in our prayers ("Om", "Allah", "AUM", "Amen", and "Tao") not only help us to connect with The Universal Intelligence, but also with The Lunar and The Solar aspects of ourselves.

For more than 4,000 years, the mantras of Buddhism, Christianity, Islam, Hinduism, Taoism, and Judaism have inspired Spiritual Knowledge. They have opened our awareness to how both of these pathways can help us resonate with The Divine Mind. But, what our religions have failed to teach us is how these two paths can work in synergy. Universal Truth would not be "Universal" if it were restricted to one religion.

The Five World Mantras can be seen a "keys". They can be put together like five pieces of a cosmic puzzle. For example, and in no particular order...

"Allah" takes our thoughts to The Eternal Realm of our existence that is without a beginning and without an end. The pure state of Divine Intelligence from whence The Universe emerges and returns.

Lunarly intermingled with Allah is "Tao". This mantra reminds us of The Universal Mother that creates and supports everything in existence – The 10,000 things. Tao also reminds us of The Five Virtues: Justice, Truth, Love, Kindness, and Wisdom.

Springing out from these two Eternal Field mantras is "Amen". It is the bridge between Universal Consciousness and Physical Matter. It is 'The Word' that created our Universe in John 1:1. If Tao is The Universal Mother, then Amen is the womb – the portal we all pass through to become physical matter.

Once something or someone passes from The Eternal Field through Amen to become matter, it is embedded with a cosmic vibration or "Om". We awaken the Solar qualities of ourselves. Quantum Science confirms that there is one universal vibration existing in all manifested things – whether it is a flower, a star, or a quasar. Deeper than the molecule or the atom is Om. It is the sound vibration resonating in electricity, gravity, and magnetism. A lot of Quantum Science is practiced with thoughts and intentions, as man too resonates with Om.

Finally, The Cosmic Vibration does not only exist on this physical and visual realm, it also exists at our subconscious and superconscious levels. "AUM" takes our thoughts deeper than the realms we can see with our five senses of seeing, touching, smelling, tasting, and hearing. AUM reminds us to also take into account our dream states and the states we are having inspired thought, hunches, and impulses. In those realms, too, we find God. The subliminal thoughts we have with AUM ultimately leads us back to Allah – completing the cycle that The Five World Mantras synergize. Starting from any point, one can trigger this cycle from any of The Five World Mantras to awaken "The Universal Tree of Light and Abundance". In other words, with The Five World Mantras we can awaken our "Inner Phoenix".

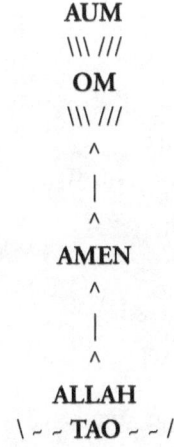

When we have a better understanding of the meanings of these mantras, and then use our new knowledge to practice the many exercises in Divine Science and Scientific Prayer, we create higher and more deeply transcendent dimensions for ourselves and for our Collective Consciousness.

What this book is supposed to help the reader to do is to learn how to pray consciously. In "Conscious Prayer" we come to a more exalted level of Thought. A level of Thought we can truly call "Divine Communion". By using the clock to pray in a more conscious and universal way, we open our thoughts and hearts to even more blessings entering our lives. Through conscious and universal prayer, we pray from a transcendent inner realm where...

We can create abundance.
We can empower our thoughts.
We can dynamize our actions.
We can intensify our aspirations.
We can create Peace in ourselves, our surroundings… and in our World.
We can generate Light.
We can evoke healing.
We can expand our Thoughts.
We can connect with God in new ways.
And… We can live in Truth.

Using The Clock of The Paired Mantras in your Meditations

As we are all spiritual beings, we have – knowingly and unknowingly – created these mantras that are all divinely charged. "Om", "AUM", "Amen", "Allah", and "Tao" are all given and re-given to us in our incarnations to help us spiritually grow. Unfortunately, it seems that many people have lost the meaning behind these potent words that can all trigger abundance within and around us. It also seems that our spiritual leaders have often done little to help. Because they have studied the scriptures, we look to them for information, understanding, and definitions. We are hungry for what these books can tell us about The Universal Consciousness we live in. But unfortunately, what our spiritual leaders often do is re-tell their own interpretations of the spiritual text, what they have been taught in Theology, or what they are told to teach by their spiritual hierarchy. No scientific analysis is brought into their laundry list of well-rehearsed spiritual sound bites. We question them and their response is "He is The Almighty" or "He is Everything!". We go to the books our spiritual leaders have written and read "God is Love, Goodness, and Kindness", "God always was, always is, and always will be", and "God is The Lord of Lords and The King of Kings". We listen to their sermons and discourses and hear "He is the life, the truth, and the way", "He is The Creator of all", "He heals the sick", "Nothing can defeat him", etc. These words and more are ALL TRUE - But, they are oftentimes blurted out to dozens, and sometimes millions, of people in such dizzying quick succession that rarely even one of them ever gets examined for what it is on its own. The audience is just bombarded with spiritually-impregnated sound bites. The result is that our heads are swimming in Light and ecstacy, but not in understanding and knowledge. Words are just blurted out to us (often with a lot of self-righteous criticisms and condemnations attached!) and at the end of the discourse the person will then ask "Can I get an Amen?".

Again... ALL of what our spiritual leaders are saying about God is true, but it would be good to sometimes stop and examine their rapid-fire litany. Science and Spirituality can operate within us as One. Understanding and knowledge can awaken an Inner Realm of Light that remains with us longer. The Pure Joy this Light awakens becomes something we can come back to to use in our prayers, affirmations, and meditations. We use mantras in all of these practices. So, it is good to examine, at least, the meanings of these divinely charged words. Electricity to a light bulb is like knowledge to a mantra. For example, in Churches and Basiliques we often use "Amen" in prayers, in song, and in sermons. But, have we ever been thoroughly explained what it means, where it came from, its power, and what deeper significance it could add to our lives? Many of our spiritual teachers don't teach – they preach. "Spreading the word of God" to many is actually "imposing my own limited view of God onto others and forcing them to believe it". Many of the richest and most influential preachers sound like TV-psychoanalysts, rather than inspired men and women. Seeing a head nodding in the pews or a hand waving in the air are signs that are easily seen. But, an inspired heart, gained from spiritual knowledge is a sign that is subtle, yet filled with enormously more light.

When spiritual epithets are blurted out in a rapid-fire way, it suggests that the divinity within is superficial. If all we ever get from our spirituality is superficiality and preaching, then, of course, that can create zealots and atheists. Both extremes are provoked from this way of "spreading the word".

When we examine any form of teaching, a student often teaches in the manner he was taught. So, when a spiritualist feels his convictions are ignored, that can create a zealot. As too, when a zealot bombards an audience of seekers with a dizzying amount of spiritual catchphrases – An atheist will shut down if none of what they hear contains any logical, practical, or scientific support. It is possible that rapid-fire "preaching" inadvertently inspires atheism and iconoclasm. Many scientists are one, or both, of these. The field of Science was inspired because people wanted proof – a small and useful way of calculating, or a mechanical way of working with, our reliable Universal Consciousness. Scientists too see this Universal

Consciousness operating in our lives. But, they want to find methods beyond prayer and faith to beneficially apply it. Scientific thought is a good balance to spiritual thought. Both help us in a more thorough investigation of The Divine Mind we are all components of.

In many ways, the field of science is more dynamic than the field of religion. For science to have gone from the penicillin to the anti-biotic in less than 100 years took a lot of dynamic and analytical thought. For science to have gone from landing on the moon in the late 1960's to exploring our Solar System in just a few decades also took dynamic thought. The discovery and varied uses of DNA also required analytical and dynamic thought. Science fearlessly updates itself. New ideas, techniques and theories are the lifeblood of Science. What The Clock of The Twelve Paired Mantras uses to activate it is dynamic thought through its analysis of the root meanings of the mantras, its variety of paired combinations and the inner connections between two, three, four, and six of the paired mantras.

Religious zealots succeed because they expect (DEMAND!) others to just fall in line and swallow everything they say whole. No questions asked. They succeed because many of us do! Before we put something into our stomachs, we examine it first. But, when we allow something into our minds, we often don't. When someone else's conviction and enthusiasm is taken as the fullest and truest interpretation of scripture, we cut the unique connection to God we were each born with. When someone else's convictions are imposed upon us, we can test their interpretations by simply asking ourselves, "Do I feel growth or guilt?". If it fills us with Light and spiritual knowledge, it is growth. If it is growth, keep it. But, if someone's spiritual interpretations guilt, anger, or fear, then their advice won't help us towards a life full of abundance and transcendent joy. Spiritual thought opens our heart, our intellect, our vision, and our mind. We just need to listen to our body to see if Light enters our being. That "A-ha!" moment is Light. A Light that touches and revives our deepest resources.

With The Clock of The Paired Mantras, we immerse ourselves in the root meanings of the World Mantras and see the synergy they create within and around us when used in pairs. Mantras are keys. They are keys in the form of a word. They unlock our resources of love, peace, joy, and transcendence. As a metaphor, imagine a millionaire with a huge mansion. A mansion has a different key to each door. One key to the front door, a different key to the back door, a different key to the garden door, a different one to the basement door, and a different one to the garage door – But… they are ALL keys into the same house. We are all millionaires with keys to our spiritual home. These keys in the form of a mantra can all trigger our highest resonance. When we understand the root meanings of these mantras, we become as abundant as a millionaire. These keys awaken spiritual ecstasy. They all help us touch our own Divinity.

Divinity is to man as the color red is to a pomegranate… or the color blue is to a blackberry. With The Clock of The Twelve Paired Mantras, we awaken a rainbow of Divinity in our Lives. We evoke a spiritual kaleidoscope in our lives.

The Clock of The Twelve Paired Mantras
Excites both Spirit and Matter

"Tao" and "Allah" take our thoughts to "The Eternal Realm" – The source of our Spirit. "Om", "Amen", and "AUM" take our thoughts to "The Cosmic Vibration" – The source of Matter. We excite them both with any of the paired mantras.

We often talk about spirit and matter as if they were two separate things. At first glance, this seems to be true. When we consider a stone and when we consider a thought, we think that they are totally different. That there is no anatomical or physical way to compare a thought to a stone. One is solid matter and the other has no matter at all. To most of us, a stone can be weighed, broken, thrown, and used as a building material. But, wait… Thoughts can also be weighed, broken, thrown, and used as building materials. As for a thought in terms of weight, there is a study showing that the human spirit has weight. When people are weighed before and after their death, these weights are slightly different. The change in weight seems to be 21 grams. That's about 21 paperclips or nine dimes. Also, when we are worried we say something is "heavy on my mind". That saying pertains to the weight of a thought. Thoughts are broken in times we say that we have lost our train of thought. Forgetfulness or trying to remember a name, for example, are also times when a thought is broken. Thoughts are thrown when we flirt, shoot someone an angry look, or give them the evil eye.

Parents and lovers throw thoughts all day. Thoughts are building materials when we are "brainstorming". In groups, when we look for a new idea or a solution to a problem, thoughts are built on top of each other. In these brainstorming meetings, they either construct themselves into something usable or they tumble and fall. Look at how many "Thought blocks" were used to build a skyscraper.

When we remember that both the stone and the thought came from the same Source, we begin to look beyond what we have been led to think they are. We see the same Source everything and everyone comes from. If we can trace a stone back to this One Universal Source, then we can trace ourselves back to it too.

That source is not hard to find. In The Bible, for example, Luke 12 :7 and Matthew 10 :30 take our thoughts to God being in every hair on our head – "Even the hairs on your head are numbered". He can count the hairs on our head because He is IN every hair on our head. Within both spirit and matter is Universal Consciousness - The dynamic realm that is without beginning and without end.

In medical science, a stem cell can become any cell in the body. In spirituality, a pure thought can become any cell in the Universe. They both contain cosmic "potentiality". Nothing manifested is as pure as pure thought. Even the air of the Himalayas is not as pristine as pure dynamic consciousness. The purity we seek at the highest peak of the Himalayas can be found in the depths of our own heart. All five of our world mantras lead us back to this same dynamic field. They are five facets of the same diamond. Each facet of Buddhism, Islam, Hinduism, Christianity, Judaism, and Taoism are all beautiful, intelligent, and important entryways into that same Universal Diamond. The 12 sides of the diamond that is The Clock of The Twelve Paired Mantras take our thoughts to this cosmic potentiality that exists within and around us.

The Clock makes you a Master of both Spirit and Matter

As is said in our religions, man is both spirit and matter. We, as human beings, are connected to both the objective and the subjective worlds – To the world we see and the world we sense. In regards to our body, it is composed of flesh and bones. The basic components of this Clock are Thought and Light. Whatever job we do or talents we possess, building a connection between physical matter and The Universal Mind is always part of our life's work here on Earth. It is because we were simply born human. We were given the rare and unique Grace of human birth and a sound mind. Through thought, we are connected to The Universe. If we can see it or imagine it… we can connect to it. We can be it. Meaning, we can be the aspects we value in it. Through thought and desire, we can become or connect to anything we choose.

When we dedicate a small part of our life to learning how to build "Bridges and Roads" throughout our inner world, we see changes in our outer world. Bridges between our spirit and matter create tremendous joy in everything we see and attract. The more bridges and roads we have laid down, the more joyous we feel, the more dynamic we become, and the more abundant we are. When we feel more, we materialize more. When our thoughts are abundant and dynamic, our lives are abundant and dynamic. The building materials of these inner roads and bridges are started from what we think and lead to how we feel and how we act. We strengthen the link between our spiritual world of Thought and our outer world of physical matter when we add conscious Divinity to both. This Clock shows you some new and old techniques on how humanity builds inner bridges and roads between the vast Inner World of Collective Consciousness and Divine Intelligence. Once more and more of these inner-infrastructures and bridges are laid down, pure transcendence, joy, and inspiration are what cross back and forth.

As children, many of us played in sandboxes. In one way, we can look at sandboxes as miniature playgrounds between spirit (our creativity) and matter (the sand). Like with clay, marble, ice, or wood, we are Little Gods when our imagination and sand come together. Sandboxes are a microcosm of our Universe. Pure Creative Thought is in constant play with the atoms in our galaxies. Each one of us is made of this divine clay. In our childhood sandboxes, we enjoyed the endless possibilities sand could be molded into by using some shovels, pails, our hands, and our own boundless imagination. However, few of us wondered what the floor of the sandbox would look like. And fewer still imagined that if we dug deep enough through this material of sand, that there might possibly be a message written at its bottom.

In some ways, how most of us live our lives can be compared to playing in a sandbox. Most of us simply enjoy carelessly playing with this malleable material within and around us. A few of us wonder what is this material is composed of. And fewer still attempt to analyze it, to see if they can trace it back to what or who created it.

Those of us who attempt to dig for answers, may first do so with our hands – only to find more and more sand pouring down over our burrowing. If we are blessed, we will meet a teacher or guide who will show us the shovels and pails we can use to help us. Meditation, prayer, and many rituals help us to see a clearer path through this divine material we are in and a part of. With practice, what we come to realize is that our spiritual activities can act not only act as shovels and pails, but also as water and glue. Working with water and glue helps us to organize the sand and see past it onto what is written for us on the sandbox floor. The dunes of sand are pushed aside and we can trace this message back to the creator. The message tells us why we were compelled to go through all of that struggle and effort. After many years of intensive work, we will finally see that the specific message we had always been searching for was within us all along.

Your paired mantra opens your thoughts to any messages there are in your sandbox. It opens your thoughts to what you are meant to achieve in this lifetime. Being regularly and consistently open to these two realms of Universal Consciousness – The Two Paths To God – awakens us as both receptors and transmitters. The 24 Exercises in Divine Science and Multiplicative Joy in the accompanying book will help build ourselves as receptors and transmitters.

Communicating with The Creator is communicating with the highest in ourselves. When we communicate, we transmit our thoughts, prayers, ideas, and aspirations to another animate or inanimate body. Someone or something with an active intelligence has to receive the information we are putting across.

The easiest route of communication is with another human being who speaks our own language. If the person doesn't speak our language, then we have to try other forms of communication to insure we are understood in order to receive an answer. But if the receptor is not even a human being, then to receive an answer to the information we have put across… we are compelled to "humanize" the receptor to get any kind of informative response back.

As humans, we "humanize" everything. We do this especially for things we do not understand. Case in point, our cellphones and computers. We put our thoughts, our lives, our contacts, pictures, and ideas into our cellphones and computers. But, very few of us understand how they work. So, we humanize them even more to make them understandable and relatable. For example, we often say our computers are "thinking". We can even say it died, it's sick, or it has a virus. Moreover, when something suddenly goes wrong with our cellphone or computer, our frustration takes the humanizing of them to a darker level. We start to think that there is some devilish, sinister entity inside it that is out to destroy us. It wants to cause havoc and ruin in our lives. But, in fact, there is no devilish entity inside our cellphone or PC. It is only our knowledge, experience, and technique that are lacking.

How we react to our computers often shows us how we react to God. When something frustrating suddenly occurs in our Life, we say that there is a sinister entity behind it. We often think that The Devil is out to ruin us. Yes, there are darker forces, but just as with our broken cellphone, what is probably lacking is our knowledge, experience, and technique. The Clock of The Twelve Paired Mantras takes our thoughts beyond our frustration into a realm where there is inspiration and Universal Abundance.

The Trinities And Sacred Hearts Found Throughout Asia's Eastern Religions

Like the Paired Mantra, Trinities are a path that lead us deep into The Heart of Divine Consciousness. They are another example of how synergy can work to alchemically inspire us.

Connected to the Trinity is The Sacred Heart. Like the physical heart, it, too, has three components. When we are praying with a Trinity, we are praying with The Sacred Heart.

In the West, Christianity, Judaism, and Islam create a Trinity. In the East, several more are found between Taoism, Buddhism, Hinduism, Confucianism, and Shintoism.

The Three Aspects Of The Sacred Heart

The Physical Heart pumps blood –
The Sacred Heart pumps Light

Arguably, the heart is the most important organ in our physical body. Even if all the other organs fail – including the brain

– we are still alive if the heart is beating. Gynecologists can see the heart beating when they perform an ultra-sound on a fetus – It's can be seen pumping nutrients through the fetus long before the brain, organs, or genitals have even developed. In addition to that, paramedics are trained to first check a person's heartbeat through their pulse when they are called to accidents and emergencies. But, as we are all spiritual beings in a physical body, there is another heart we should also remember. One that lies beyond the material realm – it is known as The Sacred Heart.

In our physical body, the heart is the source of Life.

In our universal body, the Sacred Heart is the source of Alchemy.

Blood and oxygen are the components pumping through the physical heart.

Light and abundance are the components pumping through The Sacred Heart.

The Sacred Heart connects us to The Universal Body – Divine Consciousness. Like the physical heart, it is eternally active – day and night. It incessantly replenishes and purifies every living "component" within its "body". Like the physical heart, it has a left side, a right side, and an aorta – these three parts of The Sacred Heart are the foundations of The Trinity. "As above, so below" is the Divine Law that helps substantiate that there are three components to its form. In other words, the physical heart would not have three components to it if The Sacred Heart did not have three components to it. All of the major religions remind us that we are God's children, who are made in his image.

The physical heart is the central organ of the physical body. The Sacred Heart is the central organ of The Cosmos. At one time or another, philosophic mystics might stop and ask themselves "What is the very first thing God created?". Along with asking why, when and how, mystics seemed to have also asked what? Since it could not have been anything material, the very first thing God created out of His limitless void had to be either Light or Sound. As was discussed before, our spiritual texts tell us that many ancients reasoned that the first thing God created was the sound of a cosmically charged universal vibration with the potential to become anything from a blade of grass to an asteroid. This sound is so powerful and creatively inexhaustible that not only did it become our vibrant and abundant Earth, not only did it become ourselves… but for every human being and for every blade of grass it becomes that manifestation will only exist once in Eternity. Some described this sound in the form of a word. One of the aspects of the physical heart is its incessant sound. The Sacred Heart also beats with incessant sound. It is part of the very first "body" that God created in our Universe. Of that body, The Sacred Heart is its most active component. This body is not God. If God were a body, then he would be a form occupying a space. God – the Source of everything manifested and un-manifested – is formless and eternal. The Universal body he created is, rather, a tool of purity, knowledge, wisdom, Love, and transcendence. Conscious awareness of its existence awakens joy in our lives. Habitually aligning our thoughts with its function and help awakens transcendence and spiritual power. All twelve of the paired mantras lead our thoughts deep into The Sacred Heart.

In Christianity, a Sacred Heart is formed from three components. For example, when Christians say "The Father, The Son, and The Holy Spirit, Amen", this Trinity forms one of the predominant Sacred Hearts that Christians use in their prayers and during mass. In this book, these three represent Universal Consciousness ("The Father"), physical matter ("The Son"), and the bridge between both ("The Holy Spirit, Amen"). The Sacred Heart lies with The Father. The physical heart lies with The Son. And, our thoughts, prayers, and aspirations connect the Father to the Son through the Amen mantra. When a Trinity is formed, it is defined as meaning "Three are One". The Christian Virtues of "Faith, Hope, and Charity"… The first Christian gifts of prophecy, tongues, and knowledge… The Christian values of "Faith, Hope, and Love"… are some other well-known Trinities that we can contemplate within this religion. Not all Trinities found in Christianity are obvious. Depictions of "The Three Wise Kings" is one of the more subtle and symbolic ways that it skillfully penetrates deep into our thoughts. When we see paintings of these Kings there is often Mary (Symbolizing the feminine aspect of God), Joseph (Symbolizing the masculine aspect of God), and a radiant newborn Jesus Christ (Symbolizing transcendence, Truth, Wonder, Love, and Divinity). And when we research this event deeper into the gifts that The Three Kings brought to The Newborn Christ, how they found him through the Five-pointed Star, the origins of the Kings themselves, and their arrival 12 days after his birth, we see that the Trinity is part of a larger spectrum of Divine and Alchemic Symbolism.

    Again, the equilateral triangle is the strongest shape. This strength is built into The Trinity. When we recognize a Trinity within our realm of spirituality and faith, we can then say that we have found an artery leading us directly into The Sacred Heart of The Universe. The Cosmic Body is full of arteries, veins, and capillaries.

THE TWO PATHS TO GOD

The Sacred Heart And The Trinity

Introduction

For many Westerners, their knowledge of both The Sacred Heart and The Trinity began in Catholicism. In Catholic paintings, statues, and relics, The Sacred Heart is always depicted as full of Light, radiance, and abundance. Added to that, The Master Jesus is often seen pointing to his own Sacred Heart, while looking directly out at us. It is hard to tell which is the dominate or central focus of the image, as our eyes dance between the two main focal points - A glowing, healthy-looking Master Christ and a creatively abundant, radiant Sacred Heart. In these images, we are inspired by both, as we stand momentarily entranced in front of one. Compared to other images where Jesus is on the cross or at the Last Supper, here we see a glowing and loving Master Jesus, pointing to his Sacred Heart, clearly and directly teaching us something.

For Catholics, it is the nun Mary-Marguerite who first saw a number of visions of Jesus Christ with The Sacred Heart. It was not a dream or something in her imagination she saw, it was a recurring Divine Phenomena she recounted to others. Mary-Marguerite is not to be confused with Mary-Magdalene. Mary-Magdalene was with Jesus Christ during his time on Earth. Mary-Marguerite was a simple nun who suddenly had visions of him showing her is Sacred Heart centuries after his crucifixion. Up until that time, Jesus was predominantly portrayed in paintings and sculptures as skinny, sick, and dying on the cross. However, in Mary-Marguerite's apparitions, he showed himself to be healthy and glowing. He could have stopped there – but, her visions of him went much further, by him repeatedly showing her his Sacred Heart in the middle of his chest. This was a shocking difference to how people had thought of him up until then. The Master Christ came to her several times and in many places, always radiantly displaying his Sacred Heart. When she finally told others in her convent what was happening to her, it was not an instant and joyous revelation. People doubted her – even throughout her own convent. She suffered and she struggled while these apparitions kept happening. But still, she persevered. And eventually, The Vatican and many other Catholics also began to love and accept this new image of their savior.

Not only The Sacred Heart is found in Catholicism, but also The Trinity is found in it, as well. Trinities help our thoughts resonate higher. Trinities empower our virtues and our prayers. Trinities magnify Divine Light. We are more in-tune with The Universal Laws when we are conscious of the Trinities within and around us. Faith, Hope, and Charity. The Father, The Son, and The Holy Spirit. The Holy Family. These are some of the prominent trinities found in Catholicism.

Although Christianity reveres both of these Divine Symbols, that does not mean they do not exist in other faiths. Both exist world-wide in other recognizable forms. As for the Trinity, we can begin to get a first impression of its symbolism by considering a triangle's 3-sided form. Mathematically, an equilateral triangle is the strongest geometrical shape. All of its sides and angles are equal. We can see how this form powerfully concentrates energy and power. Ancient Mayans and Egyptians probably had this in mind when they constructed their pyramids.

THE TWO PATHS TO GOD

The Sacred Heart, The Green Chakra, The Tiferet, and The Caduceus are the same

Let's first examine the location of the Sacred Heart in Mary Marguerite's apparition of Jesus Christ. The first thing we see is that it is not at all where his physical heart is located. The physical heart is on the left side of the chest. The Sacred Heart, however, is depicted in the center of the chest. We see it is a heart, but it does not look like the physical heart at all. It is always glowing, radiating, and elaborately decorated. In countless images and statues, we see one of the world's greatest teachers showing us an apparently divine and colorfully light-filled area of his body in the middle of his chest. Through the many symbolic additions that always get added to depictions of The Sacred Heart, we come to see that it can connect us to The Universe. Looking at a Messiah in all radiant display of his Sacred Heart is like looking up at a star or at a rose in full bloom. Until Mary Marguerite's apparitions, it is highly improbable that Christians would look at the middle of their chest as a source of anything relevant to their spiritual evolution. For many, this example turned their vision inwards.

Each of us is born with our own Sacred Heart. It is at the same spot that Jesus is showing us – In the middle of our chest. To find it, we put our hand on our heart and then move it to the center of our chest. As Jesus displays for us, it is one of our main pathways to Universal Consciousness. Although it is something many of us never develop or nourish further, it is still there.

In eastern religions, many spiritualists study the chakras. These are energy centers in our human body that help us to survive, connect us to various celestial bodies, and correspond to many aspects in our lives; our sexual energy, our connection to The Universe, our Compassion, our Intellect, our wealth, our communication abilities, and so forth. The most well-known chakras are commonly thought of in colors corresponding to a rainbow; red, orange, yellow, green, blue, indigo, and violet. As they are each connected to our spinal cord, we think of them starting at the base of our spine (red) and ending at the top our head (violet). The Green Chakra is located in the middle of our chest and represents our connection to The Universe. Coincidentally, it's location is in the same spot as The Sacred Heart. A description of The Green Chakra and its functions is the same as a description of The Sacred Heart and its functions. Only the label is different. The purpose, the place, and the power are all the same. People who practice yoga and meditation are often aware of The Green Chakra and use it in their meditations to help them connect to Universal Consciousness.

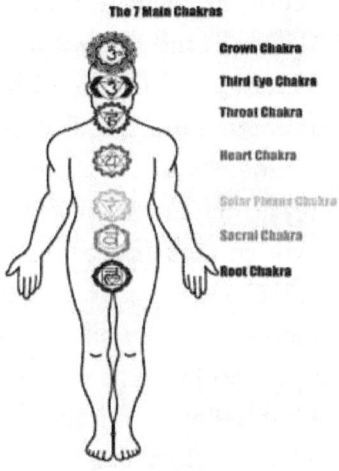

Judaism teaches about another group of energy centers that are also related to our spinal cord – The Sephirot. In our dreams at night, we can feel the exact same sensations, thoughts, and actions that we have in our physical bodies when we are awake. This happens also in our daydreams, although to a lesser extent. Dreams demonstrate that although we are not in our physical body, we have subtler bodies – our astral body and our etheric body – where we can and do operate and function. For Jewish mystics, within our astral and etheric bodies, we have 10 main energy centers that are related to wisdom, beauty, strength, mercy, etc. These 10 different spiritual centers are together known as "The Sephirot". It is "The Tree of Life", where the main trunk is our spinal cord. In some ways, The Sephirot does look like a tree – But, this tree is full of heavenly splendor and strength. As we grow spiritually, our tree develops – bearing the fruits of abundance, joy, and wisdom.

In Judaism, knowledge of The Sephirot is mainly taught through one of its most mystic disciplines – The Kabbalah. As for its 10 energy centers, the main focal point in The Sephirot corresponds to the center of the chest. It is known as "The Tiphareth" (also spelled "Tiferet"), and it too is at the exact same point where The Sacred Heart and The Green Chakra are represented in other religions. It too is thought of as our connection to The Universe and to God. As The Tiphareth is the center point, all the other energy centers are connected to it. Many detailed books have been written about The Sephirot. Each of the energy centers have been explored as to how they can contribute to our evolution. For Kabbalists, we are all born with one, and can benefit by becoming aware of the one we have – which will, in and of itself, activate its blessing on our lives.

The main "trunk" of our spiritual tree is The Tiphareth. In other Faiths it is called our Heart Chakra, our Green Chakra, or our Sacred Heart… However, its function is the same thing no matter what it's called. It is our connection to Universal Consciousness. Through it, we can and do send our prayers and thoughts into The Divine Mind, as well as receive inspiration and blessings from that same realm.

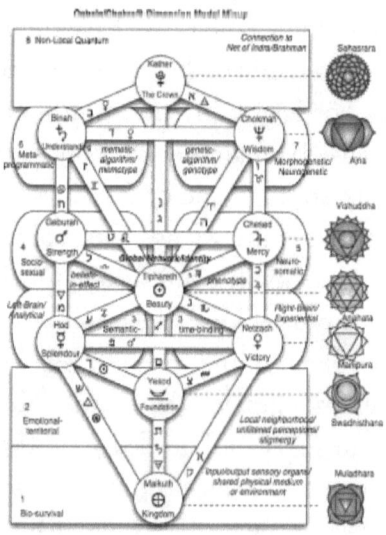

THE TWO PATHS TO GOD

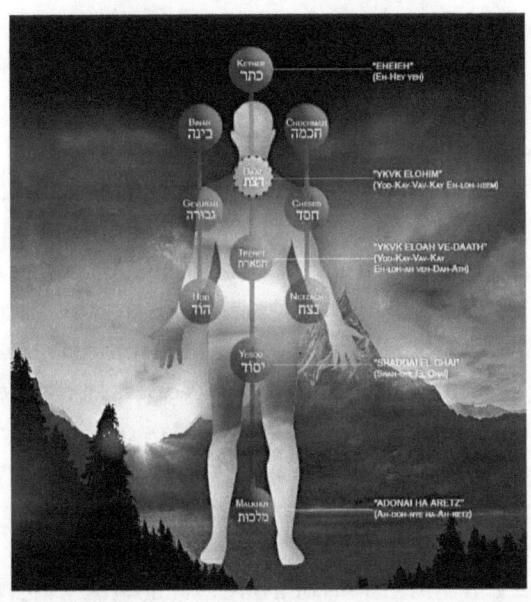

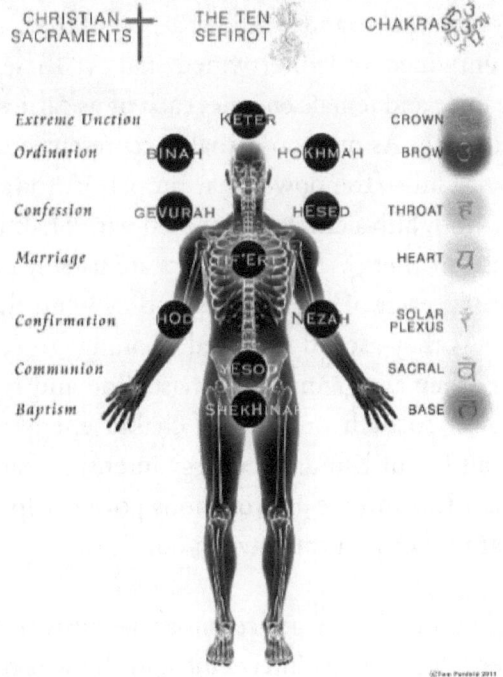

One other place we can find a representation of The Sacred Heart is in the field of Pharmacy and Medicine. The medical field is represented world-wide by The Caduceus of Mercury. There are several parts to this symbol of Health. The most prominent being the two winding snakes, the wings, the staff, and the head of the staff. Like The Chakras, The Sephirot, and The Sacred Heart, all of us are born with a Caduceus. Again, becoming consciously aware of the many signs that we are more than just flesh and bone is a valuable step in our own spiritual evolution. When we get a feeling that we have wings or that we want to fly like a bird, it is probably because the wings of our Caduceus are spiritually stimulated in some way by wonder and beauty. The Greek Sphinx, angels, and a large percentage of Catholic Icons show human beings depicted with wings. Proportionally, if we study the size and dimensions of a bird's wings, the wings of our Caduceus would be twice as big as our physical body.

Another remarkable and symbolic aspect of the Caduceus are the two entwined and intertwined snakes. These snakes represent the male and female energies each of us carries within – our Yin and Yang. As one, both snakes represent our Kundalini energy, or Chi – The power that propels us towards our oneness with God. Shiva energy combined with Shakti energy releases Kundalini energy. These serpents are usually depicted wrapping around each of our chakras as they wind their way up our spine. As they ascend from red to orange to yellow to green to blue, they are giving their masculine and feminine kundalini power to each one of our chakra energy centers. Being conscious of our Kundalini energy intensifies each color of our chakras. This intense androgynous power helps release the forces that that chakra can have in our lives.

The focal point of The Caduceus is at the cross-section on the staff, where the serpents intertwine and the wings unfold.

Again, just like we all have a Sacred Heart, a Green Chakra, and a Tiferet, we all have also our own set of wings. We are all born with a Caduceus of Mercury.

Symbolism is a prominent way of teaching in both Hinduism and Christianity. In both of these religions, Gods and saints are depicted with wings. The Caduceus wings are sometimes shown coming from the head, or Crown Chakra (our violet chakra). This is to represent the light in our intellect and knowledge, or the symbolic wings in Mercury's Helmut or in a halo. The wings are sometimes also shown coming from the Indigo Chakra (to open our third eye) and Blue Chakra (to develop power, truth, and tranquility through communication). These open wings can be shown to unfurl from any of our higher chakras – the green, blue, indigo, or violet chakra. However, one thing we never see are the wings spreading out from one of the lower chakras – The red, orange, or yellow chakra. The Green Chakra is in the middle of our spinal chakra chain – from there, there are three main chakras above it and three chakras below it. When the wings are shown spreading from our Sacred Heart, it is again depicting our connection to The Universal Mind.

We do not only have to look inwards to find our Sacred Heart. We can see it outwards, as well. There is a place where we can observe The Tipheret, remembering its beauty, glory, and abundance shining down on us – Namely, we can remember The Sun. The Sun itself is the center of our Solar System, and is seen by Spiritual adepts as our connection to Universal Consciousness. The Sun is God's greatest gift to a man or a woman on their Spiritual Quests. Seeing the Sun in this way helps us compare it with the same qualities of our Sacred Heart. What the Sun is, our Tipheret is; abundance, joy, Light, radiance, and vitality. The Green Chakra is eternal. The Sacred Heart is eternal. And in regards to the way our ancient mystics looked at the world, The Sun is eternal too. Since "Ra" in Ancient Egypt, there have always been active Spiritual brotherhoods who've considered The Sun itself as their Eternal Spiritual Savior or even as a God. Sun worshippers existed not only with Ra (or Re), but also Mesoamericans (From Mexico to South America) revered the Sun. Many Indo-Europeans (From India to Europe; Greek, Iranian…) also had The Sun central to their faith.

The Sun represents The Five Virtues of justice, truth, love, kindness, and wisdom. The Sun represents The Five Elements of The Quintessence; vitality, warmth, magnetism, Light, and electricity. The Sun represents God, as it is his greatest gift to our planet and represents everything The Father/Mother God is. Nothing on this planet would work without The Sun. It gives life to everything and is all-seeing. It is the link between here and there. Between the tangible and the intangible. The mortal and the immortal. The crude and The Divine. These attributes are the same for The Heart Chakra. Our Inner Sun is the link between the "upper world" and the "lower world".

Still, another place we can look for The Sacred Heart is in our own hand. Our hands have the ring finger, which to palm readers represents The Sun. The lines on this finger tell a reader of the glory, abundance, and divinity currently happening in our lives. Furthermore, throughout the world, when two souls unite in marriage, it is symbolized by a gold ring on the ring finger. This is a mystical tradition that is found in many – if not all – religions. The act of two souls coming together is already a profound process in and of itself – but, marriage traditions all over the world represent that whole spiritually unifying ritual by ultimately putting gold (that comes from sunrays) onto the finger that symbolizes The Sun. In its highest and most sublime sense, any marriage alliance further awakens each person's own Sacred Heart and displays their commitment to helping their partner realize The King or The Queen within themselves.

Kundalini Energy and its various representations

The Sephirot and The Caduceus of Mercury can be seen as representations of the The Kundalini Energy. Kundalini is an ancient Sanskrit term. It describes the transcendent energy that gets activated when we are consciously following a spiritual path leading us to Universal Oneness. When we follow some of our path with a spiritual guide, such as an enlightened Guru, we are more conscious of this Divine Gift that God is bestowing upon us. Our own awareness increases The Kundalini's activity. Conscious awareness gives us a boost in our spiritual evolution.

The Kundalini is known by different names, "Qi" (in Japan), "Prana" (in India), and "Shakti" (in Yogas) – However, in spite of its different names, it is still felt as the same Divine Life Force. Furthermore, since each human being is at a different point on their spiritual journey – even after coming into conscious contact with The Kundalini – The Kundalini will outwardly manifest itself in different ways. Some spiritualists will see sudden sparks of Light with their eyes open. Some will feel "kriyas", or "sudden explosions of Light and energy", within parts of their body; in their heart, head, body, eyes, and/or spine. Some people will feel the rhythm of their breathing change. Some will feel a "popping-sound" in their ears. Some will be able to see a blanket of stars in their meditations, while others will see lights of red, purple, green, and blue flowing in and out of their meditation's inner visual field. These, and more, are some of the ways that The Kundalini expresses itself here on the material plane. However, everyone will see more abundance and beauty in their lives… and, more importantly, be able to connect that beauty to its Divine Source.

THE TWO PATHS TO GOD

When depicted in paintings and symbols, The Kundalini also takes many forms. As in The Caduceus, the main elements of The Kundalini are:

- The Masculine Energy
- The Feminine Energy
- The Human Spine
- The Serpent
- Abundance
- Light
- Love
- Conscious awareness

When we look at Christianity, Judaism, and Islam we can see the main elements of The Kundalini in the depictions of Adam and Eve in The Garden of Eden:

Just as in The Caduceus of Mercury, The Kundalini is all there:

- The Masculine Energy (Adam)
- The Feminine Energy (Eve)

- The Human Spine (The Tree)
- The Serpent
- Abundance
  (The fruit from The Tree of Knowledge of Good and Evil)
- Light (God)
- Love (The relationship)
- Conscious awareness

Also, when we look at the symbol of Yin and Yang, The Kundalini is there as well:

- The Masculine Energy (Yang)
- The Feminine Energy (Yin)
- The Human Spine
  (The relationship between the dots and the "S")
- The Serpent (The "S")
- Abundance (The "O")
- Light
- Love (The two over-lapping drop-like forms that is suggested)
- Conscious awareness

The white and the black dots suggest The Sun and The Moon. The reversed "S" could have been just a straight line or even a zig-zag, but being that it is curved suggests many things to our more subtler thoughts; flow, love, union, intertwining, balance, harmony, and – of course – a serpent. All things that are more inspired when we have an abundance of Kundalini awareness.

Arguably, the most unique and mystical aspect of The Kundalini is The Serpent. The symbolism of the snake is seen with many ancient Gods; The Goddess of Crete, The Celtic God Cernunnos, The Greek God Hercules and Ganymede, The Hindu Gods Indra and Shiva, Egyptian Gods, and The Basque Goddess Mother are either holding snakes or are snakes themselves. To these ancient civilizations, the serpent symbolized Life, regeneration, and sexual desire. When the serpent is seen eating its own tail, it symbolizes The Universal Life Force itself.

It is apparent how important and mystical the snake was and is to a mystic. To many of them, every human life began with the help of a snake. Inside the mother's womb, there is a snake that gives a baby its life. This serpent connects the baby to the mother. It feeds it. It gives the baby oxygen until it can breathe on its own. The serpent tends to the baby and, for nine months, it helps it grow. Then after our birth, the snake slowly dies. Ancient seers revered the blessings and importance of this powerful and life-giving serpent – because no matter what race, gender, or religion we are, a mystic can see that each one of us had it with us inside the womb. God put it there – whether we are rich or poor – to aid us during incubation. Today, that serpent is commonly known as The Umbilical cord.

The Infinity within The Trinity is The Valentine

The Sacred Heart not only changes its names from Heart Chakra to Tipheret, etc. But, it seems that it can also change its form and combination of forms. For example, one place we can find both

The Sacred Heart and The Trinity combined is in the drawing of a Valentine. This symbolic drawing of a heart is extremely popular. It is one of the most, if not the most, popularly drawn designs in the world. It also crosses all cultures and religions. In other words, it is not banned in any part of the world. No one in the world is shocked by it, rather we all can feel how it evokes sparks of Light, Love, and Joy in the deepest resources of ourselves. The valentine looks nothing like the physical heart. However, the powerful and simple design of it may possibly represent something Divine if we examine it more closely.

There are two ways we can think of a valentine, and the mystical inspiration behind it when it was first drawn. The mystics who first designed The Valentine must have had some deep symbolism in mind when they conceived it or when the form came to them through inspired thought. In either case, for it to have lasted as long as it has, and to be as popular as it still is – it must still contain some degree of power and mysticism when it is drawn and is given away. At its base, we all accept that it represents Love. However, we can go beyond that…

When we look at the symbolic drawing of a valentine, we see its similarity in its overall shape to an equilateral triangle. The equilateral triangle is a depiction of The Trinity. The valentine sparks sentiments of Love, giving, receiving, and joy. It takes our thoughts to aspects of The Sacred Heart.

Love and the equilateral triangle are our first subconscious impressions of the valentine. The equilateral triangle is one of the handful of geometric shapes that can spark Divine Thought. It is itself the strongest shape of all. It has equal sides and equal angles. A subtly perceived Trinity is our first global impression. However, the valentine can enrich our thoughts even more. When we add the symbol of Infinity to The Sacred Heart and The Trinity, we transcend even deeper...

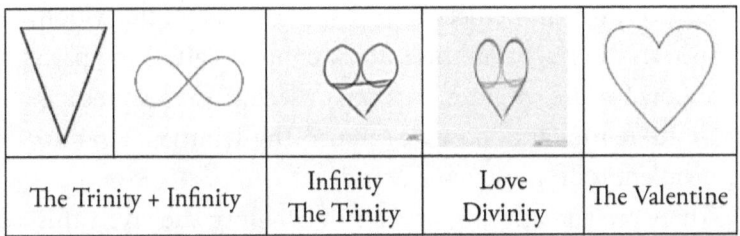

The Trinity + Infinity	Infinity The Trinity	Love Divinity	The Valentine

Every minute, countless people joyously express their Love for someone with The Valentine. This simple and deeply mystical symbol is connected to The Tipheret, Ra, and The Green Chakra. It awakens a fire within us through the giving and receiving of Love. When we examine the reasons why this power is evoked, we can see that The Valentine contains Divinity, Infinity, and The Trinity.

The Celtic Triquetra – The Trinity and The Absolute are inextricable

The Celtic Triquetra is another popular symbol of The Trinity. Like in Hinduism, Christianity, and Judaism, this Pagan Celtic civilization also saw the power of three Divine Aspects in one.

Pagans were, and still are, very close to Nature. For them, spirits are found on every level of the World around us; in various trees, stones, planets, animals, The cycles of the Moon, The Sun, and rivers. From this intense contemplation and practice of how Nature operates, wearing or seeing The Triquetra is a powerful reminder of how we can use The Trinity to tap into The Wholeness of The Divine Mind.

There are actually two aspects of Divinity shown in this one symbol – The Trinity aspect (represented by its 3 leaf-like equilateral triangle) and The Absolute aspect (represented by its circle). The inherent intertwining of its three part symbol shows that all three aspects are one. And when we look at the circle intertwined within the intertwined Trinity, we are reminded that The Absolute and The Trinity are inextricable. Both the circle and the flowing aspect of its Trinity, give The Triquetra a strong semblance to the symbolism found in The Yin-Yang symbol. The Triquetra depicts The Absolute with The Trinity. The Yin-Yang symbol depicts The Absolute with The Masculine and Feminine aspects of Divinity.

The Star of David – Involution and Evolution

Another common place we can find two Sacred Hearts is when we look at the overlapping triangles symbolizing The

Star of David. There are two Trinities found in this other popular symbol. They can be seen as two Sacred Hearts that are beautifully intertwined. One of its equilateral triangles points downwards, representing "Involution", or when God descends towards man. Blessings, grace, and almost everything about The Sun are good examples of how we can see and experience God's Hand in our lives.

Its second equilateral triangle, representing "Evolution" – is the triangle pointing upwards – reminding us of when we send our prayers, Love, and thoughts into Universal Consciousness.

Seeing how these two equilateral triangles, or Sacred Hearts, intertwine evokes Light within us. The Star of David symbolizes the unification of involution and evolution. Both happen when our Sacred Heart is activated. This, in turn, triggers its Five Virtues; Justice, Truth, Love, Kindness, and Wisdom.

Again... In Catholicism, we are taught not only of The Sacred Heart, but also of The Holy Trinity. Two of the most known Trinities are "The Father, The Son, and The Holy Spirit" (Universal Consciousness representing The Father, Physical Matter representing The Son, and The Word representing The Holy Spirit). The other is The Holy Family; "Mary, Joseph, and The Infant Christ". In these, we can symbolically see the Trinity of our Female energy (Mary), our Male Energy (Joseph), and our Transcendent/ Kundalini Energy (The Infant Christ). In Hinduism, there is also a well-known Trinity: "Brahma, Vishnu, and Shiva". These represent Creation, Preservation, and Destruction.

So just from its form alone, where that the equilateral triangle is similar to The Valentine. In esoteric terms, we can see that a Divine Trinity has already a lot in common with a Sacred Heart. It is a "Trinity of Divinity" that can be from anywhere where there is love, work, and spiritual aspiration.

The Sacred Heart itself is full of transcendence. Like a puzzle, three pieces of a Trinity come together to awaken its complete picture. Seeing its global picture awakens a tremendous amount of Light. A Light that is both dynamic and transcendent. In anatomical science, the physical heart's job is to be a pump, a tool of circulation, and a purifier. If we compare The Sacred Heart to the physical heart, we see these same functions in both. Blood, nutrients, and oxygen are the components pumping through the physical heart. Light, transcendence, and peace are the components pumping through The Sacred Heart.

The following pages outline some of the many Sacred Hearts found throughout the world. We can learn and transcend from them all. However, wherever they originate, they all lead to the one supreme Sacred Heart – The one Dynamic Universal Intelligence. God himself.

THE TWO PATHS TO GOD

The Mystic, Poetic, And Symbolic Trinities Found In Eastern Religions

As we can see, Trinities are not limited to Christianity. We recognize them in different ways. As was said before, the three Abrahamic religions form a Trinity – "Three as One". The poetic, symbolic, and mystical aspects of Islam, Christianity, and Judaism form a spiritually formidable triangular tool. Together, they form a large vein leading deep into the Sacred Heart.

Trinities are not only found in The Occident – if we look, there are also many of them found throughout The Orient. The three main distinct religions in Asia are Taoism, Buddhism, and Hinduism. Other practiced faiths like Confucianism, Shintoism, Zen Buddhism, and Sikhism descend from one or two of the three main religions in Asia. Some consider Hinduism itself not as one religion, but as several religions put together. This is because of the immense number of Gods, Goddesses, Deities, practices, and incarnations contained within this one faith. Pluralism is common among Buddhists, Taoists, Shintoists, and Confucianists. Throughout China and Japan, for example, many people practice two or more faiths simultaneously. Even a Shinto priest can bless worshipers in a Taoist temple without anyone blinking an eye! No one would think it strange. It's like imagining a Catholic priest giving mass in a Jewish synagogue to a congregation of Muslim worshippers. This is unheard of in The West, but, by comparison, very common in Asia. To many in this region of the world, we all pray to the same God. The idea of blasphemy doesn't exist when you believe that our all-encompassing God is unconditional.

Religions in Asian cultures have been intermingling for centuries. They have constantly influenced and borrowed from each other – and continue to do so. On the surface, this may seem like their societies are just very open and accepting. However, on the mental and spiritual level, this intermingling creates increased knowledge, Light, and non-judgement.

For the Trinities found throughout Asia, this section looks at some of the most historically prevalent ones. Then we will compare one of the main Trinities of The Orient to The Abrahamic Trinity found in The Occident.

Let's first take a global look at some of the various Eastern faiths…

A General Overview of Eastern Religions

	Some basic, non-exhaustive, fundamentals on certain Eastern Religions
Hinduism	A polytheistic faith in practice but, ultimately, one where all of the Deities lead to a Supreme God – The Godhead. Several rituals are involved in Hinduism – Meditation and Arati are the most common. "Yoga" is a specific practice focusing on a different divine aspect. Yoga leads to Oneness with God – or Enlightenment. It is a focused Divine art, practiced by a yogi or yogini – often under the guidance of a teacher (Guru, Avatar, Sadhu, etc..). Jnana yoga (wisdom), Bhakti yoga (love), and Karma yoga (work) are popular yogas. There are countless Deities, Gods, Goddesses, and Divine incarnations that can be prayed to, as each of these signifies a different aspect of God. The three main Hindu Gods create "The Trimurti" - A Trinity. These three Gods are Brahma (The Creator), Vishnu (the Preserver), and Shiva (The Destroyer). The main Hindu books are The Vedas, the Bhagavad Gita, and The Mahabarata.

Taoism	A Taoist learns, through thought, study, and the observation of Nature, how to come into Oneness with "The Tao" – the unborn and undying realm of The Universe. One of the definitions of The Tao is "The Eternal Field behind the 10,000 things". This Eternal Field is seen as "The Mother" of the 10,000 things. Lao Tzu was a librarian who was persuaded to write 81 brief, yet deeply probing, poem-like verses on man's quest for spiritual fulfillment. The thought-provoking book he wrote is called "The Tao Te Ching". It is comparatively short to other spiritual books, but its spiritual knowledge is very condensed. Harmonizing with the Divine Virtues is one of the paths a Taoist aims for in their quest for Oneness with The Eternal Void. The greatest teacher is Nature itself. A Taoist studies The Dynamic Consciousness we live in.
Buddhism	Buddhism is seen more as a way of Life and a way of thinking than as a religion. Central to Buddhism is Dharma. Dharma can mean many things; Doctrine, teaching, duty, Eternal Truth, law, religion, or right conduct. A Buddhist lives by two main philosophies; The Four Noble Truths and the Eight-fold Path. The Four Noble Truths are 1. Life is suffering, 2. Suffering is cause by desire, 3. Desire can be overcome, 4. Overcome desire by following the Eight-fold Path. The Eight-fold Path are our right views, right intent, right speech, right conduct, right livelihood, right effort, right mindfulness, and right concentration. The Dhammapada are verses of Buddhist philosophy. A Buddhist prays or meditates with the mantra «Nam myoho renghe kyo» (Like a Lotus flower, this mantra is to bring forth « The Eternal Buddha » deep within us). Meditating on the word « Om » helps the Buddhist control his thoughts and cravings. He harmonizes with The Mind of The Universe. The ability to do this is the most critical step before reaching Nirvana (Enlightenment), a realm where there is no suffering and no desire.

Confucianism	Much of Confucianism is borrowed from Taoism and Buddhism. It shares the same ethics as Taoism; Chinese thought, actions, traditions, and culture. However, it is much more scholastic and regimented in practice than Taoism. Some of the main aspects to Confucianism are morality, conduct, and inner harmony with Nature – very similar to some of the aspects of The Eight Fold Path found in Buddhism.
Shintoism	Much of Shintoism is also borrowed from Taoism. Shintoists want happiness here and now, rather than in the Afterlife. Shintoism is very formal and has a patriotic aspect to its practices. Cleanliness and purification rites are major parts of a Shintoist's daily rituals. To be in commune with The Natural World, with The Spirits of Nature, and to have a veneration of our ancestors are some of the major aspects of being Shintoist.

**Shintoism and Confucianism are two very popular religions in China and Japan. Since both find their origins in Taoism, this book has chosen to focus just on Taoism as one of the six major world religions for this book. Ancient Iranian religions, like Zoroastrianism, have many historic connections to both The Vedas and The Abrahamic religions. As seen in Africa and The Americas, trade has played an important role in the spread of spiritual doctrines and the birth of new faiths and practices. This phenomenon can also be seen in Sikhism and Jainism – two other popular Eastern religions. They are, respectively, the fifth and eleventh largest religions in the world. They both have a lot of geographical and philosophical similarities to Buddhism and Hinduism. For this reason, too, this book has chosen to focus on the same six major world religions – and, specifically, their five mantras.

The Trinity at the source of:
Hinduism – "The Trimurti"

Hinduism is a complex, multi-faceted, intermixed, patchwork-like, interconnected religion. A Hindu prays to one God, but actually that God or Goddess is simultaneously connected to five other Deities. There are many Hindu Gods to pray to, as

Hinduism is a form of polytheism. Because of this, it has multiple aspects and layers to it. However, central to Hinduism and to all Hindus are three Gods; Brahma (The Creator), Vishnu (The Preserver), and Shiva (The Destroyer). This Trinity creates The Circle of Life within us, around us, and throughout our entire Universe. These three Gods form "The Trimurti". Although many Hindus pray to them individually, together they create a Sacred Heart that is able to evoke Universal Light within us. This happens when we are conscious of their 3-fold power. Each of these Gods have a Goddess wife, and some even have "children". For example, Shiva and his wife, Parvati, have several children – Ganesha, Kali, Durga, and Kartikeya. Some Hindus orientate their aspirations to one of the Goddesses or child Deities, like Ganesha or Kali. However, all of these Goddesses and Child Deities too lead back to the Trimurti – The Sacred Heart of Hinduism.

Another Trinity is found in Hindu mythology, where the cosmos is thought of as threefold – made of oceans, earth and heavens.

The Trinity of:
Jainism
Hinduism
Sikhism

Of these three Indian religions, Hinduism is the oldest and Sikhism is the newest. Jainism is in the middle. Jainism was built from Hinduism, and Sikhism was built from Jainism. There are many similarities between all three. For example, all three believe in karma, meditation, and reincarnation. But, there are many differences that formed the newer faiths. The evolution of the first religion that has created two more religions, and their individually defined spiritual practices, is what forms a Sacred

Heart. It is like the trinities between Taoism, Confucianism, and Shintoism or between Judaism, Christianity, and Islam. Through conflict, three faiths are created – leading to The Sacred Heart.

The Trinity of:
Taoism
Confucianism
Buddhism

In China, these three religions have been influencing and borrowing from each other for centuries. They are known as "The Three Teachings". A Trinity of philosophies that harmonize as one.

In the 11th century, as Buddhism's popularity was rapidly rising, Chinese Taoist scholars created Confucianism as an alternate to Buddhism. However, over time, many of these three doctrines have become interchangeable. This centuries-old interchange of thoughts, aspirations, and action have created a Sacred Heart in that part of the world.

Confucianism and Taoism share many of the same views on how the goal of Life is to achieve an inner harmony with Nature. Much of Confucian thought and religious rites are borrowed from Taoism and Buddhism. Lao-Tzu is the supreme figure in Taoism. Many Taoists believe that both Buddha and Confucius were students of Lao-Tzu – Thus, depictions throughout Asia of these three guides together also lead to The Sacred Heart.

The Trinity of:
Confucianism
Taoism
Shintoism

Confucianism and Shintoism find their origins in Taoism.

All three have the same roots and spring from the same fountain. They form a Trinity, which in turn flows to The Universal Heart.

11th century Chinese scholars and The Medieval Japanese Political class adapted aspects of Taoism to form Confucianism and Shintoism. They did this to keep their followers in Taoism and to curtail the mass conversion to Buddhism. The rise of Buddhism in those countries was considered a serious threat to the centuries-long established norm. However, as a result, these three religions created a Trinity. Being aware of their trifold connection takes our thoughts into The Divine Mind and awakens our own Universal Abundance.

The Trinity of:
Shintoism
Confucianism
Buddhism

In Japan, all three of these faiths peacefully exist side-by-side. It is not at all uncommon for priests or monks from one of these religions to perform rituals in the temple of one of the other two religions. As too is it not uncommon for believers of one of these religions to practice their faith in one of the other two temples.

This inter-mingling and interacting creates a Trinity in the collective consciousness of the followers of the three faiths, as well as above Japan itself. All three offer a variety of techniques to re-connect to our innate oneness with Nature. When we are more aware of this Trinity, their Light can spread throughout the world. On a spiritual level, this Trinity merges the Two Universal Constants – The Eternal Field and The Cosmic Sound. This interweaving of spiritual acts occurs in both Temples of The Sun (Buddhist Temples) and Temples of The Moon (Shinto and Confucian Shrines). What has slowly arisen from a very deep level is respect, joy, and non-judgement. Divine Virtues are interchanged. The fact that "all paths lead to God" is both acted out and reinforced. True surrender is awakened and experienced.

Now, let us examine one of the most dynamic and multi-faceted Sacred Heart pathways of all…

The ever-changing Trinities found between Taoism, Hinduism, and Buddhism:
Taoism – Poetic/Mystic
Hinduism – Symbolic
Buddhism – Mystic/Poetic

Like Christianity, Hinduism is a strongly symbolic path to God. Not only do the various Gods, Goddesses, and Deities represent a unique aspect of God, but also the various objects these Gods and Goddesses hold in their hands, sit on, or stand on are symbolic. Furthermore, the various animals around a God or Goddess are also sacred. For instance, the peacock, the rat, the tiger, and the cobra are symbolic… as too the conch, the lotus flower, the trident, and the mala all have a symbolic meaning. As with the different Saints in Christianity, and the meaning of their various ornaments, every aspect depicted in an Icon can remind us of a different aspect of our Universal God.

As for Hinduism, its symbolism goes beyond the Deities, their ornaments, and their animal companions. The various yogas themselves represent an aspect of God. For instance, Karma yoga is the yoga of "work". Bhakti yoga is the yoga of "Love". Jnana yoga is the yoga of "knowledge". Raja yoga is the yoga of "The Mind". Since Hinduism itself, like God, is so vast and diversified, yogis and yoginis are able to focus on one aspect of it. To help themselves reach Enlightenment, Hindu spiritualists find themselves attracted to one of the yoga practices that best resonates with their karma and personality.

Like the Sacred Heart formed from Islam, Christianity, and Judaism, Hinduism forms a Sacred Heart with Buddhism and Taoism. For both Sacred Hearts, Christianity and Hinduism are their "symbolic" aspect.

Hinduism, Buddhism, and Taoism form a Trinity. As for the "poetic" and "mystical" aspects of this Trinity, the techniques found in Taoism and Buddhism interchange; There is a lot of mysticism (Divine meaning in ritual action) and poeticism (attuning to the harmonic flow of Nature) in both. Because both of these faiths have these two prominent tendencies, the Trinity they form with Hinduism is very dynamic. It leads our thoughts to an ever-transfiguring Sacred Heart. One that modifies itself in accordance to our needs.

Hindu Gods, Goddesses, and Deities – as well as Christian Saints, Apostles, and Archangels – all symbolize a certain aspect of God. They help our mind focus on a small feature of Universal Consciousness. They are channels that evoke Light as we take steps into the dynamically abundant Eternal Void.

As was mentioned above, in Christian Icons and on Hindu Statues, the ornaments that the Deity is holding or wearing also symbolize some form of spirituality or spiritual discipline. The chart below shows some the symbols found in Hinduism:

Xavier Clayton

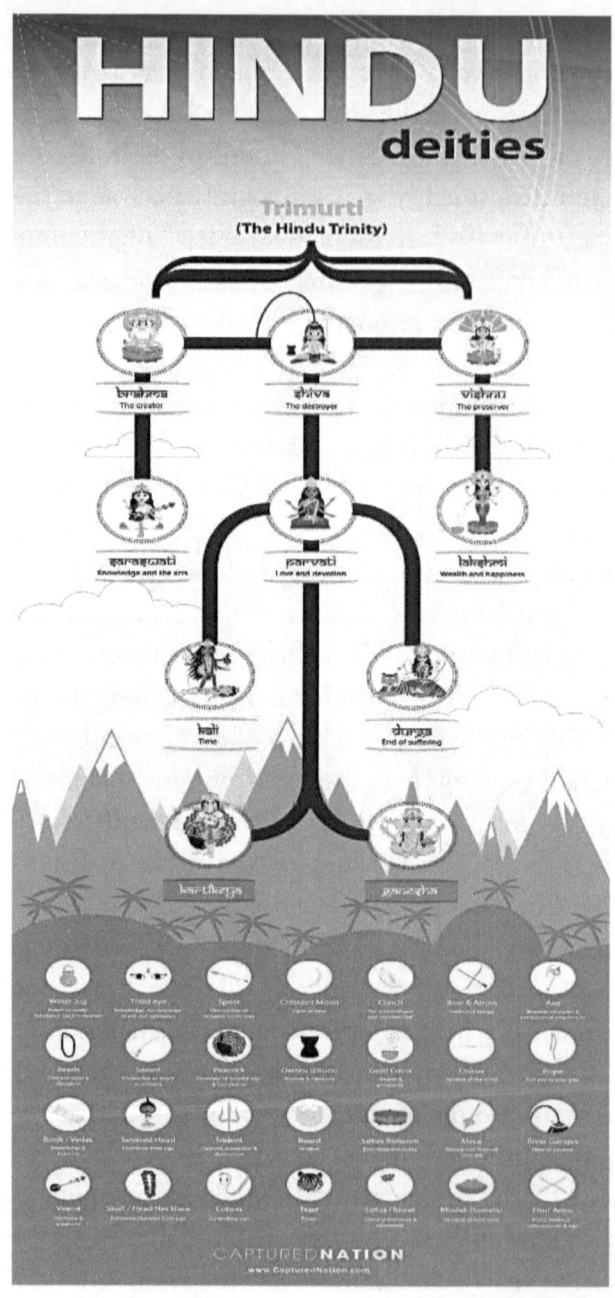

http://ultraculture.org/blog/2016/05/27/hinduism-gods-goddesses/

THE TWO PATHS TO GOD

Buddhism and Taoism are both poetic and mystic. The poeticism found in Islam, where a Muslim harmonizes their thoughts and actions to the ever-flowing aspects of God, can be related to how a Buddhist or Taoist harmonizes their thoughts and actions to Nirvana or The Eternal Tao.

The mysticism found in Judaism, where intense study and the Divine meanings behind the actions a Jew performs are meant to enhance their spiritual knowledge, can be related to the mysticism of The 8-fold path in Buddhism and the intricately formal teachings in Confucianism. As for Taoism, Lao Tzu, being a scholar and librarian, emphasized to Taoists to "study The Tao". "To study" contains many different interpretations; it is related to literature, observation, action, and Divine thought. The religious rites and rituals we perform often combine many of these interpretations in the term "to study".

Combining the symbolic aspect of Hinduism and the dual poetic/mystic aspects of Buddhism and Taoism creates two Sacred Hearts, as two Trinities can be formed.

Said in another way, Buddhism places an emphasis on regular meditation. Before we can do any spiritual rite or ritual, we have to know how to quiet the mind. This "conscious quietening of our thoughts" not only helps control our mind, but also helps open our heart. Our thoughts and our inner-vision begin to encompass the entire Universe. Both are what create peace within the Buddhist who practices placing their thoughts above their own desire and into the flow of Nature (Universal Consciousness). When a Buddhist practices daily meditation, for sometimes hours a day, it helps to put this poetic aspect of Buddhism central in their lives. One aspect of meditation is pure poeticism. By harmonizing our thoughts with The Universal Mind, we step into the realm of meditation. We close our eyes and are faced with our own thoughts. We become witnesses to the poetic dance that takes place in our own mind. Mantras, breathing exercises, imagery, and posture techniques help us to gain some control over our thoughts. As we become better at placing our thoughts above our desires, we become more "poetic" in our approach to dealing with the incessant dancing of thoughts going on in our mind. But, unlike the poeticism in Islam, the Buddhist also uses the image of their spiritual guide – namely, The Buddha - in their practice. He is their example of how to first achieve inner harmony… and then unite with Nirvana. With poetic meditation, what is happening is that we are beginning to slowly develop our own Divinity. Our individual thoughts and problems are slowly being replaced with Universal Thought and Joy. It is a form of cognitive science that the Buddhist is practicing. He or she is learning how to control the mind.

On the mystic side of Buddhism, we find The Dharma, The Four Noble Truths, and The Eight-fold Path. The four noble truths help us recognize how we can overcome suffering. To do this, we use the method found in The Eight-fold Path. Like Judaism in its mysticism, there are eight suggested rules to follow in the Eight-fold Path to be a "Good Buddhist" (Right speech, right thought, right conduct, etc..). In the Jewish Kabbalah, we find also many suggestions of right conduct, right thought, right speech, etc. The Zohar is central to Kabbalah. Dharma is central to Buddhism. Both awaken mysticism and can be defined as a doctrine, teaching, duty, or law.

Taoism places an emphasis on internal alchemy. This will naturally result when we are in tune with The Eternal Tao. Being in tune with "The Eternal Field behind the 10,000 things" will give us a philosophical maturity. Our suffering diminishes when we harmonize with Eternity. Coming in tune with this Eternal Field is the poetic aspect of Taoism.

The Tao is also described as "The Mother of the 10,000 things". The maternal aspects every mother strives to be - nourishing, listening, protective, kind, supportive, resourceful… - are the same divine aspects The Tao is. The Tao embodies The Five Virtues – Justice, Truth, Love, Kindness, and Wisdom.

Like the poeticism in Islam, where a Muslim's main focus is on "The Eternal and Everlasting Allah", a Taoist's poetic focus is on oneness with The Tao. Both The Holy Koran and The Tao Te Ching describe Universal Consciousness as "The First and The Last". They also describe it as "The Undefined". The mysticism in Taoism comes from "The Lao-Zi". This book is the Taoist Code of Ethics. A book that helps support person's spiritual knowledge and personal experience of The Tao. As with the Jewish teaching of The Kabbalah, Non-Interference is one of the main teachings of this book. However, also philosophy, the masculine and feminine aspects of The Tao (Yin and Yang), The Divine Virtues, and some sexual practices are also written about. The goal of this book is to help us find inner and eternal harmony.

"The I-Ching" is one of the most unique and mystical aspects of Taoism. It is surely one of the most unique books in all of spirituality. "The I-Ching" is different from "The Tao Te Ching". The former is partly magical, the latter is mostly mystical. The I-Ching can be read, but one of its main uses is for divination – a way of tapping into The Realm of Divinity with thoughts and questions. (In Latin, divination comes from "Divine-tion". It indicates "a state, condition, action, process, or result from an interaction with Divinity"). Questions are written and then either three stones or three sticks are tossed onto a table. Depending on how the objects land, they will tell you where in The I-Ching to look for the answer to your question. The answers you receive are quite surprising and quite specific. They are deep and thought-provoking, like the Tao Te Ching itself. The answers awaken our insight – not only into the question asked, but into ourselves and in the omniscient aspects of The Universal Mind. Practicing divination with The I-Ching only enriches and enhances the wonder you begin to feel for the dynamics of The Tao. Whether you are a Daoshi, a Taoist Master, a Daojiaotu, or just a practicing Taoist, poeticism and mysticism are very strong in The Taoist way of Life.

Taoism, Buddhism, and Hinduism create at least two dynamic and transmutable Sacred Hearts. Awareness of the interchanging poeticism and mysticism of Taoism and Buddhism, combined with symbolism of Hinduism can help us tap into The Universal Mind we are a part of. We can see these two Trinities in the following chart:

General Path	**SACRED HEART**	**SACRED HEART**
Poetic	Buddhism (Meditation, Oneness with The Flow, Learning to quieten the mind)	Taoism (Oneness with The Tao to end suffering)
Symbolic	Hinduism (Gods, Goddesses, Ornaments)	Hinduism (Gods, Goddesses, Ornaments)
Mystic	Taoism (I-Ching and Lao-Zi)	Buddhism (Four Noble Truths, Eight-fold path)

Tea Ceremonies Combine The Mystic, The Poetic, And The Symbolic Into One

Tea ceremonies provoke thought and evoke Light

Tea ceremonies are practiced throughout Asia, especially in China and Japan. There is a guest for whom the tea is prepared and an elaborate, hours-long, and extremely detailed performance by the host or master who prepares the tea. The host is usually dressed in a religious costume and there are several steps done before, during, and after the actual drinking of the tea. Steps include bowing, lighting incense, blessing of the tea, silence, kneeling, meditation, etc. Rituals involving some form of water, food, or drink are seen in other religions, as well. The steps taken have profound meanings before, during, and after a ceremony; For instance, when a priest prepares bread and wine for communion, when a Muslim washes his feet before prayer, and the many rituals surrounding the Hanukkah meal. All of these practices are done with reverence and respect. They all contribute Light into The Collective Consciousness. But, when asked about the meaning of The Tea Ceremony, often the priest performing it will tell you that it is done out of respect and high esteem for the guest. This can be, but when we remember that the goal of Shintoism, Taoism, Buddhism, and Confucianism is to become one with the Divine Nature of The Universe, we can also see that The Tea Ceremony is a display of mind-control.

To be able to carry, pour, bow, drink, and kneel with such precision during this ceremony, means that the Tea Master has a lot of control over his or her own mind. To get to that point, the Tea Master has had to come to a very high point in controlling their own will through their decades-long meditation and spiritual practices. This is truly what impresses us when we watch a Tea Ceremony performed. In the mind and in every movement of the Tea Master, he or she is focused on The Eternal Field or The Universal Vibration existing within and around us. It is a time when they can practice all they have learned; when they can be at One with Nature and place their thoughts above their own desire into the realm of Zen. By concentrating on this, the priest becomes Zen. They benefit from this ritual as much as the guest does. At times throughout this hours-long ceremony, they feel united with Nirvana. They become a conduit of Light, and this Light enters those who observe the performance.

So, seeing it in this way, The Tea Ceremony is not about tea. It is about displaying mind control in order to evoke Light. If you ever have the chance to see one performed live – please do! You will have a much deeper experience.

One Famous Example Of How Synergetic Thought Changed The World

What is possible for one of us is possible for all of us. Again… just being alive, on Earth, and in human form is a good start. Having a sound mind, an open heart, and an unbiased desire for spiritual knowledge can not only take our thoughts to an exalted level, but also that of those around us. In some cases, we've seen people who are this spiritually evolved change countries and at times even change our world. Lives such as these are the new unavoidable examples our world is heading in. Some of today's conservatives ask themselves "Why do we think diversity is such a strength?". The answer to that is simple… "Because God expresses Himself that way."

A Living Example Of The Clock At Work

The Master Gandhi

Let us, for a moment, remember The Mahatma Gandhi. He is commonly thought of as a modest Hindu who, in the early

20th century, inspired millions of people to use peaceful resistance to help change the world. Then and now, his example is often considered when there is a movement or a desire for change. The Master Gandhi dressed like a Hindu, talked like a Hindu, and taught the world many aspects of Hinduism. Yet, privately, he was inspired by not one, but by three of the world's great religions. Throughout his many travels, he always carried with him not only The Bhagavad Gita, but also The Bible and The Quran. The Master Gandhi taught of Peace and Non-violence, from the accumulated spiritual knowledge he gained from Islam, Hinduism, and Christianity. And still, he saw even beyond them when he proclaimed "God has no religion"… and reminded us that:

> "We are of God, even as a little drop of water
> is of the ocean."

All religions speak of how we, as Human Beings, are Divine. As we are Divine, religious techniques help us attune our thoughts to the one, great, source of our own Divinity – Universal Consciousness. In part, they teach us different methods on how we can harmonize our thoughts and actions with the mysterious and dynamic nature of God. The main techniques of religions are prayer, affirmations and meditation. These both direct our thoughts in different directions. With prayer, we try to harmonize our desires with God's Will. With affirmations, we try to harmonize our thoughts with one of God's numerous aspects. With meditation, we try to harmonize our thoughts with God's Essence. Prayer and affirmations are directed more outwards. Meditation is directed more inwards. Mantras are used in all three techniques. Through these basic practices, we come to realize that we, as human beings, are both transmitters and receptors. We each have the ability to send thoughts to and receive thoughts from both our Collective Consciousness and Universal Consciousness.

Collective Consciousness sustains the thoughts and ideas that we have put into it. The immense knowledge that is contain in our Collective Consciousness comes from mankind's diversity. Modern Conservatives question the power of diversity. From the handful of Universal aspects we can clearly see, diversity is one of the most apparent. There is not one type of flower, there are thousands. There is not one type of tree, rock, apple, animal, planet, moon, snowflake or human being either. No blade of grass is exactly the same. This Universal Consciousness seems like something that not only expresses eternal diversity... but an intelligence that supports it. We come closer to understanding what it is by looking at what it does.

Universal Consciousness sustains Life and the Universal Laws governing our galaxies. Each of us is powerful enough to add either harmonious or disharmonious thought into the Collective Consciousness. The overall balance contained in the collective consciousness affects us all. If there is mostly dark energy in it, we will all feel more darkness enter our lives. If there is mostly light energy in it, we will all feel that light enter our lives. We have all contributed both good and bad thought into our collective consciousness – none of which has really had an effect on the Divine Laws governing our Universe. We only hurt ourselves by what we have thought and, so inspired, done. Our individual consciousness can protect us from a dark collective consciousness. Many spiritual techniques shield us from the dark entities that are born from a dark collective consciousness we have created.

Our individual consciousness is not the collective consciousness. And our collective consciousness is not The

Universal Consciousness. The collective consciousness is what we create with our individual thoughts. The Divine Consciousness is God, and all his laws that govern our Universe. Yet still… there is a fourth dimension of consciousness – a dimension that neither we have individual control of, nor do we collectively contribute to, nor is a part of Divine Laws. There is a "Prayer-answering consciousness". That prayer-answering dimension of Universal Consciousness listens and responds to our thoughts and prayers. It is different than the many violent films, tabloid gossip, and internet junk we feed into our collective consciousness. This prayer-answering dimension is also different from the Universal Laws that keep our Earth rotating on its own axis and our hearts beating. This fourth dimension of Divine Intelligence is what The Clock of The Twelve Paired Mantras reveals to someone who experiments, prays, affirms, contemplates, and meditates with it. Consciously uniting our lunar and solar sides not only creates an inner eclipse, but also awakens our True Divine Identity.

Self-Realization supports The Spirit – Self-Actualization supports Matter

"The Two Paths to God" is the first part of a six-part series on The Scientific Prayer. In them, Self-Realization is defined as the techniques connected to our spirit; such as meditation, prayer, mantras, rituals, etc. Self-Actualization is defined as techniques related to matter; such as getting a college education, buying a home, working, family, projects that have potential growth prospects, etc… When we consciously bring both techniques into balance, we achieve a deep inner peace. Not only that, at this point, we have the ability to awaken abundance in a variety of different ways and on a variety of different planes of thought. The Clock will

THE TWO PATHS TO GOD

help you progress in both of these important Life areas. Yes, we can feel abundance spontaneously awaken throughout our spiritual world, but we can also see abundance awaken throughout our material world. We are evoking our Lunar and Solar selves to awaken our True Individuality – Our True Self.

Self-Realization has been popularly discussed for decades. Self-Actualization, not so much. However, both are needed to achieve an inner and outer equilibrium. One greatly enriches the other, and vice-versa. We get "unbalanced" when one is predominant. That is, if we live a life totally into Yoga, rituals, sacred books, churches, ashrams, and mosques, but can't support ourselves. In this situation, Self-Realization dominates Self-Actualization. Or, if we live a life full of stress about our businesses, drugs, ulcers, and deadlines, but never meditate or harmonize our thoughts with Universal Consciousness with the help of mantras. In this situation, Self-Actualization dominates Self-Realization.

When both are intertwined, we are stronger. Our hearts are stronger. Our thoughts are stronger. Our actions are stronger. Our inspiration is better. And our possibilities grow. What grows most from this is our independence, as we become focused only on The Source of both spirit and matter.

The Scientific Prayer series uses the word "God" interchangeably with other terms such as "Universal Consciousness" and "The Divine Mind". Ultimately, these terms lead us to the One Same Source. Yet, the term used depends on the subject discussed. The term used to describe our infinite Godhead is seen as a tool in helping the reader absorb the contents of the subject. If the subject discussed is rather religious or spiritual, terms like "God" or "Universal Consciousness" are used. If the subject is more scientific or intellectual, terms like "The

Divine Mind" or "Cosmic Intelligence" are used. The Clock of The Paired Mantras contains 12 pathways to the same "Realm of Dynamic Quintessence". These terms touch on different aspects of our thoughts. They trigger the subtly, different ways we can and do aspire higher. They are all One. They all lead us to the same Source because they are all different attempts to describe the indescribable.

The most important aspect about Scientific Prayer is not God. Rather, the most vital element is our own spiritual thirst. More important than God… more important than "The Devil"… more important than "Sin"… is the passion for a Divine Reunion in our spiritual thirst. God is a constant. Our spiritual thirst is not. It is a variable. Our passion for a Divine Reunion is what motivates and inspires our actions. It is what is behind our prayers, rituals, and meditations. The Pure Beauty of God is within and all around us, but it is our passion and spiritual thirst that makes us more aware of His presence. This spiritual thirst is the most beautiful part of who we are. It is what compels us to unite with the highest and most sublime Beauty. The Universal and Divine Beauty that we all emerged from, are a part of now, and will re-unite with. It is the active component, that awakens our hunger for Divine Knowledge. It will lead us to inspired actions. Realizing this, we come to see that most important component of The Clock of The Paired Mantras lies in the heart of the reader.

About The Supplementary Book "Exercises in Divine Science and Experiments in Multiplicative Joy"

When someone asks you "What was your book about?", the essence of it can be explained in a few sentences. Here are some examples:

"A scientist has researched the root meanings of words we use in prayer – "Om", "Allah", "Amen", "AUM", and "Tao". He explains how some are paths to God as The Cosmic Sound and others to God as The Eternal Field. Then he shows us how to unite both paths into 12 Paired Mantras that will work synergistically in our thoughts".

"The first part of the book explores the Five World Mantras people use in their prayers – "Om", "Tao", "Allah", "Amen", and "AUM". The second part categorizes them into Solar Mantras and Lunar Mantras. The third part unites them into 'The Clock of The Paired Mantras' – Each forming an Inner Eclipse".

"The writer is a scientist who shows how the Number 12 is found in Time, Astrology, Music, and the major religions: Christianity, Islam, Judaism, Taoism, Buddhism, and Hinduism. And, when we use paired mantras like "Amen-Allah" or "Tao-Om", we create 12 pathways into Divinity. Paired Mantras are tools to awaken Light and knowledge".

"Your thoughts are taken back 14 billion years... before Man or Earth existed... to when The Cosmic Sound emerged from The Eternal Void... and then created The Universe we now live in. Mantras resonate primarily with That Sound or with The Void. This book shows you how to use the awareness of both types of Mantra to empower prayer".

"It describes the first step of 'The Six Steps of Scientific Prayer' ".

This book, "The Two Paths to God", can be viewed in two parts: "Theory" and "Practice". This first book was "Theoretical", while the following book can be seen as more "Practical".

The Guide Chart to help navigate "The Exercises in Divine Science and Experiments in Multiplicative Joy"

Divine Science Exercises And Experiments Supplementary book	We all Pray How a Spiritualist can amplify their prayers with a Paired Mantra
	Science, Scientists, and Scientific Thought
	The Millennials and their Unique Spiritual Potential
	African Americans and The Many Historic Signs of their Paired Mantra Preparedness
	Why are the World's Strongest Economies strong? The United States, Europe, China, and India
	Three Grounding Prayer Techniques: A Tree as a tool – "I am that I am" – "I am One with.."
	24 Exercises and Experiments in Divine Science and Multiplicative Joy
	No need to look out into Space... There are Black Holes here on Earth
	The Age Of Light Not every new innovation has to be Digital Creating World Peace – The New NASA Space Program – Soap and SLS – A New Cancer and HIV Treatment – Conscious STD Prevention – Volcanoes and a Waste-Free World

An Overview of the Second Book

There are two books associated with "The Two Paths to God". The first book you have just read is very theoretical. The second, supplementary book is much more practical. Together, they are like getting your driver's license – You first study the theory and then you perform the manoeuvres.

In the second book, there are 24 exercises and experiments that involve both spirituality and scientific thought. The Twelve Paired Mantras and The Clock of The Twelve Paired Mantras are explored and practiced with more deeply. Grounding Prayers are presented to help us connect to both The Earth and Divine Consciousness.

Although these exercises and experiments are primarily meant for Spiritualists, the next book gives many individual reasons why both Millennials and African-Americans should practice them too. Both groups are in a unique and historical demographic. Many specific incentives are given as to why both of these groups should consider practicing Scientific Prayer.

At the end of the book, "The Age of Light" is discussed. An Age where science and spirituality are combined, new technologies in medicine are practiced, and ridding of our planet of many diseases and much of its pollution are acted upon. An Age where we combine the knowledge we have gained through the Ages for a better world today. It is an Age where religious wars are a thing of the past and "Conscious Prayer" is the Light of The Future.

An Age where every human being is given the tools to consciously combine science and spirituality in their own thoughts and actions. When we learn how to do this individually, we take steps towards True Abundance in our hearts and True Peace in our World.

Acknowledgements

For this book, I would like to thank Armando Acosta who started the ball rolling…

Georges Gaidon who keeps my feet on the ground…

And, my mother, Zonyia Clayton for her unshakeable faith in my talents.

Without the love and support of you three, "The Two Paths to God" would not have materialized.

I also owe a big debt of gratitude to my family, friends, yogis and yoginis who have told me my entire life that I would do "something great!".

Well… I think this is it.

Love,
Xavier

About the Author

For more than 30 years, Xavier Clayton has developed a broad and international background as a laboratory scientist and technician. As a songwriter, he has also had a long and successful music career. With decades of experience in both of these fields, he is someone who can truly claim to be a man of "The Arts and Sciences".

Born and raised in Seattle, Washington, he began his science career in The United States Army, where he worked as a Laboratory Technician and received awards and medals during his 6-year tenure in the Reserves. He also worked at The University of Washington Hospital as a Laboratory Technician and studied Biology at The University of Washington.

Following his passion for music, he left the Army for Europe in 1988. He soon settled in Antwerp, Belgium – where he lived for 27 years. During his years as an Expat, he wrote lyrics to a number of successful gold and platinum hits for various artists in Holland, Belgium, Switzerland and France. His songs have reached #1 in Europe, Asia and The United States. While in Flanders, he went back to school at 39 years old to finally finish his Bachelor's Degree in Medical and Food Laboratory Science at The Karel de Grote Hogeschool. For 9 years, he worked as a Toxicologist at The Stuivenberg Medical

Center. Part of his job included research studies for new drugs for Johnson & Johnson Pharmaceuticals.

Outside of his musical and medical careers, spirituality remained a big part of his interests. It started when a friend unexpectedly sent him "The Tao Te Ching" in 1991. Living in Antwerp's multi-religious community, he found a lot of information on Judaism, Islam, Hinduism, Buddhism, Catholicism and Siddha Shiva Yoga. The success of his music projects allowed him to travel world-wide, including to places such as China, India, Montenegro, Turkey and Africa. On these journeys, he'd take personal notes on the spiritual practices he learned. Often many of the famous and obscure spiritual centers he visited had a living spiritual master. His talks with some of these guides play an important role in the trans-faith prayer techniques Xavier writes about. "This book was just meant to be a little 20-page prayer book. But as I started writing it... it just kept growing!"

Xavier lives in Marseille, France and works as a scientist. He is married and is fluent in three languages – English, Dutch and French. *"The Two Paths to God"* took 12 years to complete. This first book describes the first step of "The Six Steps of Scientific Prayer". It is a method spiritualists of any faith can use to amplify their prayers and aspirations. It's a way to help manifest our desires from a level of synergy and transcendence.

Xavier's blog describes new topics, such as "Multiplicative Joy", "Divine Science", "The Fire of Abundance" and "Awakening The Inner Phoenix". "The Paired Mantra will not only bring Light and Abundance into the reader's life... but also, much needed Light and Abundance into our world".